THE
MODERNIST
MADONNA

THE
MODERNIST MADONNA

SEMIOTICS OF THE MATERNAL METAPHOR

JANE SILVERMAN VAN BUREN

INDIANA UNIVERSITY PRESS
BLOOMINGTON AND INDIANAPOLIS

KARNAC BOOKS   LONDON

First published in North America by
Indiana University Press
10th and Morton Streets
Bloomington, Indiana 47405

and in Great Britain by
H. Karnac (Books) Ltd.
58 Gloucester Road
London SW7 4QY

Manufactured in the United States of America

Library of Congress Cataloging-in-Publication Data

Van Buren, Jane Silverman.
The modernist madonna : semiotics of the maternal
metaphor / Jane Silverman Van Buren.
p. cm.
Includes bibliographical references and index.
ISBN 0–253–36203–2.—ISBN 0–253–20544–1 (pbk.)
1. Mother and child—Miscellanea.   2. Mothers in literature.
3. Mothers in art.   4. Semiotics.   5. Women and psychoanalysis.
I. Title.
HQ759.V295   1989
306.8'743—dc19   88–46013
                                                                     CIP

British Library Cataloguing in Publication Data

Van Buren, Jane Silverman
The modernist madonna : semiotics of the maternal
metaphor.
1. English literature. American women writers 1945–.
Special subjects. Mothers. Critical studies
I. Title
810.9'3520431
ISBN 0–946439–73–7

1 2 3 4 5   93 92 91 90 89

*Dedicated to J. G., for sharing hope and
truth amongst the other seven
servants of experience.*

CONTENTS

Preface / ix
Acknowledgments / xvii

CHAPTER 1.
The Maternal Metaphor / 1

CHAPTER 2.
The Mythology and Semiotics of Familial Bonds / 25

CHAPTER 3.
Uncle Tom's Cabin: A Myth of Familial Relations / 64

CHAPTER 4.
Little Women: A Study in Adolescence and Alter Egos / 96

CHAPTER 5.
Mary Cassatt / 124

CHAPTER 6.
Other Madonnas / 157

Notes / 176
Index / 205

Preface

The Modernist Madonna has grown from my deep interest in the signs and symbols of the parent–child relationship as they have been fashioned by biology, human subjectivity, and culture. For all of human history, familial relationships have been deeply obscured by lack of knowledge and by powerful feelings and fears. The concept of the infant has appeared over the millennia in strange and troubled ways, until this century. Similarly, the images and concepts of motherhood, mothering, and mother have been largely formed from highly idealized or debased images little resembling the human maternal figure and her functions. My concern and interest is in the dislocation of the child in all of us, as well as in the parameters of infancy and childhood as stages in the life cycle and the painful difficulties associated with mothering.

Since the last part of the nineteenth century the discovery of the structures, rules, and processes working in the mind and in language have provided us with new methods and tools to interpret and to deconstruct many of the symbolic structures of the madonna and child which had formerly been accepted as natural or divine. From the time of Freud's presentation of the theory of unconscious/conscious interactions and the processes through which we release powerful affective forces, our understanding of the manifest signs and value systems of language, myths, custom, and practice has been radically changed and opened to make accessible layered codes based on the different logics of the mind (primary process, secondary process) and their complex interactions.

Ferdinand de Saussure and Roman Jakobson probed the etiology of the manifest aspects of language and searched for the ways in which language yields meaning. Their theoretical explorations remained largely centered around the rules of language as various permutations of combination and difference. The origins of feelings, bias, and distortion were not directly sought out by them. The notion of unseen affective inclinations as "driving" the creation of the diachronic and synchronic aspects of language found in metaphor and metonymy remains outside their concept.[1] However, Saussure stated that language only exists through subjectivity—through the interaction of the mind of a subject with a linguistic code.[2] Saussure's understanding of linguistic phenomena as dynamic relational systems of oppositional difference and Jakobson's theory of a Selective Associated Synchronic and Combinative Syntagmatic Diachronic Structure allow us to imagine codes of meaning complementing each other and interacting along the sequential and relational planes.

The science of signs carries the concept of codes and signifying processes beyond linguistics; it probes all manner of communication systems—for example, bodily gestures, dress, social customs (including child-rearing practices), and systems of belief (political, religious, and scientific, among others)—and maps out the relationship of the manifest structures to their underlying meaning.[3] For Saussure and Jakobson, personal meaning grows from the relationship of a subject or culture to an object deep within the subject's mind, or as embedded within the culture's value system. As in Freud's theory, although approached from a different system, meanings not consciously known before flow into the structure of the outer or manifest sign.

Barthes extends Saussure's theory of signs beyond the structural relationship between the sound image (signifier) and concept (signified).[4] Using a metalinguistic theory of signs, Barthes opens a way of reading various social beliefs, practices, and customs, particularly in his system of mythologies. For Barthes, a mythology is not a classical mythology, in the sense of Demeter and Persephone, but an ideology created by a second order of the signifier/signified (S/S) relationship. Barthes hypothesizes that the new S/S is structured in ways that tear the old sign away from its moorings.[5] Part of the function of the new sign is to direct the receiver of the message toward an ideological perspective by subtle means of manipulation.[6] One of the examples that Barthes offers in his book *Mythologies* is detergent as a signifier to the signified spirituality or salvation. Salvation linked with soap rises from an ideology of secular cleanliness equivalent to worthiness. Barthes gives another example of a visual kind in the essay called "The Face of Garbo," also in *Mythologies*. In this piece, the nonlinguistic example is seen in the meanings of the presentation of Garbo's eyes, mouth, and make-up. Her screen image provides a conceptual or ideational screen image of beauty and mystery that offers the viewer the protection of the mask and an ideal.[7] I believe our "accepted" beliefs about mothers and children are constructed out of ideologies (mythologies). For example, think how the little Victorian sinner, to be redeemed by the domestic madonna, is replaced by a concept of the child brimming over with capacities to learn at earlier and earlier ages—a little genius. At the same time, neglect of mothers and children is a dominating theme in late twentieth-century American thought and politics. We must ask, how do these contradictory systems and beliefs coexist side by side?

Charles Sanders Peirce provided us with a method of tracking the shape and quality of the sign as it is formed out of emotional forces. He did this by adding to sign theory the notion of the sign as a triparte structure made up of the S/S relation in turn in a relationship to an "I." For Peirce, a sign, or representom, is something which stands to somebody for something.[8] Thus, Peirce carved out the relationship of the manifest images to the interior concept as a product of the mind at work so Peirce's triparte structure—interpretant or subject, object, and sign—allows us to understand the element of emotional dimensionality in the formation of the sign. Using the concept of iconical, indexical, and symbolic signs, Peirce formulated signs on a spectrum, from simple to complex abstractions or from relationships based on similarity, cause, and effect to arbitrary ones created by the interpretant. Peirce called this latter structure a symbol.[9] For him, the symbol is capable of representing multiple aspects of meaning, a complex signifier. However, Peirce did not place his theory within the domain of the mother/child dialogue.

Freud also discovered the creation of meaning out of synchronic and diachronic relations, although he did not conceptualize the functioning of the mind through sign theory. He couched his ideas mainly in the theory of the libido and of discharge. However, Freud's notion of the dream work and parapraxis is a theory of signs. Furthermore, his approach to the creation of meaningful structures most clearly and directly tracks the S/S/I relationship. Freud's theory of dreams and parapraxis is formed around the concept of the infantile wish. The drives, affects, and ideas associated with the wish are at first satisfied by hallucinations or an internal perceptual identity. However, the infant soon discovers that hunger (and all manner of desires) must find satisfaction in the external realm. At this juncture aspects of the drives are directed toward external objects while other aspects remain subterranean and find expression only through dreams, parapraxis, and symbols. The dream work, mainly condensation, displacement, and regression, forms new structures which are acceptable and bearable to the censor and the conscious mind. The newly formed manifest structure, for example, the dreams of "The Botanical Monograph" and "Irma,"[10] are built out of an elaborate S/S relationship; a sign, Irma or the Monograph, carries the coded message, "I, Freud, want to be the father who has success in the professional world and in love." The S/S relationship is determined by the latent content of passion, fear, desire, and conflict. Thus, Freud is one of several distinguished theoreticians of the turn of the century who grasped the phenomenology of the manifest code of language and behavior in the individual and in the culture. However, his concept of the infant is centered around the vicissitudes of the instincts to the extent that the infant appears nearly motherless.

Freud's theory of the infantile wish and the cathexis of the desired object presses deeply into the origins of signs and symbols. His dream work also provides us with a theory of myths. Just as the dream intertwines conscious and unconscious themes together to make personal narratives, the myth more permanently provides a people with a structure which manifestly represents their internal themes. A myth in this sense, such as the Oedipus myth, carries the significance of bonding or its failure, intergenerational and sexual strife, and important themes of the life cycle. In this way it is a cultural dream and an extended S/S relationship. Many of our notions of parenting, motherhood, and child rearing are mythic structures in this sense.

Since the days of Freud's innovations, psychoanalysis has journeyed into deeper and deeper layers of mental life. Freud himself was led beyond the theory of the pleasure principle to explore the processes of identification, splitting of the ego, and, in the case of psychotics, the implosion of libido back into the ego to the point of fragmentation. Freud's discovery of the processes which lead to the formation of the ego ideal and of the superego brought in turn a discovery of inner psychic reality made up of personas and inner dialogues. Melanie Klein, Anna Freud, and Edith Jacobson carried forward Freud's notion of the internal world and applied these theories to younger children and babies. Differing over the developmental sequences of the age and nature of internal imagoes, psychoanalytic theorists in America and Europe nevertheless understand development to be dominated by the nature of these internal characters. Loving, satisfying experiences were organized as whole and benign personas who facilitated growth and mental sturdiness. Experiences of frustration, cruelty, and indifference led to inadequate personas that filled the developmental drama with chaos, pain, and destruction. Melanie Klein held that these unconscious imagoes or internal objects were created as phantasies of self and others painted in the colors of the life and death instincts and experienced by the infant as annihilation fears or feelings of safety and satisfaction. Klein also held that instinctual life was known only as, and only in the form of, unconscious phantasies and that these structures commenced within the first few days of life.

Anna Freud, Edith Jacobson, and Margaret Mahler believed that the beginning of internal object relations came later, in the toddler stage. Anna Freud and Edith Jacobson emphasized the unconscious defenses of the ego, while Margaret Mahler stressed the separation/individuation process and the omnipotent phantasies that attended the vicissitudes of hatching.

Significantly, within all of these theories of the mind lay an expanding window to infantile mental life and mental development in its normal and pathological forms. Within this theoretical trend, W. R. Bion, Donald Meltzer, Hanna Segal, Frances Tustin, and Joseph Sandler in England; Edith Jacobson, Otto Kernberg, Harold Searles, James Masterson, Donald Rinsley, Peter Giovacchini, and James Grotstein in America; Jacques Lacan, André Greene, Janine Chasseguet-Smirgel, Joyce McDougall, and Julia Kristeva in France, to name a few, have developed theories which further penetrate the understanding of primitive mental states, as phantasy and dream on the one hand and as disorganized, explosive, and disregulated mental states on the other. Schizophrenia, psychosis, narcissistic and borderline personality disorders are today understood as disorders of the central nervous system and as faulty mental processing such as bizarre perceptions, phantasies, internal object relations, hallucinations, and the truncation of the development of thought.

To my mind, Bion in particular captures the etiology of signs and symbols and the formation of the internal world in its deepest forms. Bion maps primitive mental states, proposing phantasies not only of projection, splitting, and fragmentation of the contents of the mind but phantasies of the mind itself. He discusses the example of the formation of bizarre objects as created out of extreme mental states and primitive mechanisms. A patient believed the phonograph in Bion's office was staring at him. Bion explained that the patient was in the grip of an unconscious process in which he felt his capacity to see (to know) had been evacuated into Bion's room, specifically into the phonograph.[11]

In *Learning from Experience*,[12] Bion worked intensely on the etiology of meaningful experience. He proposed that the evolution of the contents of the mind from a simple stimulus to a meaningful realization depends on the capacity to feel and to experience. At the start of life these capacities are in part borrowed from the parental mind. Bion's idea is that as mental data are gathered and grasped, images, concepts, signs, and symbols evolve, carrying various aspects of unconscious elements along, specifically powerful emotions. He relies on Freud's outline of the exchange system between the conscious and unconscious aspects of the mind, but he departs from Freud in ways very important for this discussion. Bypassing the libido theory and the theory of discharge associated with the pleasure principle, Bion elaborates a theory of meaning or *signification*. Building on Melanie Klein's theories of internal objects, he deepens the internal drama by proposing a specific theory of thinking and signification. As each level of the mind grapples with the sign already formed, either in their simple or complex forms (from the prick of the diaper pin to the loss of a partner), the opportunity for the proliferation of meaning and significance is consummated or dissipated. For Bion the mother's capacity for reverie and thought is critical to the development of the infant's mind.

Lacan is another important psychoanalytic figure who maps the formation of the S/S relationship. He was very drawn to Freud's theory of the dream work and Lévi-Strauss's notion of a cultural unconscious—an unconscious structured like language. Following this approach, Lacan developed one of his central notions, that of the chain of signification, built out of the processes of displacement and condensation and carrying with it the deep longing of the subject. He believed that the analyst could decode the meaningful patterns of the patient's free associations by focusing on the journey of the S/S relationship in its metonymical and metaphorical transformations.[13]

Lacan's notion of the development of the mind and the capacity for language includes his theory of the mirror phase, in which the subject projects him/herself into the image of him or herself and into the mother's face or look. Lacan understood the mirror phase as based on the infant's sense of lack, anticipation, and desire. The desire is for the other self permanently alienated, or an object never to be possessed. The infant moving into language experiences desire as always displaced along the associative syntagmatic line of signification through metonymy or displacement, and through the associative paradigmatic lines of condensation or metaphor. Lacan describes a situation in which the subject never grasps the object of desire itself and is never able to integrate his/her two halves. The forming subject creates or initiates the signification of his/her experience and at the same time becomes enmeshed in the already existing signifying system within his or her culture.

At this point in his thinking, Lacan left both women and the maternal figure in an inferior place, as nonexistent in the symbolic order. He interprets the world of language or the symbolic order as a system of culture created out of male unconscious structures, the legacy of the Oedipus complex. This theory bifurcates the mother and baby signs from those of symbolic culture. Though Lacan broke free from the constraints of the biological determinism of Freud, he remained faithful to Freud's notion of culture as the product of male sublimations, leaving behind the infantile perceptual and sensual body talk of baby and mommy. Lacan's theory depends largely on the superiority of the present object, the phallus, not unlike Freud's notion of the castration complex. Lacan described the resolution of the Oedipus complex somewhat differently, however, as the fall into language.

For Lacan, a multiplicity of meanings and significations originate in the play of the signifiers in substitution and combination. Umberto Eco discusses Lacan's emphasis on condensation and displacement and the play of the signifier in this way: "If the sign can only be known through the signifier, and if the signified emerges only through an act of perpetual substitution of the signifier, the semiotic chain appears to be just a chain of signifiers."[14] Eco, interpreting Lacan, suggests that the chain of signifiers can be manipulated by the unconscious if the unconscious is understood to be linguistically constituted.

Lacan's concept of "jouissance," defined as the original satisfaction which will be sought again and again, is essential to understanding his notion of desire or sexual motivation. As Catherine Millot suggests in her article "On Hysteria, the Phallic Function, and Jouissance,"[15] Lacan's concept of the jouissance of the other is much like Freud's first experience of satisfaction, an experience which is soon to be lost and which all psychic activity will be aimed at rediscovering. Freud suggested that the mark left by the initial experience of jouissance left a trace, "A." Lacan followed Freud in this way and underlined the impossibility of the psychic apparatus's effort to re-find "A." Millot explains that Lacan emphasizes that the second experience "A" can never be the same as the first, so there will always be a failure, since that first experience is forever lost. The effort to rediscover jouissance is the painful, driving motive that carries the semiotic chain along. Another difference between the first jouissance and the second is that the first is the subject's experience of fusion, and the second is the effort to relocate it or reinscribe it. The mark of the first experience is a commemorative mark. This loss Lacan calls "Petit Objet A." Therefore we can see that Lacan's unconscious in many ways is not Freud's; for instinct, he substitutes the effort to recapture the first jouissance, and for biological determinism, he substitutes the separation from the mother's body as leading to a chasm between the mother-infant experience and the symbolic order.

Recent infant-observation theorists have brought a fresh perspective to bear on the subject of psychoanalytic semiology. Daniel Stern proposes that the response of the infant to his/her caretaker is the source of the development of the core self.[16] Following the English Middle School, such as Winnicott and Bowlby, and recent Self Psychologists such as Kohut, Goldberg, Stolorow, and Tolpin, Stern innovates on their notions of bonding and attachment as the foundation of epigenesis. He further theorizes that the gradual development of the core self grows out of built-in perceptual capacities, affects, and, later, memory of self and other, interacting in an episode. He gives the examples of a breast-feeding episode and a peek-a-boo episode. Out of these little events with an *attuned* other, self-experience, a sense of continuity and regulation, develops. Furthermore, the many repetitions of these episodes grow into what Stern calls a RIG— a Representation of Interaction Generalized—what other theories term a primitive sign, which codes conscious and unconscious experience. The core self is built from these structures in positive and negative tones. Stern suggests that many possible RIGs flow into the intersubjective field; for example, mother's RIG with her mother, positive or negative, or herself with father, siblings, and so on—the permutations are infinite. Stern emphasizes strongly that the RIG is a *lived* experience, growing out of the interactions of already structured RIGs constantly changing and combining in new ways. From this theoretical perspective, we are offered a different approach to infantile mental life. It seems attractive to hypothesize that Stern's notion of infantile representations of RIG experiences are early signs of the subject's mental life.

The relationship of psychoanalysis with semiotics may be understood as the bringing together of different disciplines. At the same time, however, explorations of the processes that create dream, myth, painting, and text display considerable overlap in the mind at work. It is from this area of the overlap that I explore the signification processes of the madonna and child.

Acknowledgments

There are many people to whom I feel much gratitude and thanks: my father, Leo Silverman, for sharing his fine sense of humor and his passion for people; my mother, Lilian, for her early feminism and her great political sense; Donald Meyer, who "turned me on" to women's history in 1966, which he presented with considerable elegance, originality, and depth; Stephen Thernstrom for shepherding the early versions of this work; Frances Tustin, for much support, much lucidity, and brilliant ideas; my colleagues at UCLA and California Institute of the Arts, Jeanette Gadt, Bonnie Engdahl, and Martin Van Buren, for their creative, insightful and stimulating talks on women's studies and critical theory; my children, Kevin, Beth, and Chris, who have given me much encouragement, support, and many fine talks; my psychoanalytic supervisors, Richard Alexander and James Gooch, for generously sharing their long years of clinical experience; Joan Catapano, Women's Studies editor at Indiana University Press, for believing in the book; Karen Oblom, for patiently providing so many versions of the manuscript; my friends at the Sisterhood Book Store for providing wonderful books and friendly support; Alfred Silver, for contributing extensively to my understanding of psychoanalytic semiotics; and finally, Jim Grotstein, who shared and integrated so many important adventures with me.

T H E
MODERNIST
MADONNA

CHAPTER

1

THE MATERNAL METAPHOR

Let us note that by establishing itself as the principle of a symbolic paternal community in the grip of the superego, beyond all ethnic considerations, beliefs, or social loyalties, monotheism represses, along with paganism, the greater part of aggressive civilizations, and their ideologies, women and mothers.

—Julia Kristeva

The modernist madonna as a signifier is a particular shape and form of the beliefs and affective forces which gather around the concepts of mother and child. Each culture or society organizes mothering, pregnancy, birth, and child care to fit the economics, religion, and scientific beliefs of that time and place. Moreover, whatever the pattern or structure, the emotional origins of the madonna and child configuration lie within themes of survival, potency, and mortality. The writers Harriet Beecher Stowe and Louisa May Alcott and the painter Mary Cassatt constructed their madonna and child out of the materials of the Victorian era, a time of new heightened interest in personal relations, the accelerating creation of the concepts of the individual, and the discovery of inner life.[1] As is well known, mainstream Victorian culture focused on an ideal woman in the family. Anxieties about political upheaval, the psychological implications of secularization, and the radical transformation of work and lifestyle appeared in the form of a quest for control and purity staged within the family around a cult of a domestic madonna. I believe that Stowe, Alcott, and Cassatt working as writers and artists were responding to the madonna's claims on their own psychic lives. As mothers to their work, and as expressive children within it, they worked to transform the madonna and child inside their minds and in the society. The parameters of their sense of self began with a supernatural, idealized icon of mother and child but gradually were transformed into the flesh-and-blood mother and living, feeling infant. Stowe's struggle to overcome her childhood mythic narratives took place in her writing around a dialectic of Calvinist oppression and slavery opposed to the values associated with liberty and love. Alcott's and Cassatt's explorations began in the sentimental field with the ideal mother and daughter and developed toward a full concept of personhood. Alcott's little Victorian women, the models of a perfect pilgrimhood, gradually explored the tempestuous feelings and sensuality of female adolescence. Cassatt's portraits of mothers, infants, and children, while still enclosed in a somewhat ideal and segregated female world, made a radical departure from the concept of sanctimonious motherhood and the idealized child.

The work of Stowe, Alcott, and Cassatt challenged the existing codes and myths of women and children, and in this way anticipated avant-garde art of the later twentieth century, setting itself against existing tradition. As women artists, their rebellion was against a culture manifestly dominated by male personality; in addition, their work was set against the restraints of the myths of motherhood, which as I will discuss, are organized structurally through horizontal and vertical divisions. The important unconscious aspect of the vertical split is seen in the separation of women and family life from the male-dominated public sphere. A horizontal bifurcation is seen in the attempt to banish from conscious life infantile emotions associated with need, desire, and helplessness. Thus it can be interpreted that mythic narratives of maternity and codes of sexual difference are structured by both repression and the splitting apart of the affectual links which carry sexual and emotional feelings between men and women and those which tie parents to their children (and the reverse).[2]

Psychoanalytic feminists finding their personality and identity profoundly defined by myths of motherhood and of sexual difference have made the concept of woman as mother a central focus of their work. Their deconstructive efforts at dismantling and decoding myths and ideologies which signify women and motherhood in peculiar ways (vertical split) and omit or distort much of the infant's experience with the mothering one (horizontal repression) have uncovered important structures of Western thought and culture. Though the psychoanalytic feminist theorists work with Freud's theories of mental functioning seen in dream and symptom formation and the relation of the conscious and unconscious, they find in his theory of the Oedipus complex a distorted coding of female development and character which is structured along the lines of male privilege in its vertical and horizontal superiority. Men are in the forefront of society, placed in the public sphere versus the domestic one and are privileged within the symbolic order, though the placement of men in this way tears them away from their little baby selves.

Feminist scholars on both sides of the Atlantic are critically probing the asymmetry of sexual difference as it is signified in history, literature, and language.[3] Their analyses examine the connections between women's development, particularly in the context of Freud's theory of the Oedipus complex, cultural and social expectations of women, and the designation of women as the primary caretakers of the race. Americans Nancy Chodorow and Dorothy Dinnerstein interpret the coding of sexual difference and draw from object-relations theory and Melanie Klein's emphasis on the pre-Oedipal as well as from the writings of Freud. Chodorow uses object-relations theory and research to explore the effects of separation/individuation processes on gender arrangements and the reverse within the individual and the group. Dinnerstein applies many of Klein's ideas about the archaic phantasies of the infant in the human drama of helplessness and dependence. Both women emphasize the effects of mother-dominated child rearing.

Members of the French school (which includes the Americans Jane Gallop, a professor of French literature and women's studies, and Mary Jacobus, a professor of English literature and women's studies, and the Europeans Julia Kristeva, Luce Irigaray, and Hélène Cixous) work with a psychoanalytic Lacanian perspective but also criticize Lacan's notion of the symbolic order (language) as made up of male sublimations. As part of their critique they explore Lacan's privileging of the metaphor of fatherhood or the etiology of the phallus as the transcendental signifier. The American and French schools come together around their mutual objection to the cultural codes and values which structure sexual differences as inequity, leading to the mutilation of concepts of parenting and of sexual identity.

Although Simone de Beauvoir and Adrienne Rich did not approach their interest in motherhood from a formal psychoanalytic perspective, they anticipated the work of the American and French psychoanalytic critics, unmasking cultural assumptions that assumed female gender to be equivalent to motherhood and as given by nature rather than culture. De Beauvoir and Rich[4] argue in Barthian fashion that women are not destined by biology or nature to fulfill themselves as the servant of the race, either as mother or as man's alter ego. De Beauvoir calls attention to women's status as other, while Rich wants to extricate motherhood (which she feels to be far more powerful than culture allows) from its banalization in modern culture.

Roland Barthes has called our attention to mental processes which structure cultural values in *Mythologies*.[5] Barthes argues that "mythological beliefs" spring from cultural bias. He believes that the cultural assumptions that appear in contemporary sign systems are drained of their primary meaning. In the original relationship between the signified and the signifier, meaning accrues from the rich experience of history (social, psychological, and personal), which are then contained in the structural relationship between the subject, the object, and its connotation for the subject in culture. Mythologies, on the other hand, are signs drained of the historically significant relations between aspects of the sign. Thus, in Barthes's perspective, "woman," or "mother" as a popular mythological construction, is drained of the historical and emotional significance of the experience of pregnancy (fetus or mother), birth, or nursing. The infant subject is cut off from its relationship to the mother as part of her/his sign and the relationship's meaning is replaced by a skewed idealization more powerfully exemplified as the madonna and pathetically as the mother of Mother's Day. A myth, on the other hand, found in classical culture or in anthropological artifacts and in the dream work[6] signifies more completely the passions of the human life cycle and of familial relations. Freud's *Totem and Taboo* provides an example of an analysis of a psychoanalytic cultural myth based on the principles of the dream work, condensation and displacement, and makes connections to the deepest strata of human existence. De Beauvoir and Rich argue in accord with Barthes that both gender and motherhood are contrived concepts accepted as though given and natural.

More recently, Chodorow and Dinnerstein have continued the effort of demythologizing cultural notions of motherhood. Chodorow emphasizes that mothering in its present form makes claims to stem from nature or innate tendencies. She supposes that in nontechnological societies the need for women to mother and for men to protect their family, pregnant woman, or mother and infant, necessitated by defense of the group and for the provision of food, no longer is viable.

> We can draw several conclusions concerning the biological basis of mothering. The cross-cultural evidence ties women to primary parenting because of their lactation and pregnancy functions, and not because of instinctual nurturance beyond these functions. This evidence also suggests there can be a variety of other participants in child care. Children of both sexes, though more often girls, often perform caretaking functions in addition to women. The prehistoric reasons of species or group survival which tied women to children have not held for centuries and certainly no longer hold today. Women in contemporary society do not bear children throughout their childbearing years. There is almost no work incompatible with nursing, and bottle feeding is available and widespread, either as a total source of food or for occasional feedings. Societies no longer need women's mothering for physical reproduction. The evolutionary functional account does not explain why women mother today.[7]

Chodorow suggests that mothering, as organized in contemporary culture, is structured through a formidable separation of the sexes and is self-perpetuating. She places her criticism of female-dominated child rearing within Freud's interpretation of the Oedipus complex, particularly as it is privileged for boys. Freud argued throughout his writing that women's growth is stunted by the complexity of her development. He thought she must change not only her desired object from mother to father but also her genital zone as well. Male children maintained both object and zone consistently throughout their development. More crucially, Freud's anatomical destiny argument is often interpreted to mean that women by nature are fit only for home and family.

However, Chodorow departs from Freud by drawing on object-relations theories of the pre-Oedipal period and the vicissitudes of separation individuation. From this perspective she makes distinctions between the achievement of boundaries or sense of self in female and male children. In a culture or society that dichotomizes gender identity and roles, boy infants are experienced early by their mothers as destined for an autonomous and separate public life. Within these conditions, female offspring are in danger of massive and confused identification with mother, who interfaces with them as an aspect of their own being and a sign of limited womanhood, the characteristics of which are an overemphasis on the welfare of others, on caretaking, and the sacrifice of individual needs.

Furthermore, Chodorow explains that both male and female offspring growing up in a sex-segregated culture in the nineteenth and twentieth centuries suffered the imbalance of a fatherless home. Emphasis on male parenting diminished as fathers turned their interest and energy into the work world and withdrew their ties to family life. It seems to me that the separation of work and home was one aspect of the vast breach between domestic life and social life that had been developing since the early reorganization of society in the industrial age. Under these conditions, male children had to scrounge a sense of maleness and achieve their identity by differentiating themselves from their female caretakers more than by identifying with their fathers. Instead of immersion in the murderous Oedipal rivalry that Freud described in *Totem and Taboo*,[8] male children found themselves either pushed by their mother into premature separation individuation or fighting off their mother's desires for a male partner at home.[9]

Female children, destined for domestic life and motherhood, might find their identity or sense of self by not finding it. Drawn into a merger with mother or prescribed as her alter ego, the only escape was in the relationship with father; but this access led back to truncation and confinement. As daddy's girl, the little girl or adolescent young woman might rehearse the role of wife and mother. Freud had stressed the compensatory functions of the daughter's turn to her father: recognizing her castration she turned to him, searching for the penis = baby substitute. Chodorow, on the other hand, stresses the new interest in the father as a way of escaping the engulfment by the mother. But neither theory points to the achievement of an individuated adult personality for women. Chodorow interprets the perpetuation of women's special development:

That these issues become more important for girls than for boys is the product of children of both genders growing up in families where women, who have a greater sense of sameness with daughters than sons, perform primary parenting functions. As long as women mother, we can expect that a girl's preoedipal period will be longer than that of a boy and that women, more than men, will be more open to and preoccupied with those very relational issues that go into mothering, feelings of primary identification, lack of separateness or differentiation, ego and body ego boundary issues and primary love not under the sway of the reality principle. The girl does not simply identify with her mother or want to be like her, rather mother and daughter maintain elements of their primary relationship, which means they will feel alike in fundamental ways.[10]

Although Chodorow emphasizes the impact on women's development when only women mother, both male and female development is skewed. Primary bonding processes are disturbed if the male infant is phantasized by mother as the hero of separateness and individuation. Moreover, the little boy subject is further burdened by the necessity to play a character in his mother's inner world rather than evolving as himself. Analogously, girl infants and children are prevented from finding their autonomous and assertive potential.

Chodorow's critical theories focus primarily on the phenomena of the perpetuation of family and gender arrangements. As she deconstructs the "reproduction of motherhood," her analysis remains at the level of the interaction of social patterns and the formation of the parameters of gender. In part the etiology of the separation of the sexes is an aspect of the internal world of identification, with splitting of the self as well.

The creation of gender dichotomy emphasizes complex internal processes as well as cultural ones. Boys raised by women but encouraged to become public, active, striving types, split themselves. They projectively identify with their mothers and sisters, allowing them to carry or be their feminine self. They are thus consciously distanced from a large part of their personality (horizontal split). Girls raised primarily by women and encouraged to be a replica of their mothers, domestic, caretaking, and even self-sacrificing and passive, would necessarily split off their male side and male qualities allowing men to carry them albeit bifurcating their self structures as well. Under this system, each gender is tied to the other not in a complementary way; each is in search of the recovery of its lost self and also in fear of the brutal return of the disavowed, which leads to fear of the other sex.[11]

Thus, in their totality both men and women are merged with mother and separated like father. Furthermore, aspects of the self and of the two parents that remain unconscious are doomed to repetition until integration and acknowledgment take place. In addition, gender and family patterns reflect deep motivations that are known to us in their biased forms of social and personal mythologies. In her book *The Mermaid and the Minotaur: Sexual Arrangements and Human Malaise,* Dorothy Dinnerstein analyzes mother-child, male-female familial relationships through the prism of infantile phantasies. She states that as infants are reared and nurtured by mothers almost exclusively, they associate the infantile experiences of helplessness and intense experiences of pleasure and pain with the partner of their early symbiosis.[12] Dinnerstein, following Freud and Melanie Klein, understands the infant's affective phantasies to be the structure of the infant's mental life. She proposes that the bifurcation of mothering and external public affairs is rooted in the bifurcation of the infant's mind.[13]

> The male-governed, world-making enterprise has had as its heart then, our ongoing struggle against our own infantilism, our ongoing struggle to carve out and fence around a realm for the exercise of sober self-reliance. It is true that this realm, insofar as we have succeeded in carving it out, is polluted in important ways, increasingly polluted as the enterprise goes forward, with bluff, with death-ridden pseudo-activity. It is true also that to counterbalance our own boldness and daring even feebly to try to grow up we go on paying heavily hostile, costly, magic homage to the original magic protector; not to woman herself but an abstraction of woman as captive goddess of an archaic realm. Still the attempt to grow up, however equivocally made—is in each life a step forward.[14]

Dinnerstein goes on to propose that the fear of mortality is associated with contact of one's own body with the flesh of the mother's body in all its delightful and terrifying ways.

> That we are born mortal now gets its meaning from other grievances against the body which develop before we discover that it was born and will therefore die, and which later meld together with this discovery into one global rage. For this rage, woman, who both bore and raised the body, is at present the natural target.[15]

In Dinnerstein's view, the exclusivity of female child rearing is a method for splitting the responsibility of bearing the force of infantile affects of helplessness, fear, and rage. The fallout from primitive emotions attaches almost exclusively to mother's image. In this way the memories and derivatives of infantile experience are segregated and associated with mother, home, and personal family life. However, Dinnerstein notes that their absence from the public world of politics, economics, and foreign affairs promotes policies of indifference and noncontrolled violence. The "male" individual, creating history and culture, cut off from his vulnerability, desires, and phantasies (they are left at home, inside the woman's circle or inside the internal "woman" aspect of his self), seeks the satisfaction and consolation of his feeling body self through greed and megalomania. Following this pattern, he has never reconnected with his lost child self and attempts again to "find himself" in projects of mastery and self-aggrandizement.[16] The masculine character described here is a cultural tautology. Clearly, unemployed male workers may believe in male superiority but find little opportunity to enjoy these kinds of omnipotent phantasies, while "successful males" in fact increase the danger to their longevity in several significant ways.

Though Dinnerstein's hypothesis works from a theory of unconscious phantasies, she like Chodorow believes that changes in parenting arrangements would bring about changes in attitudes toward motherhood and mothering and toward infants and children. She believes that as both men and women assume the responsibility of parenting, the deeper archaic contents of mental life (characteristic of but not exclusive to infancy) will not be segregated (repressed) from the public sphere. She believes that culture will then be changed through the integration of personal and public aspects of that culture.

It seems to me that Dinnerstein's and Chodorow's hypothesis that the restructuring of child-rearing customs will modify concepts of gender, family relations, and ultimately social values is useful but incomplete in that their analysis assumes that external change might in turn change deep unconscious structures that in part grow from innate programming for survival, attachment, and the quest for meaning. At least Dinnerstein's analysis leads us into the processes of phantasy and the signification of passionate and primitive feelings. Infants live at the edge of intense experiences of pleasure and pain. These experiences are powerful and antithetical to conscious civilized life, as Freud had already maintained in his theory of infantile amnesia. Furthermore, unconscious structures are associated with emotional intensity that is persistent and difficult to transform in the individual personality as well as in the group. These feelings and phantasies are repressed, but they remain associated with women and are denied and/or distorted, surfacing in the public sphere as grotesque opposites. Chodorow, on the other hand, relies on certain aspects of the psychoanalytic theory of pre-Oedipal development and modern developmental theory of separation individuation. She uses the notion of the infant's early boundary relationships to mother to explain the profound ways that a girl or a boy is made into a culturally defined woman or man.

My view is somewhat different. The "man" or "woman" that family and culture requires develops out of the individual or group needs for assurance of survival and potency. This leads me to suggest that the notion that only women mother needs to be investigated from other perspectives. I would like to raise the idea that the fear of not being mothered is the latent motivation that creates rationales for perpetuating female-dominated child rearing of the next generation. All societies have had serious difficulties caring for their young, but modern secular society raises the new concern of individual selfishness known in ideologies of the quest for personal fulfillment. The new ideologies reflect the possibility of freedom for mothers, posing a painful and fearful question. What would hold them, then, at home? The history of the nineteenth century makes clear both new realizations of child nature and the need for special nurture and intense worries that human mothering in its previous forms would not be adequate to the new knowledge and circumstance; hence the obsessive concern for what motherhood should be. The twentieth century has seen a deepening of the appreciation of infants' nature and their needs, but also at the same time the anxieties surrounding the new knowlege of infants' intense requirements and women's liberation which opens the door for women to escape from enforced domesticity have greatly disturbed the old myths and ideologies. In modern life, as the universal passion play of separation from mother's body into individuated life becomes ever more understood and encouraged, the intense need for the maternal matrix increases.[17] The desperate rationale for women's limited and specific nature reflects not only the manifestation of ancient themes gathered together around the formation of the maternal goddess icon as the source of life but also new themes growing out of the increasing consciousness of the depth and complexity of human mental life commencing at birth or before. It seems to me that the first priority for "deconstructing motherhood" in its limited and possessed forms is to uncover the full range and potency of maternity hidden within the codes and myths which disguise its underlying meaning and full power.

The French feminist psychoanalytic critics Luce Irigaray, Julia Kristeva, and Hélène Cixous approach the concept of motherhood in this way. Using Lacanian theories in addition to those of Freud, they propose that the metaphor of maternity and of the mother's body locates a richer meaning that precedes the signs of language. They believe that the language spoken between infant and mother carries the living meaning of signs and symbols which the law of the father represses too brutally. The French school trio applies the metaphors of the madonna, maternité, écriture féminine, and Kristeva's notion of the infant semiotic to explore the nature, function, and power of the mother's body and mind in relation to the mother and infant's experience of pregnancy, birth, and nursing.[18] They suggest that the potency and efficacy of the mother's early mental symbiosis with the infant and the archaic hermeneutics of that relationship are the wellspring of culture; but they charge that the emotions and values associated with these deep states of mind have been dammed up or barred from the symbolic discourse of society and civilization to the extent that the symbolic order of Western civilization operates on a phallic-centered bias. In Irigaray's book *Speculum of the Other Woman,* she in fact argues that the fallacy of presence and certitude dominates the values of Western thought and defines woman's place in culture as nonpresent, nonexistent, or that of the "other."

The new French feminists employ many of Lacan's central theoretical notions to release the exiled and imprisoned elements of pre-Oedipal or prelinguistic experiences. But at the same time, they employ his ideas to deconstruct his notion of phallocentrism. Lacan followed Freud in interpreting outer culture as a creation of male sublimation. Freud's theory of the resolution of the Oedipus complex in some aspects followed the values of Western logocentrism based on the system of binary oppositions, for example, in which one of the terms, man/woman, is valued at the expense of the other.[19] Qualities of presence, familiarity, and wholeness are valued over those of absence, strangeness, and secrecy or mystery. Freud and

Lacan developed a myth of psychosocial development based on presence, though the theory of the unconscious allows for an exploration of the unseen and the unknown. Freud theorized that only male sexual development led to full intellectual and emotional realizations. Boy children repressed their desire for mother's body under the dread of castration. The boy's superego developing out of fear of the father's wrath in competition for mother's body prohibited his desire and demanded repression and sublimation. Freud emphasized that the potential actuality of castration challenged the ego in alliance with the superego to achieve sublimations of a worthy sort. Girls, on the other hand, met with difficulty in the phallic stage. After suffering the disappointment of the discovery of an inferior organ, they were brought to a resignation in which they reconciled themselves to their inferior anatomy. Additionally, rather than being motivated by the fear of castration, they suffered the sadness of its actuality. The feminine superego, formed out of less terror and more subtle fears of loss, was itself less intense and less demanding, such that the superior sublimations of art and science fell to men. Furthermore, women suffering the pain of "inferior" anatomy turned to the father in search of compensation for the lost privileged organ and found it later in marriage and babies. Civilization was then built from the encounters of fathers and sons, as visibility and familiarity determined a superior and more complete maturation with a full invitation to enter the public world.

While Lacan understood the Oedipus complex in somewhat different terms than did Freud, Lacan shared with Freud the notion that society and culture are manmade. For the libidinal phases and the installation of the superego, Lacan substituted the law of language or the law of the father. Lacan arrived at his theory of culture through the notion of the symbolic ordering of individual mental life and of the group. He was influenced by Ferdinand de Saussure's linguistic studies and Lévi-Strauss's work in anthropology, the latter applying the universal laws of language to cultural coding. Lévi-Strauss determined that all societies are regulated by a series of signs, rituals, and mythological structures which organize and signify through language-like laws of relational differences.[20] Lévi-Strauss called the signifying system "the symbolic order." He stressed that the rituals, rites, and belief systems not only order culture but reflect the functioning of the human unconscious, which he described as a symbol-forming organ. For Lévi-Strauss, laws regulating kinship and the exchange of women and prohibiting and defining incest develop out of the innate structuring capacities of the physiological mental apparatus.[21]

Lacan, extrapolating from Freud and Lévi-Strauss, transformed the founding laws of society from the law of incest to the law of the patronym. The law of the father is based on the authority of father's name, le nom, and his no ("non"), in which both familial and social identity are invested.[22] Lacan also designated these laws as the symbolic order, which he believed is already in place in society itself and must be accepted and internalized by the child in order to function adequately as a social subject. Through language the subject internalizes the values, sets of rules, and behavior given by the language system, codes, and myths of his or her society.[23] At the same time, the capacity to code his or her experience and to create laws for him or herself contributes to the field in such a way that the values of the next generation are added to the existing motivations and values of societal preferences.

Both Freud and Lacan believed that certain structures of the symbolic order are universal and enduring. One of the eternal structures is the Oedipus complex, which the feminist theorists suggest is structured on the boy's experience of the Oedipal situation while underestimating the girl child's struggle with this developmental crisis.[24] The whole problem of how the Oedipus complex is resolved for males but never for females is the central question which the feminists have taken up against both Freud and Lacan. Lacan suffered from the same blind spot as did Freud in formulating the idea of a woman in society and culture. Lacan believed that woman as a concept could never come into existence because the Oedipus complex brings the little girl into *masculine* unconscious structures, masculine because they are created by the acceptance of patriarchal law.[25]

The French feminists enter their protests at this point in Lacan's thinking in order to break the imperfect closed cycle of patriarchal culture producing only full development for male children. They also set out to rediscover female epigenesis in all its aspects. In their search for female development, Irigaray, Cixous, and Kristeva found a bifurcation between the language of the early mother-infant relationship and the symbolic order. Lacan had explained that the law of language stands outside of the mother-infant experience until the Oedipus complex intervenes, confronting the child with the awareness of separation and "not-me" phenomena.[26] Winnicott used the term "not-me" to designate the awareness of phenomena and objects which took place outside the narcissistic self. Falling from paradise into the laws of time and space, the maturing child became socialized and acculturated. In this way, Freud's patriarchal superego, the legacy of the libidinal phases, is superseded by Lacan's notions of the signifier/signified relationship (including abstraction and representation) and ultimately the loss of the tactile relation to the mother's body.[27] The old criticism against Freud's bias that women were destined by anatomy and nature to a defective development led to a feminist argument against biological determinism. Lacan's theory of the resolution of the Oedipus complex as a fall into language and its laws allowed for feminist arguments to unfold in the realm of semiotics. Although they find Lacan's notion of the symbolic order flawed, Kristeva, Irigaray, and Cixous direct their new criticism toward the area of the play of the signifier. The construction of meaning, values, and myths as part of the signification process can be deconstructed or demythified in contradiction to values etched in the flesh. As part of their new strategy, feminist writers oppose the very ordering of the symbolic order.

Lacan's notion of the phallus as a transcendental signifier[28] is a central focus of their deconstruction of his theory.[29]

Jane Gallop's essay "Of Phallic Proportions: A Lacanian Conceit" provides us with an example of deconstruction from inside the Lacanian system.[30] In considering the organization of sexual difference in language Gallop focuses on Lacan's use of the phallus as "a privileged signifier." Lacan had described the phallus as the signifier intended to designate as a whole the effects of the signified in that the signifier conditions them by its presence as signifier.[31] Gallop takes umbrage at Lacan's notion of the transcendental signifier and asks the reader: by what right does this portion signify, or represent, the whole? She develops her discussion around the play of the words "whole" and "hole," and the use of a metonymy to contrast the phallic conceit: the part standing for the whole, standing for the hole. In elaborating the phallic conceit, Gallop interprets male fears of women exploring their deepest sources. She contrasts the intimidating phallic mother who is felt to be "whole," omnipotent and omniscient with the fear of the hole—castration imagined or complete[32] and suggests that Lacan's phallus reiterates Freud's skewed understanding of the human family and of sexual difference.[33] She stresses the bifurcation in Freud's theory, with women and children on the one hand associated with the domestic realm, and men with the development of culture and civilization on the other.[34]

As part of her analysis of Lacan's concept of the phallus, Gallop elaborates the importance of presence and wholeness associated with sighting. "Sexual difference takes its actual devise of significance upon a sighting. The privilege of the phallus as presence for the concomitant disappearance of any female genitalia under the phallic order is based on the privilege of sight over other senses."[35] The fears associated with separation from mother's body are denied and turned into a triumph of the penis while the concept woman is designated with the onus of the hole (incompleteness) for both sexes. Gallop calls our attention to Freud's theory of the relationship of civilization and the senses. She explains that he believed that the creation of higher civilized culture was linked with the higher order sense of sight, while smell was understood as a carry-over from early, archaic sexual patterns.[36] According to Freud, before the triumph of the eye over the nose, the menstrual process produced an effect on the male psyche by means of olfactory stimuli.[37] The visual mode is associated with abstraction and representation and the mastery of instinctual forces. The "odor di femina" becomes odious because it threatens to undo the achievement of repression and civilization and threatens to return the subject to the experience of powerlessness, intensity, and anxiety of an immediate and unmediated connection to the mother's body[38] (or the loss of it).

Extrapolating from Freud's theory of male civilization, Gallop suggests that men in culture are thus doomed by the repression of the olfactory to sublimation of their basic sexuality to an incomplete satisfaction. Lacan describes this sacrifice of complete satisfaction as castration.[39] This sacrifice is necessary to the attainment of social gender identity. Thus cultural man is sentenced to an endless metonymic search for satisfaction which will always be incomplete.[40] Gallop explains that, for men, desire is metonymical impotence—the frustrated search along a decentered chain of signifiers. Feminine sexuality is not structured in the same way:

> the difference is that desire is metonymical impatience, anticipation pressing ever forward so as to close signification. Whereas feminine sexuality is a *jouissance* enveloped in its own contiguity. Such *jouissance* would be sparks of pleasure ignited at any point along the line, not waiting for closure, but enjoying the touching.[41]

From one point of view, Gallop and other feminist theorists misinterpret Lacan's metapsychology and overlook Lacan's emphasis—that he is always talking about the way in which sexual difference comes to be *signified*.[42] In fact, Lacan insists that sexual difference is known only as a symbolic structure—based on the juxtaposition of the signifiers man/woman. Lacan theorized that the subject is constituted through language. In the space after separation from mother's body, incompleteness (lack), desire, and identity are represented in an order outside the subject, as the subject becomes the subject of speech (Lacan's parler-être). Desire for wholeness, for the "other," promotes concepts of sexual identity whereby each sex mythically offers completeness and gratification to the other.[43] Furthermore, the phallus as a signifier "stands for that moment when prohibition must function,"[44] in the sense that seen through the function of language, the presence or absence of the phallus figures sexual difference rather than the reverse.

The flaw in Lacan's theory that disturbs the feminists is an emphasis on difference with the superiority of presence over absence. While Lacan thinks that the phallus is purely a symbolic structure and that the paternal metaphor stands for the symbolic function itself—*representation through substitution*—he cannot overcome the logic of the polarization of mother/child/presymbolic—father/child/symbolic order. Lacan cannot free himself from the traditional notions of sexual difference even as he insists on its fabrication through the symbol process.

Thus, the critical analysis of Cixous, Irigaray, and Kristeva focuses on the dichotomy between phallocentrism (made up of male sublimations) and maternal or female *jouissance*, including the mother-infant experience.[45] The feminist disagreement with Lacan's theory of the symbolic order therefore changes the parameters of the discussion about sexual difference. The old formulas regarding the place of men and women in society and the nature of the cultural web of values, customs, and language structures which carry concepts of difference are unmasked as based not only on hierarchical oppositions but also on a denial of experience with the mother's body.

The French critics found an ally and a methodological approach in Derrida, who in his way opposes Lacan's notion of the symbolic order as phal-locentric and logocentric.[46] Derrida's deconstructive efforts go so far as to challenge Western metaphysics and philosophy. Also, his notion of *différance* upsets the system of hierarchies which holds that something exists prior to differences; something exists in and of itself as origin, as giver of meaning, as transcendental signified, explaining and organizing and ordering everything else.[47] Instead of the superior/inferior value system, Derrida put forward a theory of equal relations. In addition, he insists on the dismantling of the notion of one subject and the basic assumptions on which any text is based. Through Derrida's critique of the assumptions of the binary conceptual system and the belief that there is one meaning, feminist writers found a way to deconstruct Lacan and even psychoanalysis itself. As they found themselves within a system of thought which defined woman as outsider, strange, inferior, or weird[48] they challenged the values of language and signification of women. They stressed that "woman," associated with pregnancy, birth, and child rearing, is placed in a category outside social discourse; then the full meaning of woman is repressed along with the sensual and archaic relationship to the mother's body.[49] Thus, following Derrida and challenging Lacan, Irigaray, Cixous, and Kristeva invent a new form of writing called écriture féminine which is opposed to the system of binary difference and the existing coding of sexual difference. Écriture féminine speaks from the babybody discourse.

Irigaray, Cixous, and Kristeva seek their release from language by diving into the internal world, pressing deeply into the area of the preverbal of their own minds and into the preverbal underpinnings of their culture. Each woman discovers there the potency and functions of the maternal figure and sets out to bring its value into the cultural discourse through the restructuring of their writing which "flows from the experience of the infant-mother's body experience."[50] Thus, not only do they recuperate their own subjectivity through the acts of writing and thinking, but they initiate a search for a cure for a culture which in their view is ill with the principles of phallocentrism. Their metaphor of maternity encompasses many themes opposed to cultural codes based on presence and the erection of ultimate authority. The maternal metaphor acts as a semiotic instrument to invoke the unrepresentable and absent aspects excluded from the mainstream of "father"-dominated culture.[51]

Unlike the American writers, the French feminists construct their notion of maternal difference on the symbolic and the imaginary rather than the "real" of the historical.[52] Irigaray argues that in order to achieve cultural innovation women must call for another syntax, another grammar of culture. In "Le Corps à corps avec la mère" and "Amante Marin"[53] she declares the murder of the mother to be the foundation of Western culture and society. "Thus, to think of the mother in every woman and the woman in every mother is a forbidden act that will undermine the patriarchal culture and bring about a revolutionary ethic of sexual difference.[54]

Irigaray's *Speculum de l'Autre Femme* (1974) is a massive project for the deconstruction of the concepts of woman as found in culture. Her scrutiny of Western thought from Plato to Freud describes the blind spot of symmetry which defines women as other or the negative to the positive of maleness.[55] The process of Irigaray's deconstruction reiterates the content of her attack. She accomplishes this by refusing the authoritative reading approach to the text and by intimating a plurality of meanings and fully exploring the possible ambiguity in language; in other words, substituting a new kind of symbolic or new use of language.[56] Irigaray argues that women's sexuality, desire, and style of language differs from the male counterpart. Rejecting the notions of deficiency and lack, Irigaray explains women's mental functioning as based on a different experience with the world. "Woman's desire most likely does not speak the same language as men's desire and it probably has been covered over by the logic that has dominated the West since the Greeks." She argues that in fact women's desire is less confined and sets the model for écriture féminine. "The geography of woman has sex organized just about everywhere and thus her pleasure is much more diversified, more multiple in its difference, more complex, more subtle."[57] She suggests that the nature of women's relating and thinking is not based on hierarchical oppositions and the known but rather on associations, simultaneity, and equality.

Irigaray then goes on to pose the serious question, "How are women to find themselves as equal subjects and to discover their difference from men if they are socialized in the symbolic order?" She reminds women that they might find their subject selves through a common discourse. She encourages a mother-daughter discourse as a source for the new speaking subject. In "The One Doesn't Stir Without the Other"[58] she reveals the misuse of the mother-daughter relationship and its future potential as well. In this paper Irigaray unpacks the sort of mother figure whose mothering covers the gaps of her limited existence. The daughter confronts her mother with women's cloying fusion, the merger which denies personhood. The daughter asks her mother how the discovery of her individuality affects her? "If I leave, you no longer find yourself. Was I not the bail to keep you from disappearing? The guardian of your non-existence?"[59] The daughter urges her mother to break the confinement and silence of women and to find the language of women to forge a new symbolic which includes the mother's body and mind and all sorts of female experience. "But we have never, never spoken to each other and such an abyss separates us that I could never leave you whole, for I am always shrouded in shadows, captive in our confinement." As the daughter concludes with an urgent plea—that they both live—she states: "And what I wanted from you mother was this: that in giving me life you still remained alive."[60]

In "Our Lips Speak Together," Irigaray proposes the etiology of woman's language or "l'écriture féminine" through the discovery and recitation of the language between mother and child. In this context, Irigaray devises a challenge to formal syntax and grammar which she replaces with the use of double or multiple voices, broken syntax, and repetitive rather than linear structure.[61] The speaker speaks to her double about the dangers of speaking and thinking within the male symbolic order. She says,

> If we keep on speaking the same language together we're going to re-produce the same history, begin the same old stories all over again. Don't you think so? Listen. All around us, the same discussion, the same arguments, the same scenes. . . . If we keep on speaking sameness, if we speak to each other as men have been doing for centuries as we have been taught to speak, we'll miss each other, fail ourselves again. Words will pass through our bodies, above our heads, they'll vanish and we'll be lost."[62]

The subject speaker proposes that her partner come out of symbolic language and plunge into the experiences of the preverbal, immediate, and sensual contact. Two mouths stand for multiple channels of connection. "Open your lips, don't open them simply. I don't open them simply. We-you-I are neither open nor closed. We never separate simply; *a single word* cannot be pronounced, produced, uttered by our mouths. Between our lips, yours and mine, several voices, several ways of speaking resound endlessly back and forth."[63]

Irigaray's persona seeks to break the authority of the one subject which she connects with male superiority and the logic of hierarchical opposition. She says:

> We haven't been taught, not allowed to express multiplicity. To do that is to speak improperly. Of course we might, we're supposed to exhibit one truth while sensing withholding muffling another. Truths are the side and its complement; its remainder stays hidden, secret.[64]

The speaker proposes to invent a new language to find a body language as the mode of signifying and experiencing another truth, the other truth. Irigaray employs *parler femme*, speaking as a woman, as the means to reach into the underside of the symbolic order, and applies the metaphor of maternity to the experiences underneath the cultural signs in order to replace the concept of woman as either nonexistent or an object of exchange (as sign). *Parler femme* resurrects the concept of woman as a subject or transcendental being with a consciousness and a voice who generates meaning on her own.[65] Irigaray believes that the woman subject can only be birthed by breaking the old syntax and finding a new language.

Hélène Cixous develops her theory of écriture féminine around the contours of the metaphoric maternal body. She challenges the symbolic order as articulated by Freud and Lacan defining woman as lack and suggests instead that culture stems from the mother's body, out of the abundant life forces of pregnancy and nursing and the processes of the rhythms and images of the unconsious.

> She is giving birth with the strength of a lioness, of a planet or a cosmogeny of a woman . . . a desire for the text! Confusion! What possesses her? A child! Paper! Intoxications! I'm overflowing! My breasts overflow! Milk ink. The moment of suckling. And I? I too am hungry. The taste of milk. Of ink.[66]

Cixous emphasies the pre-Oedipal in a way that overcomes undervaluation of the languages of experiences taking place in the body ego of the infant with mother's body while privileging the logical discourse of the adult coded in the symbolic order.[67] Freud had touched on the prehistory of woman and the deep attachment to the mother of early years. He argued that girl children had great difficulty getting past their primary love and attachment to their mothers. He proposed that the original satisfying relationship with mother was never finally given up and was brought to the marriage bed. Freud applied the pre-Oedipal "Mycenaean Civilization" to females only. Strange that we now call the earlier time "pre-Oedipal."[68] Although today we appreciate the notion that infants of both sexes pass through the odyssey of a preverbal, presymbolic relationship to the mother then through the resolution of the Oedipal crisis to the realm of symbolic laws, until very recently only male development has been thought to reach the destination of outer culture. Cixous, like Irigaray, resuscitates the notion of the pre-Oedipal to provide the function of an incubator for the future feminine.[69] Her description of the female pre-Oedipal is as a burial as well as a promise of the future.

> As if they were buried alive between the breasts under the clay curtains, in the chest, behind the fertile lungs, a woman in the cradle hardly conceived, already perfectly formed, a living presence . . . daughter of woman, a female in gender without father, fruit of mother love, the kind that can be conceived *naturally* only in the regions of preoedipal culture.[70]

Cixous insists that women, abducted and buried alive like Persephone, must delve into their archaic origins even within their tomb while emerging then to the surface where discourse takes place. Cixous believes that the deep and the past of the mind can be recaptured for a rebeginning through the de-repression of unconscious archaic memories.[71] Cixous, like Irigaray, employs écriture féminine as a mode of subversion of the symbolic order. The feminine or maternal voice (as literal speech) contains the mother's song, "a song before the law—before the symbolic took one's breath away."[72]

Women's writing or voice is opposed to male writing because it maintains a connection to the infant or child with mother as known through both breast and voice.

> In woman there is always more or less something of a mother, repairing and feeding, resisting separation, a force that just does not let itself be cut off but that runs codes ragged.[73]

The meanings which flow from the mother's body are linked by Cixous with ongoing giving and nurturing; she designates great significance to the pregnant woman as the source of life and of the original spring of meaning.[74] Cixous urges that women silenced and obliterated by the particular split between the pre-Oedipal and the symbolic order struggle to speak of and from themselves and challenge the profound chasm between men and women, infant and adult, and between language and unconscious discourse. Cixous works to release underlying forces and to allow their entry into language itself.

Julia Kristeva also explores the pre-Oedipal as a source of subversive activity. She formally defines the language between mother and child as the semiotic (le sémiotique),[75] a prelinguistic, sensual activity which sets the body rhythms of poetry against the linear structures and codified representations of the symbolic.[76] Kristeva understands le sémiotique as the mode of communication at the time of the infant's intense attachment to the mother's body before clear differentiation is achieved. The semiotic or primitive sign[77] reflects and draws on the rhythms of sensual contact and the forces of the drives expressed between infant and mother. Kristeva proposes le sémiotique as a structure of meaning which precedes those of the symbolic order. Lacan's mirror stage, in which the mirror image of the self introduces the infant to the awareness of absence and his/her own lack initiates the space of representation and the capacity for abstraction which in turn allows the signification process to develop in its mature form. Kristeva adds that the thetic (giving meaning through gesture and enunciation) develops only within the new psychic space (the opening vista of differentiation) and ends the exclusive reign of le sémiotique while initiating the child into language.[78] Le sémiotique now works in a dialectical relationship to the symbolic. Much like the model of Freud's dream work, le sémiotique continues by emerging in various forms as the compromised formations of secondary revision or as its alter ego seen in slips, puns, and dreams, and also in psychosis.[79]

The semiotic disposition as designated by Kristeva is language before language, which carries forces and meanings so powerful that neither obliteration nor integration is entirely possible.[80] However, Kristeva suggests that the representation of the unrepresentable is possible under different rules than the ones that guide the symbolic order as spoken under the law of the father. Kristeva proposes in the present system prelinguistic experiences suffer exile alongside the figure of the pre-Oedipal mother.

Kristeva explains in her theory of *le sémiotique* that the semiotic originally draws from other elements of mental life that are at the edge of the abyss of meaninglessness or the horrors of strange forces which she designates as the abject. She explains, "The abject confronts us on the one hand, with these fragile states where man strays on the territories of the animal." She adds that primitive societies show us these unconscious links between the animal totem and sex, murder, the polluted and the unholy.[81] Kristeva states that *le sémiotique* gathers meaning out of formless and meaningless states. Before this process begins the earliest self is drawn into a place where meaning either collapses or never comes together. Primary narcissism bringing the organization of significance through phantasies and dreams pulls the infant out of distant galaxies into the sphere of human mental life.

Thus the abject is found at the edge of primary repression, the place where the at-one-ment of mother and baby is rejected by the infant in his/her struggle with the overflowing delights of merger and in an act of mental birth, *le sémiotique* begins and initiates phantasy and primitive thought. In other words, Kristeva proposes that meaning as it evolves at the boundary of what can be known grows from the wellsprings of biological presocial, deep affectual sources.

Kristeva theorizes that *le sémiotique* as the transitional structure between the abject and sane meaning is the underpinning of language and that its contents and forces challenge the language of "men" used in public discourse. She notes that it is only in regression, in privileged moments of art and creativity or in psychosis that the subject re-enters this prelinguistic field of archaic processes.[82] Kristeva argues that phallocentrism as it is constructed is maintained at the expense of the archaic and prelinguistic contents of the mind. Her interpretation of maternity as the gateway to the presymbolic invites a challenge to the existing bifurcation between the maternal metaphor and the paternal metaphor.

Kristeva's own interpretation of the meaning and functions of the icons of maternity seen in the madonna (the mother's mind and body) is that they function as organizing structures against preverbal chaos and as an anchor for the nonverbal modes of signification close to primary process.[83] From these ideas she outlines the concept of a fundamental discovery crucial to the understanding of the history of parent-child relations. Recent psychoanalytic theories of mental development and current interest in the myths and realities of family life have made clear some aspects of the etiology of the bifurcation that these French feminists are responding to.

Western history of childhood tells us that a notion of the development of the infantile mind and the parents' function in that development has only very recently become conscious. Pre-modern, pre-twentieth century concepts of child rearing were filled with superstition and fear. Partly because many babies died in the first year and many more died before the age of five, parents showed little personal attachment to their offspring.[84]

Until recent times motherhood was a concept closely associated with death.[85] Not only did many infants and children die early, but epidemics and lack of good nutrition and medical sophistication meant that a large portion of the family might be cut down within a few days. Although infant mortality has fallen steadily for the past 200 years, it remained relatively high until early in this century.[86] The effects of such constant and severe loss worked as a powerful inhibiting force on parents' feelings for their children. In this regard, Lloyd Demause reveals peculiar and cool attitudes throughout human history. He states that empathy for infants and children is a recent phenomenon and that the record shows not only an awkward insensitivity to infantile experience but clearly hatred and indifference.[87] Infanticide, abandonment, and swaddling[88] were common modes of treatment of babies. Ariés suggests that concepts of childhood and infancy were slow in emerging, but secularization and modernity provided the material for more defined categories of the stages of the life cycle. An attachment to this world, confidence in survival, and the discovery of personal will and need led to the appreciation of personal parent-child relations and a concept of children as special and in need of gentle, segregated training.[89]

Lloyd Demause's essay "The Evolution of Childhood" implies, as the title suggests, some improvement within parent-child relations. He hypothesizes that each generation of parents incorporates from their parents more benign attitudes toward children accompanied by a gradual increase of the capacity to tolerate, interpret, and soothe the infant's primitive states of mind which include intense needs and fears as well as perpetual passionate engagement. Recent studies in psychoanalytic theory of infant development including infant observation[90] posit that the mother-infant relationship as a team is the heart of the baby's development. Without the partner as selfobject or maternal environment or container,[91] the infant's epigenesis is severely changed, and in extreme cases leads to premature aging and death, as Spitz's studies on marasmus make clear. In this way, "mothering" is a function of survival, both for the individual and the race.

Melanie Klein, an early explorer and archaeologist of the pre-Oedipal and archaic levels of mental life, made important discoveries about primitive mental states. In a series of spectacular papers written from 1919 to the early 1960s,[92] Klein mapped a developmental exploration of the archaic deep substrata of the infant's mind including infantile phantasies of mother and child relations. Powerfully influenced by Freud, she elaborated on his theories of the unconscious and the influences and functions of the instincts in mental development, both supplementing his notions and challenging them. Klein's interest lay not only in the child in the adult, but in the chronological infant him- or herself. Through her own family experiences and her clinical work with children[93] as young as two, and for over forty years, Klein formulated a theory of mental life dating from the earliest days of postnatal life.

Following Freud's theory of phylogenetic knowledge encoded within the instincts or drives, she theorized that the infant was endowed with biological potentials that were lived out in phantasied relations between the baby and the mother. She also drew on Freud's notion that instinctual knowledge made itself known in universal phantasies such as the Oedipus complex. Klein, however, believed that these phantasies of Oedipal triangulation surfaced not at three years of age but along with the emergence of mental life itself. While Freud's archaeology led him to notions of the primal scene, castration anxiety, seduction, and death wishes,[94] Klein added images based on an early relationship to the mother's body and father's and siblings' relation to it as well. She believed a group of diverse phantasies rose from the ground of innate instinctual forces and the infant's experience seen through the lens of the life and death instincts. She believed that the death instinct, mobilized at birth and felt as annihilation anxiety, stimulated phantasies of attack. The life instinct, realized through gratifying experiences of nurture and safety as well as innate potential, proliferated images of a beneficent breast and a loving relationship with an aspect of mother signified by body parts. Klein named the period of early phantasied object relations to part aspects of the primary objects the paranoid-schizoid position.[95] The designation grew from her notion that the infant not only builds up internal characters (objects) out of the processes of projection and introjection of instinctual forces, but split the good image from the bad inside the early ego (self).[96] These imagos, the good breast and bad, were also cyclically reprojected into the external figure, seriously modifying the experience between mother and child externally as well as internally.

Thus, according to Klein's theories, the infant sends messages to mother based on instinctual knowledge or codes built into the infant's perceptual, cognitive, and motor apparatus.[97] Klein tended to emphasize the inevitability of the dark influence of the death instincts, but Wilfred Bion, an English psychoanalyst who trained with Klein, emphasized the manner in which mother receives, detoxifies, and participates in these primitive experiences of body and affect.[98] Klein's emphasis on the innate influence of the infant's destructiveness was probably influenced by her era and the culture's distrust and confusion and even ignorance about the infant's nature. Victorians including Freud himself openly distrusted the passion of the body associated with sex and immaturity.[99] Klein emphasized the infant's constitutional nature in managing the instincts and separating the good from the bad more than she emphasized the environmental factors, including the empathy and devotion of the parenting ones.

According to Klein, the infant subject is an active, vigorous participant in the creation of his/her phantasies or semiotics. The death instinct, Klein felt, was experienced and interpreted by the infant as a battle with not-me experiences. These were depicted according to the seriousness of the constitutional or environmental trauma as a pageant of penetrating, devouring, and robbing activities toward the enemy which was kept separate from the beneficial persona by splitting. Klein supposed that as the infant phantasized a real attack had been made in or on the flesh, he or she felt persecuted by the object's wish to retaliate. Klein suggested that in time, as the infant matured and gained ego strength and was able to integrate the evil and the beneficent images, he or she realized that the beloved mother was the same entity as the hated one. Here guilt replaced persecutory anxiety and reparative impulses replaced those of attack. At this time, reality became more viable and phantasies were tempered by a sense of otherness.

In Klein's theory of infantile mental development, the infant's release from the prison of his/her instinctual endowment and preconceptions depended on ego strength and good parenting. Good enough mothering, stressed by Winnicott and Bowlby, was not powerful enough to break Klein's cycle.[100] The solution lay in the ego's integrative capacities. In the second quarter of the first year, the infant's ego developed the capacity for integration. Also, appreciation of reality challenged the fantastic omnipotent images of the paranoid-schizoid position. Klein designated these new capacities as taking place in the depressive position. She stressed that in this phase the integration of negative and positive imagos takes place. The infant no longer lives in a world of extreme witches and angels without moderation in him/herself and his/her internal and external characters. Klein emphasized that primary anxieties associated with internal object relations shifted from paranoia to concern. For her, the outcome of the developmental journey into the depressive position was largely a constitutional one.

Klein's remarkable archaeological forays into archaic phantasies and codes emphasized the role of the instincts over the mind's capacity to create new meaning, particularly in the field between mother and child. However, Klein leads us into the deep contours of early semiotics as they appear out of the infant's capacities, innate and developmental, to create meaningful structures of experience. Klein's notion of affect and body sensations coded for the communication between mother and child suggests infantile semiotics much as Kristeva defines them.

For Kristeva, mother and child, as participants in the discourse of preverbal significance, are witnesses to the infant's struggle to extricate him/herself from the powerful grip of undifferentiation.[101] Kristeva explains that the infant semiotic or phantasy emerges only after the wrench of the achievement of some differentiation. At this point the baby needs the mothering one to receive the communications of his/her states of mind coded and recoded, processed and reprocessed, shared, detoxified, and organized. Through containing, holding, and empathetic functions, the infant's primitive affective structures of experience are made meaningful and manageable. If the infant's epigenesis is to unfold normally, the parents must loan their signifying capacities to the process.[102] The absence of mental bonding produces mental deficiencies and defects: autism, psychosis, or death. The bifurcation of the symbolic order and infant semiotics splits away the fears of exile, abandonment, and deficits in mental functioning which are the legacy of failed bonding.

In this context, the signifiers of maternity, motherhood, and mothering explored by Kristeva and Klein yield untold multilayered narratives of survival and escape from mental chaos. The diverse cultural forms of mother and mother and child in the figures of ancient goddesses, the madonna of medieval Christianity, and the more recent ideology of the domestic madonna attempt to hold and signify deep anxieties about infantile helplessness, meaninglessness, and lack of mental organization.

Klein's notion of infantile phantasies and Kristeva's theory of prelinguistic semiotics (*le sémiotique*) are ways of explaining the infant's organization of random experience. Although the infant subject is endowed with inherent codes for survival, they must be supported and encouraged by the mothering one (ones). The infant has many capacities to process experience at birth or soon after. At as early as three weeks of age, its ability to organize sensory data and to discriminate between mother and other faces and voices is clear. The new infant observation studies show that infants discriminate cross-modally. Given pacifiers with bumps and another group without bumps, the infants of each group were able, at three weeks of age, to choose the visual analogue, a picture of the pacifier which had been in their own mouth. Infants shown the mother's face accompanied by another woman's voice become anxious, yawn, and avoid the confusion of that experience.[103] Stern also shows that infants can discriminate using elements of time as well. "Using heart rate and behavior as the respondent measure, these investigations show that infants recognize that an auditory temporal pattern is correspondent with a similar visually presented pattern. Temporal properties can be transferred cross-modally. It is becoming more obvious that the infant from early in life is exquisitely sensible of and sensitive to the temporal features of the environment."[104] Another feature of the infant's inborn apparatus is the mature visual motor system which is virtually intact at birth, making gazing available, which is a potent form of communication.[105]

However, without the support and regulation of the "mothering one," the capacities that make sense out of experience break down. If the normal bonding processes of the infant to his/her primary objects are not derailed by either constitutional difficulties or environmental ones, the development of a core self begins to come together between the second and the sixth month. This early core self rests upon the working of many interpersonal moments of diverse modes of relatedness which include care, play, and communication of all sorts. Normally, after the discovery of the domain of core relatedness, the infant, somewhere between the seventh and ninth month becomes aware of subjectivities other than his/her own. This in turn deepens the sense of self as well as the capacity to relate. Sensorimotor events, affectual experiences, and memories are then organized into more complex structures of rhythm, intensity, image, feeling, and thought, which are used for the purposes of communication systems and self-knowledge. Mental life at this time is taking off, bringing vitality and continuity to the infant's mental experience.[106]

Mother's task is to share her organizing capacities in order to hold, regulate, and translate the baby's unorganized experience. Primary process and the instincts normally code and organize the vast waves of primary raw data which are at first experienced as meaningless forces.[107] The phantasies and defenses of Klein's paranoid-schizoid position and Kristeva's semiotic are the structures which grow out of the mind's capacity to dream, phantasize, and mythify raw data into manageable narratives. The unbonded infant lives in a mental landscape of dread, chaos, and randomness and is subject to fragmentation, the feeling of being in a black hole, and the feeling of being mutilated.

Infantile semiotics or phantasies code and mythify infantile mental experience, and they also carry the various narratives of the womb, birth, bonding, and individuation. The development of the human mind is a narrative in itself and the development of diverse structures of meaning that potentiate that development are part of the narrative. The transformation of deep, unformed mental life into meaningful forms takes many detours. Many of the elements of early emotional experience are buried, lost, dismantled, or destroyed on the way. This book investigates the mythic semiotics of the mother-infant relationship over the course of these processes of transformation as they appear in three American women artists. Stowe, Alcott, and Cassatt are critical figures in the discovery of the maternal metaphor and the infantile metaphor which yield and hold together sanity and significance. Not only does their work center around the new themes of familial life, but their work was done at a time in the modern Western world when inner life and emotional attachment were emerging from deep repression and disavowal. The deconstructive efforts of the American and French feminist writers has led to the realization that infantile phantasies and semiotics carry the possibility of birth or abortion of the internal world and the elements of mental life. *Uncle Tom's Cabin, Little Women*, and Cassatt's paintings reflect these processes, and in the next chapters, using my own psychoanalytic deconstructive efforts, I will focus on the emergence of the human infant with mother in regard to the evolution of the human mind.

CHAPTER

2

THE MYTHOLOGY AND SEMIOTICS OF FAMILIAL BONDS

> If one inquires to know her ultimate origins, the oldest textual remains and images can carry us back only so far, and permit us to say "Thus she appeared in those early times; so and so she may have been named; and in such and such a manner she seems to have been revered." But with that we have come to the end of what can be said; with that we have come to the primitive problem of her comprehension and being. She is the Primum mobile, the first beginning, the material matrix out of which all comes forth.
>
> —Joseph Campbell

The internal and external dimensions of family life are known through their mythological forms. The structures of significance that convey and interpret birth, parent-infant-sibling relations, and male and female relations are organized in mythic narratives based on the events of the life cycle and the growth of the individual mind. Cultural and personal myths grow from the deepest aspects of mental life, from levels which precede thought and language but which extend to include complex systems of narratives well known within culture.[1] Themes of existence and survival are coded, recoded, condensed, displaced, symbolized, and revised like a dream which culminates in the manifest content[2] through mediation of unconscious desire and the imperatives of conscious life. Lacan's theory of the symbolic order draws on Freud's theory of the dream work and those of Saussure and Lévi-Strauss for their contribution toward a theory of the laws of the unconscious. Saussure introduced the ideas of the organization of language through binary oppositions and the signifier/signified relationship.[3] Lévi-Strauss applied Saussure's theory of language to culture and argued that cultural myths are structured like language, organizing both mind and culture through myths structured in binary oppositions. Lévi-Strauss understands the Oedipus myth in this way, as will be discussed later in the chapter. Finally, Lacan's theory of a symbolic order and of individual development implies that both are known only through the signifying structures of language or through the chain of signifiers.

In particular, the Oedipus myth, centered on generation and sexual difference, has appeared in many guises over the whole span of human culture, its elements being found whenever and wherever humans signify their existence.[4] The mythic configuration designated the Oedipus myth is a structure which maps out and contains realizations of family life of the child's relationship to his/her ancestral heritage, to his/her immediate family, the parental couple and their values, and the course of his/her development into his/her destiny. Its elements are held together by the emotional linkages which pass back and forth between the characters and between the hero/heroines of the piece and the challenges and demands of individuated mental life.[5] Its elements can also be found isolated if not fragmented; for example, the great goddess, the mother of all things, represented as Athena or Diana with a multitude of breasts may be read as one aspect of the narrative of familial relationships and emotions, a manifestation of early infantile experience or dream.[6]

The Western version of the Oedipus myth that comes down to the present from Sophocles to Freud manifestly is a myth of male development and power. The Sphinx proves the exception, signifying bizarre maternal potency or the phallic mother, though her authority is soon toppled by Oedipus's cunning and talent. Jocasta, despite her royal privilege, signs the failure of exogamy as an object to be fought over by the men of the clan.[7] However, as Freud's dreams of self-analysis suggest, a son's passionate attachment to mother is not exclusively sexual, but one of longing and nostalgia for the comfort and security of mother's body. The Oedipus myth maps not only the fear of incest and parricide, but primitive family culture before the repression of the later "Oedipus complex."[8] Helen Bacon, writing on the tragedy of Sophocles, emphasizes the presence of the mother's body as a foundation supporting the narrative.[9] She suggests that the underlying force of the myth lies in an attempt at integration of female potency which resurfaces in the theories of *Oedipus at Colonus*. Though the manifest Oedipus myth can be read as structured around the intention of undervaluing female power and employs signifiers of women which have been drained of many-faceted significance, this particular structural configuration is a mirror of splitting in culture: men visible, active, privileged; women hidden and mysterious.

From another perspective, the placing of maternal force in an underlying position reiterates the pre-Hellenic concept of the notion of mother as Mother Earth, the life creating womb force which brings forth fertile gifts from the ground. Joseph Campbell gives examples of the concept of the earth as both a bearing and a nourishing mother. The fertility aspect is seen in the artifacts of the archaic hunting and agricultural cultures. Hunters believed that animals derived from the mother goddess's womb, and agricultural lore held that it was in the mother's body that the grain was sown.[10] Another extension of these concepts is that of the woman giving birth to the world from her body.[11] The Oedipus myth as we know it denies female goddesses their capacities, just as post-Hellenic culture denied it these figures to the advantage of male divinity.[12] The female goddess's power of transformation connected to birth, death, and rebirth and integration is reduced to separate functions or to degenerate powers. Hera becomes troubled wife; Athena loses her matrifocal origins, subsumed by male militarism, and becomes father's daughter;[13] Aphrodite becomes the responsible beloved. Eurydice and Themis, the oracular personifications of the earth's continuity and being and the spirit of group bonds, are replaced by father God's dominant rule.[14]

The transformation from cultural myths woven out of maternal bounty to myths of exclusive male superiority and power is interpreted in Jane Ellen Harrison's exploration of Greek religion, *Themis*, as a felt incompatibility between infancy and tribal activities of survival. She elucidates the belief system that obliterates the significance of women as the source of life. In terror of the possible dissolution of the self, fusion states, and of seduction, associated with continuing undifferentiation and unawareness under the rule of the pleasure principle, male children, the warriors, hunters, and workers of the future, are purged of the taint of the maternal birth through rituals and rites. The ritual of the *second birth* gives the boy child a new soul, the soul of his tribe. From that crisis onward, he is mother's child no more. Through the use of symbolic activities, the group contrives a second birth; the child emerging from the cultural male womb is transferred from a "woman thing" to a "man thing." In banishing physical pregnancy, birth, and infant care, the rites of the second birth tear culture from its origins, establishing a rift between internal and cultural experience.

In primitive matrilinear society mother occupies a position of respect as the mother of the tribesman-to-be. Religious imagery complements the notion of mother as a great social force—as the source of future tribesmen—of strength and continuity. In the matrilinear vision, the earth is a focus of religious awe rather than the heavens.[15] In the transition to patrilinear structure, the festival of the same mother named *Apatoria* is transformed into the festival of the same father. The complementary myth of *Trilogenia* developing out of this new emphasis obscures motherhood. As Athena springs from the head of her father Zeus, "she is turned into a diagram of a motherless birth."[16] Apollo makes this clear:

This too I tell you, mark how plain my speech. The mother is not parent of her child, only the nurse of the young seed within her. The male is parent, she as outside friend cherishes her plant, if fate allows its bloom. Proof will I bring of this argument. A father needs no mother's help. She stands child of Olympian Zeus to be my witness, reared never in the darkness of the womb, yet fairer plant than any heaven begot.[17]

The shift from the maternal theory of birth to the paternal one continues the polarization of sexual difference, but reverses the underestimation of paternity previously held. A two-parent theory of conception and child care requires toleration and integration of difference. Segregation perpetuates discontinuity between the infant's mental experience and societal affairs. As outward culture springs from the paternal body, the mother's body is the secret vault of inner reality—closed within the burial chamber of cultural structures.

The severe repression of mother-infant experience within the template of the Western Oedipus myth inhibits its functions, which are to signify many levels of mental growth and to map the integration of infantile phantasies or semiotics into the discourse of the symbolic order.

Campbell challenges the notion of the ritual second birth and the splitting apart of male and female, mother-father, adult-child, personal-social. He believes that myths themselves are a second womb woven from cultural, interpretive constructions of innate programming of phantasy and external affairs. Campbell explains that myths and rites, or culture itself, grow from the necessity of sheltering the long-dependent human infant. As Campbell develops his notion of the mythological womb, he suggests that its symbolism is geared for the protection of psyche and soma, and for growth and awareness.[18] He describes it as both a vast network of attempts to protect the infant from his/her fears of aloneness and mortality and at the same time, to initiate the child into the experiences of life and death. Campbell's concept of myths as a kangaroo pouch resembles Winnicott's theory of transitional objects as providing companionship for the odyssey beyond mother's body.[19] Myths, acting as transitional phenomena, provide comfort and reassurance, but they also provide a sheltered space for the creation of lively phantasies and rituals of initiation, which in turn function as stepping stones to separate mental life.[20] Mythic narratives, cushioning the infant or child within their network of symbols and signs, reiterate the functions of the earth goddess, who as creator and protector of new life contains and perpetuates not only the bounty of the physical universe, but the flowering of the infant's mind.[21] Myths, as cultural dreams and historical explanations within the parental cultural mind, hold together meaning just as the soil holds all plant life or the universe holds its planets.

Campbell believes that the infant mind unfolds within the postnatal womb of mythology. He explains that cultural myths are part of humanity's biological adaptive endowment. He theorizes that they function as part of epigenesis.

> A functioning mythology can be defined as a corpus of culturally maintained sign stimuli fostering the development and activation of a specific type or constellation of types of human life.[22]

Campbell compares the mythological image to the innate releasing mechanisms of other species described by Tinbergen, for example, the red dot that imprints the baby duck to attach to and imitate mother duck. He says:

> In every primitive society on earth, whether of hunting or of the planting order, these inevitable imprints and conceptions of infancy are filled with new associations, rearranged and powerfully imprinted, under the most highly emotional circumstances, in the puberty rites, the rites of initiation, to which every young male (and often every female too) is subjected.[23]

In this view, myths are adaptive and epigenetic structures which not only channel the psychic forces of the individual and integrate him/her into his/her cultural group but are also symbolic way-stations for a second birth in which the infant journeys safely from symbiosis to separate existence. Campbell describes the second birth as made possible by the function of mythic symbols as guides which point the way to maturation and self-knowledge in the journey through the phenomenal world to the universal and transcendental world.[24] In Campbell's view, myth-making works similarly to Freud's dream work to release and create meaning. Harrison's interpretation of the second birth suggests a more neurotic and at times deeply disturbed process in which certain experiences and their meanings are disavowed rather than sublimated.[25]

The Oedipus myth, as it has appeared in culture over thousands of years, is an epigenetic structure organizing through displacement, condensation, and secondary revision the significance of family life and relations. However, as it appears in Sophocles, Freud, and later Melanie Klein, it is a tragic and violent narrative more revealing of grave neurotic difficulties than of epigenesis. The realization of the myth as it appears in Sophocles' *Oedipus Rex*, *Oedipus at Colonus*, and *Antigone*, is heavily weighted with violent and tangled relationships, yet the cycle of plays can also be understood as a coding of the great odyssey of the life cycle and the various states of mind that accompany birth, survival, parental and sexual bonding, generational strife, sibling relations, and those of the end of the life cycle, which arise with the approach of death, such as ecstasy, terror, and anxiety. In Sophocles' *Oedipus Tyrannus* (or *Oedipus Rex*), Oedipus's physical and cultural births (first and second births, respectively) are cursed by the sins of his ancestors.

The Oedipus myth or legend derives its narrative force from generational impiety. Cadmus, the founder of Thebes, and Oedipus's paternal great-grandfather, overturned the order of things when he murdered the dragon Ophion, who originally mated with the Eurymone, the Goddess of all things. The dragon, as one of the animal gods sacred to Hera and earlier valued in the ancient matriarchal pre-Hellenic pantheon, signifies the relation to mother in her immediate and background functions. Labdicus, Cadmus's son, blighted by the sin of his father, died at an early age, leaving Laius orphaned in his first year. Laius, Oedipus's father, contributed to the curse on the family through his seduction of the youth Chrysippus. His homo-sexual act further disturbed the balance of Theban society and endangered the Labdacid house. In Oedipus's generation, the sins of the father in-creased to the extent that Oedipus's birth and death were cursed. Yet Oedi-pus was fated to play the role of the messiah or the sacrifice in order to free his family from the dreaded curse.[26] Thus, it fell to Oedipus to enact the drama of both the odyssey and the curse of human experience and human development. As the one destined as the messiah, who ends the transgenerational sins of the father, Oedipus suffers and dies and finds reconciliation only at the end of his life. The defilement and destruction of the maternal deities is the fundamental offense underlying the mythic narrative. Cadmus's act of slaying the dragon signifies lack of respect for the maternal goddesses. As the narrative is structured on or emphasizes the sins of the male line, descended on a male child separated from his mother's care, it conveys the splitting off and disavowal of maternal pres-ence and potency as well as female development.

Oedipus, born into a family warned by the Oracle of the danger of procreating more children of the Labdacid house, is rejected at the first birth while his second birth is revised into a human sacrifice. The response of Laius and Jocasta to the warning from the Oracle at Delphi is to abandon their child and implement his infanticide. The abandonment and murder of their child signifies parental hatred of a child as he or she signals their own cursed existence. From another perspective, Oedipus's fate is repara-tive. He is designated as the one to break the hereditary cycle by expunging the sins of Cadmus, Labdacus, and Laius. The character Oedipus's meaning is largely derived from the chain of transgenerational victims and avengers. Oedipus's murder of Laius ends the cursed line of men who violated the matriarchal deities to found Thebes. Oedipus's life takes on the meaning of savior. His ultimate self-discovery and self-knowledge lead him to the Grove of the Furies, where he is able to find reconciliation through the acknowledgment of the disavowed maternal deities.[27]

Oedipus's odyssey through his life cycle also represents survival of the child despite the troubled culture which had already dishonored the ma-ternal figure of the early Oedipal or preverbal experience. Additionally, the symbolic order into which Oedipus's second birth ejected him contains condensations of the elements of infanticide, a rupture in maternal bond-ing, the transformation of the mother into the Sphinx, child abuse, child sacrifice, incest, and parricide. These are the elements of his culture which gather around the structure of the second birth.

In this context, the Sphinx represents the return of the split off or dis-avowed phantasies of the mother with the baby who is symbolically or actually deprived of attachment experience. The Sphinx appears to Oedi-pus as a cannibalistic monster after the unknowing parricide of his father, King Laius.[28] The Sphinx as a highly condensed figure has many aspects or dimensions. Her manifest form, a woman's head, the wings of an eagle, the body of a lioness, and the tail of a snake dragon, suggest a compression of many totem animals from archaic matriarchal cultures[29] and of female early goddesses themselves. Her name means "strangler," or "she who squeezes," connoting a dangerous female threat to the body of the infant.

The Sphinx is a figure associated with powerful, grotesque, and reversed images of infant and mother bonding and adult sexual bonding. Ancient myths present her as a horrifying bird of death who flies into the other world, kidnapping the bodies of souls of its mortal prey, who clasp her convulsively in a parody of an embrace.[30] Belonging to the class of witches, demons, or the Medusa, the Sphinx's mythic narrative unfolds in several lurid portrayals, all utterly destructive of human life. Her lover (or baby) seduced into a relationship is slain or cannibalized. As Empusa, she drinks the blood of her victim, or as the barren Nampia, she devours the children of other women.

The Sphinx is a horrible dream or phantasy that arrives in the face of emotional or physical danger. She is a part of the pageant of experience that the infant witnesses helplessly without the protective support of the parent's mind. In that situation, the baby's fear and rage, combined with preconceptions of danger transform the maternal image into the Sphinx.

The deadly Sphinx of the Oedipus legend is a signifier of an infantile catastrophe in which the infant's mind fragments or breaks within a failed mental symbiosis.[31] In the absence of the "mother" and the mother-baby semiotic dialogue, chaos, fragmentation or an explosion destroys the infant's mind and epigenesis. The Sphinx figure originates out of the debris of the break. She is also the maternal monster who appears when mother is gone too long or never connects.[32] On a cultural level, she also appears to punish by castration or cannibalism the sins of the male line associated with the violation of the maternal deities.[33]

The riddle of the Sphinx and the fatal ritualistic demand that it be solved presents to Oedipus in condensed form the monstrous mother of scarred epigenesis and a distorted infant-mother dialogue. The infant, bereft of maternal sanity and empathy, must solve the riddle of his/her own safety and survival. In Oedipus's case, his normal curiosity and epistemophilic instinct are denied satisfaction and are transformed into parricide and incest. The answer to the riddle, which is to solve the problem of human history and to pierce the meaning of the life cycle, is blocked, and the answer sent back to the infant in particles of anxiety, dread and fear.[34]

Jocasta is another aspect of the Sphinx. Her first failure as a protective shield can be seen in her seduction of Laius and her disregard for the Oracle's decree. After her infant's birth, she allows him to be carried to Mt. Cytheron, his ankles pinned together, and left to die uncovered and unprotected. Jocasta's character conveys the danger of untrustworthy sexuality in the person of the mother, who cannot structure the infant's or child's proper passage into individuation and adult sexuality. The act of incest which ruptures the law of exogamy suggests a disturbance in development.

On a deep level of meaning the act signifies the lack of clear boundaries between parent and child and between generations leading to madness and death.[35]

In one of the plays of the trilogy by Sophocles, *Antigone*, Antigone, as the female child of the fifth generation of the curse, resists its spell. A woman of compassion, she is loyal to her father in his exile and to her brother Polyneices at his death. In her generosity and love, she opposes the monster mother archetype and thus begins to heal the rift between men and women as well. Her refusal to obey Creon's decree that her brother Polyneices be denied a proper burial ends in her own interment in a crypt. Her death is a sacrifice, like her father's, that cleanses the impurity and blasphemy of her lineage. Another meaning of Antigone's role in the house of Labdicae is that with her the Oedipus myth expands to include women and the relationships of the siblings.

Sophocles encodes the parents' failure to solve the riddle of their own generation, and that failure becomes a hereditary curse. He grasps the Oedipus myth as a template for the gradual attainment or expansion of self-knowledge and the possibility of reconciliation between family members. Thousands of years later, Sigmund Freud, deeply attracted to the Oedipus legend as he was developing a theory of the unconscious, discovered an unconscious structure for organizing generational and sexual differences.[36] Freud's monumental *Interpretation of Dreams* is a work born out of his own self-analysis in which he discovers his own unconscious Oedipal legend or myth. A fair number of the dreams analyzed in *Interpretation of Dreams* reveal themes of desire, conflict, and longing of the child Freud for his mother and his rivalry with his father. Out of his explorations in which he located his personal myth, Freud read the hieroglyphics of symbolic structures of universal myth. He proposed that dreams and myths, as well as neurotic structures, are part of the signification capacities of the human mind, that the unconscious wrote experience through displacement, condensation, and the channeling of the drives, desires, wishes, and memories as part of the project to make the unconscious content compatible with the conscious mind and to assign meaning to experiences. In this way, Freud discovered the processes of signification as well as symbolization processes[37] which are the underpinnings of language, culture, and family arrangements such as kinship structures. Thus, as Freud discovered the Oedipus complex in his dreams, he saw into the universal structure which organizes familial and personal experience much as the scientist looks into the molecular structure of a new chemical compound.

Freud's interpretation of the Oedipus complex, while based on the myth of Oedipus the King and his family, is confined to the themes of unconscious sexual wishes and parricide. In Freud's Oedipus complex, incestuous feelings for the contralateral parent and hatred for the ipsilateral parent dominate his understanding of several of his dreams and of his theory of development. In chapter 5 of the dream book, in a section called "Dreams of the Death of Persons of Whom the Person is Fond," Freud carefully uncovers possessive and hostile impulses within the dreams of children and repeated in myths and legends.

In terms of individual development, Freud discovered in himself and in his patients a profoundly ambivalent layer underneath the surface behavior of children. He explained that while children depend on their parents' goodwill and love for their survival, nevertheless, their dreams and fantasies (phantasies) are filled with a great many tempestuous feelings toward the parents which might not be included in what is known conventionally as childish affection. Freud particularly noted the presence of death wishes of children against the parent of the same sex.[38] He added that hostile impulses against dearly beloved parents found their force in fact in sexual rivalry, indicating the onset of a highly charged triangular relationship at an early age (about three and a half).

Freud theorized that the chief part played in the mental lives of all children who later were to become psychological neurotics was found in the nature of the child's feelings about his/her parents. Being in love with the one parent and hating the other, he said, were among the essential constituents of the stock of psychical impulses which are formed at that time and which are of such importance in determining the symptoms of a later neurosis.[39] He added that it was not his belief that psychoneurotics differed that sharply in this respect from other human beings who would remain normal. The distinguishing feature of those children who are to become psychoneurotics was that they exhibited on a magnified scale feelings of love and hatred toward their parents which would occur less obviously and less intensely in the minds of most children.[40]

Freud found the combination of universality and normality of this constellation of feelings in the powerful legend of Oedipus the King. The power of these contrasting feelings, he thought, made up the tragedy of Oedipus rather than the classical interpretation which until the time of Freud's explorations had been understood as the tension between the supreme world of the gods and the vain attempt of mankind to escape the evil that threatens them. In this view, the lesson to be learned by the "deeply moved spectator" in viewing the tragedy is submission to the divine will and realization of man's own impotence. Freud takes exception to this view and warns that Oedipus's plight is our own, since we are all cursed by the same decree which comes down from the Oracle before our birth, as upon Oedipus. Freud goes on, "it is the fate of all of us, perhaps, to direct our first sexual impulses towards our mother and our first hatred and first murderous wish against our father."[41]

This quote makes clear Freud's bias in interpreting the Oedipus myth as rooted in universal themes structured around infantile sexuality and its destiny to bring on conflict and tragedy. "It is the fate of all of us" emphasizes the universality of infantile sexual wishes, but the rest of the sentence, "towards our mother and our first hatred and our first murderous wish against our father," implies the limited view through which Freud perceived the Oedipus configuration as a male drama. Thus, as Freud sifts through mythology for examples of his theory of infantile sexuality, he finds many more examples of males pitted against their father than of girls in a hostile and competitive rivalry with their mother. Later, in *Totem and Taboo* and *Moses and Monotheism*, he would argue that outer culture was in fact formed out of the father-son relationship, and he suggested that the obscure information which is brought to us by mythology and legend from the primeval ages of society gives an unpleasing picture of the father's despotic power and of the ruthlessness with which he made use of it.[42] Freud gives the examples of Kronus's devouring his children just as the wild boar devours the sow's litter and another in Zeus, who emasculates his father. This latter example is taken up in *Psychopathology of Everyday Life* in which Freud uses the example as a case of his own slip. In the chapter "Errors," Freud corrects his mistake. He says, "I stated that Zeus emasculated his father Kronus and dethroned him. I was, however, erroneously carrying this atrocity a generation forward; according to Greek mythology, it was Kronus who committed it on his father, Uranus." Freud then explains that this slip had to do with his own unconscious hostility toward his father as part of his Oedipus complex.[43]

Freud was not unaware that the emphasis on male sexuality and the relationship between fathers and sons neglected the issue of female sexuality and the relationship between mothers and daughters. He explained in *Moses and Monotheism* that culture grew from the relationships between males and that the relationship to mother in particular had to be left behind in order for the formation of culture to take place. "This turning from the mother to the father points to a victory of intellectuality over sensuality that is an advance in civilization since maternity is proved by the evidence of the senses while paternity is a hypothesis based on an inference and a promise." Freud added that giving preference to thought processes over sense perception has proved to be a momentous step.[44] We can observe that in Freud's thinking the development of language and symbolic structures of all kinds left behind the infantile experience of the mother, which he emphasized as largely sensual.

However, Freud's meeting of the Oedipus myth yields more than an analysis of male experience. Freud's interpretation of the Oedipus myth expands beyond his limited vision of female development to a universal theory of personal myth and of the functioning of the psychic apparatus. He understands Sophocles' tragedy as a legend that sprang from "some primeval dream material" which has as part of its structure and content the distressing disturbance of unconscious family life.[45] In these terms the Oedipus complex or myth is an internal diagram for emotional growth and a template for the assemblage of meaning. Infantile sexual wishes, particularly incest, and the primary phantasies of castration and parricide can be extended to be understood as manifest aspects of a dream or signifiers of internal object relations of pain and fear, the meaning of which has been disguised by condensation and displacement in the dream work.

As will be discussed further on, relationships to parents and relationships to oneself are revealed in the Oedipal structure. In the process of the dream work and myth making, the mind is revealed as creating meaning at all levels, which transcends concepts of sexual discrimination. Many of Freud's papers are structured on a paradox. On the one hand, he describes women's limitation; on the other, the almost unlimited creativity of the mind. It did not occur to Freud that maternal empathy and the capacity to contain the infant's projections were the bulwarks or the ballast for the growth of that creativity. However, Freud's originality drew him toward many aspects of human culture, particularly those which elaborate the origins of culture and of the family and of the value-laden images of mother, father, and child.

Totem and Taboo is Freud's greatest account of the evolution of the Oedipus complex. While his interest is in tracing the drama of the libido through its crisis and denouement leading to the resolution of the Oedipus complex, he is also searching in this paper for the mental processes that create Oedipal structures in the mind of the individual and the group. In *Totem and Taboo*, Freud elaborates a series of transformations of Oedipal beliefs and customs which provide a historical and mythic account of the Oedipus configuration from its origins in primitive hordes to its later forms in religion and morality. In *Moses and Monotheism*, Freud reveals that he is thinking of history as myth, or as the dream work:

> An essential part of the construction is the hypothesis that the events I am about to describe occur to all primitive men; that is, to all our ancestors. The story is told in an enormously *condensed* form as though it happened on a single occasion, while in fact it covered thousands of years and was repeated countless times during them.[46]

Paul Ricoeur interprets Freud's theory of the Oedipus structure as a theory of signs and symbols rooted in the life of the species:

> Energics or even hydraulics are articulated only in semantics; the vicissitudes of the instincts can be attained only through the vicissitudes of meaning. Therein lies the deep reasoning for all analogies between dreams and myth, dreams and works of art, dreams and religious allusion; all these cyclical productions belong to the area of meaning and are connected to the question;, how do desires become signified?[47]

Ricoeur believes the motivating force of sign-making to be the interpretations of one's existence. He suggests that the individual must make signs, in order to give form and meaning to his/her existence.[48]

Following Ricoeur, the totem is interpreted as a mythic signifier and the taboo as a symbolic rite; and in this context they may be read as realizations of innate patternings of family relations. In that regard, Freud's Oedipal myth functions as a theory of development. At the preverbal or presymbolic phase, phantasies are experienced as actual events; actual parricide and actual cannibalism are believed to take place. In the second phase of the development of an infantile neurosis, patricide (or original sin) is repressed and returns symbolically as the totem and its taboos. In the last phase of transformation, further capacity for signification develops. The external totem is replaced by or transformed into the internal superego. The individual identifies with the primal father figure and imaginatively constructs a replica of that figure within his/her mind. The superego, or ego ideal, is condensed and displaced out of countless emotional exchanges between parent and child. Today psychoanalytic theorists believe parental imagos to be present in the early months of infancy and become slowly representational throughout childhood years. According to Freud, with the birth of this figure at the resolution of the Oedipus complex, mental life operates at the level of representation. The individual and the group in culture create the symbolic system of the obsessional neurosis. Signs of deep mental experience replace concrete action.

In *Totem and Taboo* and in *Moses and Monotheism*, Freud's Oedipus myth is dominated by male protagonists. Women are cast in the narrative as objects of their desire. In these accounts, Oedipus's feelings for his mother are limited to sexual possessiveness understood as adolescent and adult sexual rivalry. Infantile affection and dependence and female authority are deleted from the mythic tales.

It is well known that in Freud's Oedipal developmental scheme, little girls fare badly.[49] The female child, inevitably suffering from the deficit of her biology, falters along the developmental pathway. Freud's perspective on sexual difference leads to the conclusion that women are imprisoned in a biological destiny which inhibits the achievement of higher symbolic functionings. Women are banished from complex semiotics and from the interpretation of cultural forces due to their incapacity to sublimate.

Though Freud believed that he came upon the inherent biological Oedipal configuration, in fact he found and interpreted a distorted realization of family relationships, skewed by turbulent psychological growth and by cultural symbol systems. Freud's emphasis on lack as signified by the presence or absence of the penis reflects the bias of Western culture. The papers on the Oedipus complex reveal a particular realization of the Oedipus myth in which dependence and attachment are undervalued while male sexual rivalry and violence are given privileged weight. Similarly, culture is seen as deriving from male motivations, desire, and activities. Mother/infant, mother/daughter, and mother/son relationships are disallowed their contribution as forces of personal and cultural meaning.

This distorted realization perhaps is bound up with the universal dilemma of culturally structuralizing experiences of separating into selfhood, moving into one's own life cycle toward maturity, and finally toward one's death. The task of separation and of mental birth, of experiencing the turbulence of one's own mental life, is terrifying as well. As the exhilarating ordeal evokes murderous feelings (parricide) or the desire for merging (incest) as well as love and curiosity or their opposites, stupor, withdrawal, and ignorance, each culture is challenged with the task of managing all these experiences.

Freud's culture, fin-de-siècle Vienna, was a culture of tempestuous birth, enduring the ordeal of the transition from feudalism to modernism. Enlightened progressive experiments with liberal reform were immediately threatened by the forces of reactionary backlash. The anti-Semitism of the Christian Socialists and the Catholic working class expressed the hatred for the new and explosions shattered the infant possibilities for rationalism and liberal reform appropriate to a modernist culture.[50] As the vacuum left by the crumbling of feudal authority grew more ominous, faith in enlightened reforms began to appear pathetic.

Gustav Klimt's paintings at the time of Freud's early papers capture the turbulent and painful spasms of European cultural change. "Jurisprudence," "Medicine," "Philosophy," and "Music" provide visual metaphors of a universe in dissolution and deterioration reminiscent of a psychotic vision.[51] In contrast, Freud's writings do not attend directly to cultural fragmentation, but allow his theory of the id and its fulminating instincts to probe the turbulence of crumbling authority.

Klimt's painting "Jurisprudence" suggests, as do Freud's new theories, the discovery of the dynamics of inner life. But Klimt juxtaposes more specifically the relation of the inner and cultural realms. In this painting, he portrays a situation in which all boundaries are dissolving. Earth and sky, heaven and hell, fragment and dissolve into each other while humanity appears as drifting eternally in an open space. The old baroque container/structure, Theatre Mundi, in which the drama of life may properly take place, slips into oblivion. Consciousness is barely represented by a blind sphinx peering out of the nothingness of an eerie cosmos and by the hint of a prompter at the base of the painting.[52] The painting contains many elements of a mental breakdown and suggests that the functions of mental integration personified as a benevolent caretaker, interpreter, or cohesive authority, is overwhelmed and fractured. Klimt's vision investigates the loss of old illusions and structures in his transitional culture, a situation which follows the fault line of painful disruption.

Klimt's "Siren," "Femme Fatale," and "Monstrous Eve" illuminate cultural symptoms of these changes. Under conditions of cultural upheaval, the hieroglyph of women as harmless, stable creatures was to soothe anxious souls. Yet the bifurcation of the maternal goddess spawned and released the angel's opposite. Klimt discovers and interprets the other woman who does not appear clearly in Freud's interpretations of his dreams. Think of the "Irma Dream" or the case studies in hysteria. The women of these papers are bourgeois Victorian women whose sexuality has been stultified. In "Water Snakes II" (1904–7) and "Judith and Holfernes" (1901), femaleness emerges in sensual, mysterious, and threatening images. Woman, strongly linked with archaic sexual desire and ancient magical powers, finds expression in "Pallas Athena" (1898).[53] In these works, Klimt portrays sexuality emerging and overcoming asceticism and idealism but always personified as dangerous femininity.

Although Freud associated his newly discovered unconscious and its instinctual life with mother, sexuality, and the archaic, he dismembered his characterization of women. The women of *Interpretation of Dreams* appear as background characters and as vehicles for the action of male agents. The dreams of the Botanical Monograph and of Irma's Injection disguise and bury mother's significance. The themes, as Freud analyzes them, center around Freud's career, his fear of failure in the public world, and his anguished fear that honor and recognition might fall elsewhere or that his grandiose quest might fail completely.[54] Thus, manifestly Freud's interpretations are focused around recognition and approval in the public sphere of male activities.

The Dream of the Botanical Monograph is structured in a parallel fashion in a vertical split between the early Oedipal presymbolic layer of experience and the more manifest strata of the symbolic order characteristic of his culture. However, Freud, while experiencing these splits in a personal way, made forays into the repressed through his dreams and associations that begin the tasks of integration and recovery for himself and for his society. The manifest Dream of the Botanical Monograph is as follows: "I had written a monograph on a certain plant. The book lay before me and I was at the moment turning over a faded colored plate. Bound up in each copy there was a dried specimen of the plant as though it had been taken from an herbarium."[55]

Freud's associations lead to an oppositional structure, male-female, which parallels the separation of the sexes found in late nineteenth-century Vienna. The two oppositional spheres gather around the associations to flower, monograph, colored plates, dried specimen, and herbarium. Flowers appear in both contexts; first Freud's thoughts move in the direction of favorite flowers as a token of love. He reproaches himself for forgetting to bring Martha, his wife, such a token. The difficult relations between a man of worldly affairs and his domestic spouse is highlighted by a case which also illustrates Freud's theory of forgetting. The young husband forgets the customary bouquet honoring his wife's birthday. The figure of the wife, Frau L., through displacement, crosses back and forth between the male and female spheres. Standing for the man's feeling for a woman (a man forgets his tie to a significant woman), she also leads to Freud's professional life as an example of his new explanation of forgetting as repression or as an aspect of the break-up of repression and also as an ex-patient. The last association is to Frau L.'s meeting with Martha, Freud's woman.

The Monograph leads by association to a daydream which again crosses by displacement back and forth between the external professional sphere and the sphere of domesticity or women, family, and personal feelings (and between conscious and unconscious feelings). Though Freud had not pursued his research to its conclusion, a dissertation on the coca plant (Freud, 1884) had drawn a colleague's attention to the anesthetic properties of cocaine. Freud's daydream associated to cocaine. "If I ever get glaucoma, I had thought, I should travel to Berlin and get myself operated on incognito in my friend's (Fleiss's) house by a surgeon recommended by him." Freud would remain incognito and bask secretly in the surgeon's praise for the discovery of a new anesthetic.[56]

Freud's need for narcissistic praise and attention struggled to the surface in this daydream. He craves praise and attention but finds them missing. Associating to his father's glaucoma and the resultant eye operation, Freud points to the theme of male colleagues and their rivalry. The three men present at the operation of Freud's father were the people responsible for furthering the use of cocaine as an anesthetic, although Freud received no credit.[57] The daydream leads to deeper associations. The eye operation suggests the tragedy of *Oedipus Rex*. In Freud's daydream he has glaucoma, too. Both father and son have eye trouble, connoting an eye for an eye[58] and the eye as the organ of knowledge and a displacement for the male sexual organ associated with castration. The longing for possession of the mother and her body is implied and disguised.

Thus, the flowers appear once more and take on new forms and associations. Freud associates the word blooming to a conversation with Professor Koller in which they discuss a Festschrift and an intensely important matter for Freud. They were then joined by Professor Gardener and his wife. Freud congratulated them on their blooming looks.

His next association leads him to the specimen of the plant. Cruciferae is connected to Freud's difficulty with botany and to Compositae. The family Compositae includes the artichoke, which Freud names as his favorite flower.[59] Artichokes are clearly associated to a childhood screen memory of pulling colored plates from a book leaf by leaf. Though the book was released for the purpose of childish destruction by Freud's father, it is also linked with his father's disapproval of his favorite hobby, collecting and owning books and with sexuality linked with tearing out leaves. Leaves work as a signifier of the labia minora. Didier Anzieu interprets the incident of the artichoke book as sexual play in which Freud's younger sister Anna took part and was the object of Freud's desire. Anzieu also connects the theory of sexual play with another of Freud's screen memories in which such play with his contemporary niece and nephew and flowers carries the associations that make up an Oedipal structure. Here botanical classification structures Freud's screen memories.[60] Dandelions of an early screen memory and cyclamen, which are pink mauvish brown in color, carry the associations of a woman's body—in the latter case by memory, in the former by sexual play. Pink mauvish brown is reminiscent of the interior of a woman's body as it appears in Irma's open mouth in the Irma dream.

Freud's outward analysis, however, returns to the outer layer of professional pride. He explains, "Once again, like the dream we first analyzed (the dream of Irma's injection), the dream turns out to be in the nature of a self-justification, a plea on behalf of my own rights." Freud explains that the Botanical Monograph dream continues the theme that began in Irma. "What it meant was, 'After all, I'm the man who wrote the valuable and memorable paper on cocaine.' Just as the earlier dream said on my behalf, I'm a conscientious and hard-working student, in both cases what I was insisting was, I may allow myself to do this."[61] Though Freud is focusing intensely on his desire to be the discoverer of psychoanalysis and of deep mental life and to claim just recognition for his original and creative journey into the self, his desire for love and recognition in the personal realm of mother-child relations and his personal feelings for the beloved mother and the parents of infancy and childhood years remains unpronounced. The dream of the Botanical Monograph gives a botanical classification to the search for sensual closeness and sexual knowledge. The coding of these elements are the background of the dream. Plant genera are diffentiated from one another by structural differences in their flowers, i.e., in their reproductive systems; such differences structure the binary opposition of the dream. Why are there two sexes and what distinguishes between them?[62]

The structure of the dream also suggests through the juxtaposition of flower and monograph the repression not only of Oedipal passion or of primitive Oedipal feelings but of those which are linked with needs for empathy, support, and mirroring.[63] Freud's interpretation of the Botanical Monograph Dream points to a major structuring displacement or allusion from flowers associated with his wife's preferences to his theory of forgetting and to "Festschrift" linked to honor accorded to professional colleagues.[64] Another reading of the dreams suggest the displacement moving in the opposite direction from honor in the world to preference in the world of domesticity, to be chosen (not overlooked or forgotten) as mother's favorite flower. Freud's emphasis obscures the alternative structure associated with a child's attachment to his or her mother.

The earlier dream of Irma's Injection also follows a similar structural configuration.[65] Irma is a highly condensed figure that gathers together many of the vicissitudes of the modernist experience. From his own point of view as a male physician, Freud proposes that the signifier, Irma, develops out of the precarious position of the modernist voyager. As a secular figure montaged over the older figure of the priest or shaman, the scientist Freud holds within his will and powers of creativity a godlike responsibility.

As he comprehends the possibility of his expanding individuality, Freud shares his experience of groping in the dark, vulnerable to grave errors in judgment. A dear friend misuses cocaine offered by Freud as medication for nose and throat problems (Fleischel). A woman is given an overdose of an inappropriate drug. A young man is allowed to travel to Egypt despite Freud's intuitive understanding that his diarrhea was hysterical and required psychoanalytic treatment. And behind all these figures is the woman, Emma, who nearly hemorrhages to death, endangered by his surgical collaboration with Fleiss.

The attention to vulnerability, human frailty, and the bias of merely human judgment is seen through the eyes of a male subject, caught up in the activity and rivalry of the professional sphere. It is as if this subject is suspended in the symbolic order, severed from his origins in primitive mental life. Adopting the perspective of Irma, the inner damaged self appears in the various troubled and tender orifices of her body. Her mouth, throat, vagina, and skin speak of neglect, pain, disease, and extreme penetrability. In opposition to the male god of secular prowess and certitude, Irma's person exposes vulnerability, tentative will, and narcissistic rage. Furthermore, Irma either cannot or will not be cured by psychoanalysis. In refusing to open her mouth, she expresses distrust and dissatisfaction, and like Emma, who is condensed into Irma, her hemorrhaging orifices signify the victim entombed underneath the structures of the second birth, acted upon in rituals that banish the narratives of birth, infancy, and children's growth.

Irma is a code name for Emma, who was a patient treated by both Freud and Fleiss. Fleiss treated both Emma and Freud. Fleiss cauterized Freud's nose for the treatment of sinus trouble, and he was called in to treat the hysterical young woman Emma, as Freud had consulted him about Emma's abdominal pains to ascertain if they were of nasal origin. Fleiss cauterized Freud's turbinal bones, and also operated on Emma. He bungled the operation badly by leaving a piece of gauze in the cavity, nearly causing her death.[66]

The appearance in the dream of Freud's examination of Irma's mouth as well as the doctor-patient episode signifies sexual phantasies of copulation and the possibility of Martha's latest pregnancy and abortion. Emma and Irma as they appear in the dream of Irma's Injection signify many dimensions of male/female relationships, particularly in the context of Victorian Vienna, a bourgeois society which was cracking open,[67] and as part of the discovery of the child's feelings and phantasies about the mother's body.

The structural allusion of the dream of Irma's Injection that is reversed in the manner of that of the Botanical Monograph is revealed in the sentence, "If you still have pains, it's your own fault."[68] Here, Freud conveys his strategy to bypass the experience of victimization and dependency. He places his child or victim self onto the person of Irma, and then contrives the freedom to condemn and judge the victim for her pain, much as Western culture has condemned the real child and the child in the adult to exile and scorn.

In Freud's formal theory of Oedipal development, built out of the signs of a second birth, women are linked with failed development. The vagina figures as a hole, or lack. The little girl with a hole, who will never be whole, alone carries the weight of human imperfection and immortality. She also connotes the underestimation of the birth canal and womb, with their associations to life and death. The image of women as creators and keepers of life shrinks down, much like the earth goddesses and mother goddesses who were transformed into harmless shadows of themselves in post-Hellenic culture.[69]

The Freud of the dream of Irma's Injection personifies the transcendent individuated subject appropriate to post-revolutionary culture. Hopes for the full flowering of political and religious reform are linked with new concepts of self-knowledge and self-awareness.[70] Modernists begin to understand culture as made up of varieties of relations and renounce the notion of society and culture as created by apriori forms and laws. Such understanding unmasks the abyss of uncertainty. The doctor of Irma's Injection, confronted with individual existence, splits away his mortal self into Irma. Klimt's images are prophecies of maternal potency threatening to resurface;[71] the contents of the tomb promising to return, as in the Judgment Day. The concepts of the fulminating instincts and the inferior girl with a lack, the privileged male superego, the monstrous siren, and the neurotic woman are realizations that grow from the effort to dilute the significance not of forceful sexuality alone, but of the underlying preconceptions of aloneness, fragmentation, and mortality in a cosmos without God.

Freud worked with these issues in a fascinating, elegantly argued paper, "The Theme of the Three Caskets."[72] He suggests in this paper that a theme is found in several fairy tales pertaining to the hero's odyssey. The hero is offered three choices as part of his access to progress and to adulthood. The choices are personified and symbolized as women, or the Fates or goddesses whose task it is to educate the hero. In this context, the Minerva forcefully warns man that despite his accomplishments he is inevitably a thing of nature and subject to death. Freud traces the transformations of these mythic themes in his terms as the recognition of both aspects of the mother goddess—the mother who gives birth, and the mother associated with death—Aphrodite as opposed to Artemis/Hecate. In this piece, Freud explores the workings of these universal powerful fantasies of the archaic functions of the mother. "The great mother goddesses of the oriental people, however, all seem to have been both creators and destroyers—both goddesses of life and fertility and goddesses of death."[73] Freud also elaborates on the function of choice in relation to these maternal images. He suggests that choice stands in the place of necessity. Through wish fulfillment, man evades the acceptance of his death. In reality, the three choices signify the three inevitable relations that a man has with a woman: the woman who bears him, the woman who is his mate, and the woman who destroys him; or, to put it another way, there are three forms taken by the figure of a mother in the course of a man's life: the mother herself, the beloved one who is chosen after that pattern, and lastly the mother earth who receives him once more, the third of the Fates, the goddess of death who will take him into her arms.[74]

At this point, Freud acknowledges the maternal figure as powerful and unavoidable, linked with the function of giving and protecting life as well as associated with its end. Life and death are women, yet this passage still very much speaks of the male subject experiencing women. Also, the ideas in this paper are not well integrated into the discussion of the Oedipus complex.

Following the logic of Freud in the *Theme of the Three Caskets*, vulnerability and aloneness are experiences which need to be mythified. The Oedipus myth as interpreted by Sophocles is a tale of a baby without a mother who becomes a sacrifice[75] to his parents' inability to tolerate the infantile.[76] Thus, Oedipus is Christ as an infant sacrifice and as a prey. The disavowal of the infant's plight is often overlooked in favor of an emphasis on incest and parricide, as the version of the myth delineated in *Totem and Taboo* makes clear. The human infant as a prey involves more than the experience of helplessness. Realizations of one's own death, or the danger of it, are part of our adaptive endowment. Knowledge of death and life is possible through our adaptive endowment in the form of phylogenetically honed bundles of knowledge which aid the individual as innate releasing mechanisms or preconceptions.[77] The life instinct can be thought about as an inherent organization whose task it is to keep the living organism alive by helping it to recognize its need of nutrition and safety.[78] Similarly, the death instinct, as it has been conceptualized by James Grotstein is in fact an inherent undifferentiated defense organization, which preserves the life of the organism through defense maintenance and repair. The death instinct as a defense organization has access to the inherent preconception of the prey/predator series as one of its functions so that danger is known and knowable.[79]

Paradoxically, human beings are plagued with the images of the inherent warning system; to the human infant the signal of danger appears as a life-threatening and horrible presence when bereft of the parent's reverie, which transforms the panic into signal anxiety as well as providing comfort and common sense.[80] The untranslated signifiers of danger surface as part of the experience of being victim or prey. The individual and the culture respond to these images of the predator in many complex ways. In *Totem and Taboo*, Freud represses the mother goddess themes and they return in a reversal of the prey/predator relationship. The underlying fear of being a prey, either to one's own parents, or to be unprotected by them, is presented as a male competition for the woman of the horde. The story of young males with sexual desire is substituted for that of the infant, who, requiring assurances of bonding with mother's body and mind as a guarantee of survival, desires her *presence*.[81] In Melanie Klein's discovery of the early Oedipus complex, she came to the realization that children of both sexes covet the mother as their source of survival. Infants' emotional links to mother are affectionate, curious, and needy rather than exclusively erotic. Later on, the boy changes his more dominantly dependent relationship to the mother's body for a sexual one which looks forward to a mature relationship with a woman. The little girl, as is well known, must give up her dependent relationship with mother for an erotic one with father, which will set the stage for the entrance in the girl's life of a mature sexual partner. In Freud's discussion of the Oedipus complex, this early relationship is not yet uncovered. In *Totem and Taboo*, it is eliminated. The possibility of sacrifice is delegated to the father, not the child, thereby bypassing the anxiety and helplessness of infancy. The myth in this form, as it is passed down from generation to generation, is a hermeneutic spiral which attempts to deny prey anxiety by transforming it into predator anxieties which are more vigorous, public, and are appropriate to a later stage of development.

Nevertheless, the theme of sacrifice remains as an important element of the myth, which Freud worked with as the theme of the abandoned child in *Moses and Monotheism*. In the essay, he purports to be discussing the legend of the birth of the hero, but despite the grand origins of the little aristocrat, Freud's portrayal is of an infant cursed by fate.[82] He draws on Rank's theory of the birth of the hero in which the curse appears as difficulty in conception, barrenness, societal disapproval, and danger to the father. As a result of this last element, the child himself (Freud speaks of boy babies) is condemned to death or to exposure, usually by order of his father or someone representing him.[83] Freud ends his discussion of infantile exile with a return to the theory of *Totem and Taboo* and a reference to that interpretation of the Oedipal configuration. He draws on Rank's Birth of the Hero to make his argument: "The hero is someone who has had the courage to rebel against his father, and in the end victoriously overcomes him."[84] Freud cites the totem and taboo theory as the source of monotheism; the monotheistic God is explained as a further transformation of the primal father→totem→God. The contradictory attitudes of hostility and loving reverence toward the father are reconciled in an act of cannibalism, by which the father is both eliminated and taken in. Freud's manifest mythic narrative submerges the themes of exile and infanticide under the ordeal of male competition and combat. Neverlehess, the latent content of myths dealing with incest and murder may be the thoughts and feelings about survival in the face of danger and death. The signifiers of the "second birth" appear out of a dubious relationship to the signified. In this case, the latter is the passions of being and attachment mythified and dreamt, formed within timeless mergers of parent-and-child, parent-in-child, child-in-parent, in the immanent poetics of the confluence of life and death.[85]

The notion that death is not only the enemy of life but an integral part of it is not always split away but is expressed in several creativity myths. The hero or heroine dies as he or she creates gifts for personkind and provides them with a means to survive. Creativity myths put forward the idea that the plants on which man lives derive from the death or murder of the mythic persona, oftentimes a woman who is buried in the earth or who descends into the earth and becomes a sacrifice which brings fertility. Persephone is one of these figures; another is the divine maiden Hainuwele of New Guinea legend.[86] The notion that life feeds on death is encountered in all cultures. Campbell points out that the appearance of death in culture is balanced by the notion of procreation—sex; the sexual organs are mythified at the same time as is the appearance of death. Campbell adds that the juxtaposition stands for the idea that reproduction without death would be a calamity, as would death without reproduction:[87]

> We may say that the interdependence of death and sex, their import as the complementary aspects of a single state of being, and the necessity of killing—killing and eating for the continuance of this state of being, which is that of man on earth and of all things on earth, the animals, birds and fish, as well as man—this deeply moving, emotionally disturbing glimpse of death as the life of the living is the fundamental motivation supporting the rites around which the social structures of many early cultures are composed.[88]

The very stuff of life is interpenetrated with death. The task of acknowledging the various interfaces of life and death is awesome. Ritual murder can be thought of as an enactment of an attempted mastery of these contradictions and the inevitable death of the individual. The mythic configuration of a god who demands these sacrifices is a divine personification of the realization of the monstrosity and cruelty of the everyday world and the inhumanity of the order of the universe, heightened exactly by the monstrosity of things.[89]

The notion that some must die to appease the god who has died for the good of the group finds its way into the culture in certain concepts of parent/child relations. The birth of the child signals the death of the parent and the passing of strength from one generation to another. The child, born out of mother and father's biological capacities, resents and fears their power to bestow life, but at the same time dreads the cost of his/her birth to his/her parents. If life is dear, and birth is intense and painful, what damage has it perpetrated on mother's body; what has been stolen from father's? If these experiences are not recognized and received by parental understanding, they mingle with signs of external danger, of hunger and lack of protection, and stimulate the inherent undifferentiated defense organization. The infant then feels him/herself to be a prey, a sacrifice to the god-parents. Guilt and the terror of death are enacted and ritualized between the generations and down the generations. A spiral of prey-predator relations enters culture, for example, as war at one end of the spectrum and puberty rites at another. The puberty rites designed for both boys and girls dramatize to the participants the experience of little murders through mutilation and endurance. Campbell has found these mythic themes in the rites of the primitive Australian tribes as well as in Greek mythology.[90] These myths serve several purposes for instructing the next generation: they reinforce the lawful authority of the parents and bind the child firmly into the values and customs of society. Subincision, circumcision, fasting, and other ordeals teach the child the relations between life and death but also warn of the dangers of rebelliousness and independence. Body mutilation, ritual murder, and war announce the parameters of the young individual's development and aid his/her integration into the community as an adult.

Rites for both boys and girls provide guides for helping the child to undergo the death of their child-selves. Circumcision and subincision ritualize father/son rivalry as well as cutting off the mother. While the boy is allowed to merge with her symbolically by transforming his penis into a vagina by a subincision, he is separated from her forever; his adult life is among men and purged of the mother culture.

Female children are initiated into their adult destiny of child rearing upon their first menstruation period. They enact rituals that symbolize the blood and its relationship to the mysteries and the power of fertility.[91] They also part with their childhood selves but are not pressed to detach from their mothers; and they will not, as a rule, enter the world of men.

The ways in which the child-bearing, child-rearing sphere is juxtaposed to the domain of public activities are organized differently in various cultures, but often safety and survival are mythified as male/protector/provider and female/child-bearer/caretaker. This conceptual connotation has been accompanied by considerable rigidity in modern times.[92] While some few cultures value the fertility of womenkind, many modern societies have associated the sphere of childbirth, nursing, and child rearing with weakness. The culture of the mother goddesses of ancient times designate a robust power to women.[93] Furthermore, female/child culture is not always segregated off into private pockets, but continues smoothly out into the public sphere.[94] Joseph Campbell describes the overthrow of a balanced male and female society in this way:

> Before the violent entry of a late Bronze Age and early Iron Age nomadic Aryan cattle herders from the north and Semitic sheep and goat herders from the south into the old cult sites of the ancient world, there had prevailed in that world an essentially organic vegetal non-heroic view of

the nature and necessities of life that was completely repugnant to those lionhearts for whom not the patient toil of earth but the battle sphere and its plunder were the sources of wealth and its joy. In the older mother myths and rites, the light and darker aspects of the mixed thing that is life had been honored equally and together, whereas in the later male-oriented patriarchal myths all that is good and noble was attributed to the new, heroic master gods leaving to the native nature powers the character only of darkness, to which also a negative, moral judgment was now added.[95]

Campbell suggests that the counterpart for the Greeks was the victory of Zeus over Tithon, the youngest child of Gaea, the goddess earth, by which deed the reign of the patriarchial gods of Mount Olympus was secured over the earlier Titan broods of the great goddess mother.[96] The victory of the masters grows from the inability of culture to integrate weakness and strength.

I would like to suggest that the underlying configuration that maintains the dichotomy male/external/strong/vital/capable versus woman/internal/weak/treacherous/limited is connected to prey-predator anxiety, which in turn is related to the dilemma of the management of the dread of either of these possibilities. My notion is that cultures often make this dichotomy far more rigid than it needs to be despite its obvious attractions. In our recent past, the temptation to cloister or trivialize the mother/child culture and to glorify and appropriate to males the external sphere of defense, politics, religion, and economics has been powerfully compelling. This division maintains a separation between life and death. Death is intimately linked to weakness and fragility associated with the infant, but the connection is disavowed from consciousness in culture and transformed into manic claims of omnipotence and strength. The invulnerable figure of the young male warrior is used as a pawn in this way. External life is claimed exclusively for the male adult realm and severed from its roots in infancy and childhood. The prey experience is associated with a mother/child dyad but cut away from awareness. Maleness then becomes equated with predator activities and femaleness with the prey experience. The Oedipus myth, as a myth of the hero, tragic though it is, becomes a myth that tries to understand or unravel these oppositions. It is a legend that reflects the male "consciousness" that grows out of this "solution." Freud, in his discovery of the Oedipus complex, seemed to be accepting this defensive pattern, but began its dismantling for which a modernist culture provides the opportunity.

Melanie Klein intuited the presence of anxiety about danger and death in the child's or infant's mind. She came to believe through her work with young children that primitive, passionate relationships with parental imagoes existed in the infant's inner world almost from the beginning. She explained that the phantasies of self and others were already highly developed in a child of two and a half or three years of age, suggesting that the antecedents of these imagined relations began in the first year. Klein believed that the Oedipus complex commenced with the phantasies of one's relationship to mother's body and the rival that appeared even at the breast. In her earlier papers Klein moved the onset of the Oedipus complex back to the end of the first year.[97] In her later work, "Schizoid Mechanisms" (1946) and "Notes on the Emotional Development of the Infant" (1952), she theorized that the Oedipus complex began with mental life itself within the first few weeks.

Klein had already departed from Freud in her emphasis on the phantasies associated with the libidinal phases. Freud's theory of development was based on the journey of the libido through the oral, anal, and phallic stages until reaching the genital stage, its ultimate destination. He emphasized that the presence of libidinal tension at each stage stimulated phantasies about the self and object in the currency of the zone. For example, the libido centered on the penis stimulates the phantasy of castration. Klein, following Karl Abraham, her mentor, particularly the ideas in his paper "A Short History of the Libido" (1924), began to formulate the Oedipus complex as made up of phantasies of self and other filtered through each of the libidinal zones. However, Klein's phantasies were not based on discharge or satisfaction (from the principle of constancy). Though she thought that the life and death instincts were the basic firing pins for infantile phantasies, she understood the underlying force to be survival itself. Furthermore, the drama enacted in each of the zones was one of the need or dependence on the object. The infant needed the maternal object to be fed, cared for, and to be buffered from disruptive separation.

However, Klein did believe in the inevitable difficulty in the infant's instinctual endowment. Although the baby's phantasies were guarded by the life instincts for the purposes of survival, the death instinct was also the snake in the garden which appeared in the form of destructive impulses. According to Klein, just as the infant's loving, bonded relationship was guided by the life instinct, the infant responding under the aegis of the death instinct to excessive frustration or a poor holding environment felt tremendous anxiety from the threat of annihilation. Klein emphasized that some infants were constitutionally endowed with a particularly low threshold for danger. Even an excellent or good enough mother or environment would not reassure the thin-skinned infant. Autism and psychosis may have their origin in a situation in which the infant can only try to destroy what he or she feels to be utterly unhealthful. Klein thought that the innate death instinct must be deflected toward the primary caretakers in order to escape the feelings of annihilation anxiety. She described a dreadful closed spiral under these conditions. The infant projects out its fear of dying onto an imagined image of the mother who is then felt to be life-threatening or disturbing. If the balance between the environment's contribution and the infant's subjective coding of both internal and external perturbation is weighted in favor of persecutory anxiety, the infant will become extremely troubled, even ill. Also, aspects of the primary caretakers take on grotesque shapes and qualities. Klein explains that during the oral stage, as the infant's first object relation is the relation to the mother's breast (part object) and as the mother's contributions are introjected and take root in the ego with relative security, the basis for satisfaction and development is established. Under the dominance of oral impulses, in good circumstances the breast is instinctively felt to be a source of nourishment and therefore in a deeper sense "life itself." Mental and physical bonding partially restore the lost prenatal unity. Fear, manifested at times of frustration as destructive impulses, is modified.

Under difficult circumstances, the phantasies signifying experiences that take place in the mouth by incorporation become ferocious, biting, devouring and cannibalizing, and are attached to the image of the breast within the infant's mind, and if not modified by human interaction or intersubjectivity, the infant lives in an unending paranoid situation. Only if the good breast is experienced may this cycle be broken. Similarly, anal and genital phantasies are colored by the balance between the life and the the death instincts according to Klein. Dramas of loving possession and merger are in tension with those of violent possession and intrusion.

Klein's theory of phantasies makes clear infantile mythology about the inside of the mother's body as the first labyrinth or stage of the infantile odyssey into separation. Also, the mother's body is the dream screen and the scaffolding for mythology. Thus, the mother's body as well as the bodily zones is a staging for much of the infant's mental life.

For Klein, the Oedipus complex begins in relation to aspects of mother's body, breast, and caretaking capacities. The early rivals are experienced as anything that disrupts the infant's felt needs for bonding. One Oedipal rival may be felt to be the other breast, who snatches the nipple and milk away, or the breast may be felt to be feeding the other breast, excluding the baby. The inside of mother's body is felt to contain other rivals: the inside babies, who are undisturbed and always fulfilled, and the father's penis, which is in a privileged position and stands in the way of the infant's exclusive possession of mother's body. Under conditions in which the infant feels threatened, the death instinct colors the intersubjective field with dark and hostile affects. The early Oedipal triangle, baby breast and rival, eggs or penis, develops along the lines of the infant's sense of safety and danger.

Klein theorized that the superego is formed under the aegis of the life and death struggles of infancy. Her notion of the superego differs from Freud's. Rather than being structured at the resolution of the childhood Oedipus complex under parental prohibition at four and a half or five years old, Klein believed that the archaic superego developed out of the destructive impulses directed at primary objects projected and introjected and if not well-contained, developed into greedy, envious, and unhelpful personas inside the ego.

Klein acknowledged, as did Freud, that the instincts were the motivating force for the construction of phantasies. She also emphasized his theory of narcissistic identifications in which self and other were mingled and an internal cast of characters came to life.[98] A spectrum developed which began with a breast-mouth relationship to one with a whole object, far more in keeping with external experience. However, the early dramas, Klein thought, were fleshed out from the first experiences of the body and primitive phantasies and were highly fantastic.

Klein believed that the Oedipal drama begins with the infant's struggle with instinctual awareness of danger and the longing for security. Possession, need of care, rivalry, longing, love, and hate are played out in the early months.[99] The nature of the later whole-object Oedipus phase is heavily determined by the exchanges of the archaic intersubjective field. Klein's understanding of the early Oedipal saga pierces the underpinnings of myth and legend of cultural dreams as do Kristeva's infantile semiotics, the stuff of preverbal, presymbolic languaging.

Wilfred Bion,[100] deeply inspired by Klein's notions of mental development and primitive mental states, explored the implications of her theory, proceeding even deeper into the origins of mental life. Bion departed from Klein in one very significant way. He gradually came to realize that the infant's intense communications were not based so dominantly on an instinctual program, i.e., the inevitability of the mark of the death instinct, but instead he felt that explosive and violent feelings, and dark and hostile images, appeared in the wasteland of the failure of infant-mother relatedness. Bion understood Klein's theory of projective identification as a communicating signifying system. He explained that as the infant communicates internal experience to the mothering one, he/she can provide regulation, soothing and meaningfulness by sharing the maturity of adult mental capacities. Thus, the fear of dying as a wild, raging breast in the tummy would be tamed by consolation, understanding, and the appropriate response. The primary caretaker's inability to participate with attuned responses, to experience the experience with the infant, and to reject the message leaves the infant helpless and driven crazy by the random and chaotic content of his or her mind.

Bion conceptualized the "mother"-infant communication system as the container-contained and proposed that all mental life worked on this principle.[101] In his theory of the evolution of a thought, he proposes that sensory data (internal and external) and innate preconceptions are contained and transformed into mental elements which can be dreamt and mythified and made into phantasies out of which are developed concepts and words and later abstract scientific systems fit for ever more complex representations.

Bion emphasizes that the infant at birth requires a mental partnership to support his or her immature mental apparatus.[102] He suggests that the parents transform the seeds of the infant's archaic experience into thinkable elements with his/her capacity to dream, think, and signify. Bion calls this "maternal reverie" (or paternal reverie); the capacity for transformation, alpha function; and the thinkable elements, alpha elements. He emphasizes maternal reverie, but in fact he is describing a function which creates meaning out of random or concrete experience. Pregnancy and nursing bring the infant-mother into a closer empathetic communication system, but father's participation in the birth and the early infant care allows his capacity to contain and detoxify to develop inside of him. In fact, both parents are needed for infant care, not only one to protect and one to provide, one to nurture and one to rest, one to papoose the infant but also one to contain the other parent, all in order to adequately translate, interpret, and detoxify the infant's intense, forceful emotional communications. The Oedipus myth in its familial form portrays a situation in which the the infant is denied the container-contained relationship, and the parents deprived of a rich, satisfying familial interaction.

Bion understands the origin of personal group myths as beginning with mental life itself or before. He explains that the unconscious stores not only memories of self and others but mythic significances of past, present, and future. Inherent meaningfulness, purposefulness, and a template for self-discovery are stored in structures identified as preconceptions. They are innate and contain the ultimate coding for self-knowledge and expressiveness, but known only as earthly manifestations of their full transcendence and complete meaning.

In addition, preconceptions work adaptively. In this sense, preconceptions may be also understood as inherent releasing coordinators, as Bowlby discusses them,[103] which carry genetically coded information that facilitates the infant's bonding capacity and learning processes. Preconceptions also function as keepers of the hero or heroine's destiny. The latter is carried in the genetic coding of the individual's unique talents and predispositions. Preconceptions range from the primitive and biological such as breathing and eating to complex and eventually more conscious ones. For example, a divinitory hypothesis that supposes that a husky-voiced, bearded person is a Da-da. This, in turn, can evolve into a scientific deductive system such as: babies have two parents, of different types.[104] Preconceptions have a destiny, which is to mate with their counterpart in conscious awareness, thereby bridging the gap between the archaic occult world of dream and fantasy and the world of conscious thinking.

According to Bion, the Oedipus myth (or any myth) is an extended complex preconception which serves as an innate template for the questions and emotions integral to family experience: How did I come here? How was I made? How do I fit in as one of three? What is my importance to myself and to these two others? The Oedipus myth originates as a preconception which, when mated with an external realization, is transformed into a conscious myth,[105] understood first by the individual and then by the group, and shared in specific ways in culture. However, the evolution of the individual myth depends significantly on the emotional interaction between the infant and the parents, extended family and culture. The realization as it appears in Sophocles' *Oedipus Rex*, *Oedipus at Colonus*, and *Antigone* is a tale of entangled, doomed relationships, and appraisal or warning in which Oedipus suffers, and is chosen to be sacrificed for the sake of others in the group. He is a near infanticide, a victim to his family's fear of meaning.

Thus, for Campbell, Freud, Klein, and Bion, the surface narrative of the myth is constructed not only out of cultural/social interpretations of developmental tasks and experiences, and out of biological innate mapping for survival, but out of the emotional experiences of need and desire. The surface events of Oedipus's journey into anguished self-discovery are created out of many elements in mental life: the arcane, the instinctual, the preconceptual, the perceptual, cognitive, and conscious, which are transformed and symbolized by the force of meaning seeking its birth.

The thrust of the mind honing its signs and symbols is fueled by the emotions to create structures which link structures with other structures or thoughts with images and ideas. The links move in all directions in synchronic and diachronic patterns.[106] These are the transformations of emotional significance. Experience of all kinds can be mythified in this way; natural phenomena, events of the life-cycle, such as initiation and marriage ceremonies, and lastly, emotions themselves.

Bion's theory of transformation of mental experience from the somatosensory to abstract systems of thought clarifies the relationship of the imaginary or *le sémiotique* to the symbolic order. Rather than oppositional or dichotomous, Bion conceptualizes them as structured by the container-contained principle. In this way, the experience of infantile phantasies or the semiotic of primary process is transformed and contained in conscious language. The conscious structures are charged by the originary, unconscious images and feelings. However, the conscious mind linked with the symbolic order of language, ideologies, and social customs and values, make up in part the content for the container of the dream process or myth. Through reciprocal exchanges and signification processes, the symbolic and the preverbal inform each other and are interwoven into the other's fabric. Freud's notion of the dream process and the role of the day residue, the infantile wish and childhood memories suggest a dialectical relationship between conscious thinking and unconscious mental processes. Recall Freud's idea that the drives, linked with a powerful childhood wish, pull down the left-over thoughts of the preconscious to camouflage themselves as part of the search for discharge. From this perspective, neither the maternal nor the paternal metaphor needs to be privileged at the expense of the other. Signification processes are based on the complementary relations between the presymbolic and the symbolic and between what has been designated the maternal and paternal respectively. The toleration of difference depends intimately on the containing function of the parents. Paradoxically, in the absence of the toleration of difference, the containing function is undermined. To head off a closed circle of meaninglessness, the adult mind must tolerate the contradictions in the infant's mind that are at first polarized as love and hate, good and bad, full and empty, presence and absence, life and death. Klein theorized that in early infancy, the baby sorts out experiences through splitting into categories. Splitting used this way is an important organizing capacity for the infant. Gradually, the splits are integrated, and cognition and thinking replace phantasies based on dramatic splitting as methods of organizing the data of experience.

Mythic structures function as containers for the individual's meaning about his or her feelings, parents, siblings, larger family and culture. Unconscious emotions and desires patterned into phantasies and dreams mingle with external reality. The myth directs the innate and deep forces towards their conscious destiny. At the same time, then, the myth presents cultural symbols and values to the developing individual of the new generation. Thus, for example, the Sphinx represents eternal phantasies of a primitive, unsatisfying relationship to the breast. Oedipus signifies the baby's frustrated yearning to bond with his family throughout his odyssey. The good mother and the good mating on any level are split out of the play of *Oedipus Rex*. Oedipus's reconciliation and integration are not achieved until *Oedipus at Colonus*, and then they come to him only at the end of his life. The cultural values and systems of the Sophocles plays are presented in the Oracle's decree of the curse and the moral offense. From our cultural perspective, we would find the moral dilemma of the Oedipus legend strange. At the same time, however, the themes of attachment and desire are universal and are found in every culture.

Myths function to present emotional or public catastrophic change. For example, the infant's moving from a symbiotic relationship to one of separate, individuated mental life. Or, in culture, from a hunting to an agricultural society, or from a culture in which raw food is replaced by cooked food. Myths stage dilemmas, crucial changes, and contradictions in several ways. The processes of signification working inside the myth are several and operate according to different laws of the mind. The first is the manifest, or narrative element, structure associated with historical narrative, operating within time and moving in an orderly, progressive fashion and organized by cause-and-effect logic which moves toward a goal or solution. Oedipus leaves his second family under a misapprehension, and returning toward Thebes, meets his father, etc. However, Lévi-Strauss has expanded the notion of the narrative. He believes that the processes of signification are structured horizontally and vertically or associatively.[107] Lévi-Strauss conceptualizes the associative as bundles of units, "mythemes," as he calls them, or structures which are organized by the mind to sort the polarity of experience and to solve universal dilemmas such as: How was I born? How will I survive? The mythemes function synchronically and the linear narrative diachronically. The synchronic patterns work eternally outside the laws of time and reflect the operations of the mind itself and its contents as it sorts and organizes meaning. Lévi-Strauss defines the unconscious itself as a symbol-making organ "reducible to a function." He explains the symbolic function as characteristically human.

In the overture to *The Raw and the Cooked*,[108] Lévi-Strauss details this function further. He explains that he believes myths are based on secondary codes which are transformations of primary ones, or inherent ones. He conceptualizes the inherent codes as similar to Bion's theory of preconceptions. Lévi-Strauss states that myths bring people face to face with potential objects of which only the shadows are actualized with conscious approximation of inevitably unconscious truths. He understands these primary things, like Bion, as before language and uses the phrase "the primary stuff of language." The level of mental life before language is connected to the natural laws of the mind and biology. In this way, Lévi-Strauss develops a notion of myths as do Campbell and Bion. To make this argument, he proposes a comparison between music and myth. He says:

> Like a musical world, myth operates on the basis of a two-fold continuum. One part of it is external, and is composed in the one instance, of historical or supposedly historical events of theoretically infinite series from which each society extracts a limited number of relevant incidents with which to create its myths. And in the other instance, the equally infinite series of physically producible sounds from which each musical system selects its scale. The second aspect of the continuum is internal, and is situated in the psycho-physiological time of the listener, the elements of which are very complex; they involve the periodicity of cerebral waves and organic rhythms, the strength of the memory, and the power of attention. Mythology makes demands primarily on the neuro-mental aspects because of the length of the narrative, the recurrence of certain themes.[109]

Through his analysis of mythological transformations, Lévi-Strauss has made a connection between the meanings associated with the universal and the deep structures of the mind and culture.

Lévi-Strauss's structural analysis of the Oedipus myth provides a map for discovering eternal or universal emotional polarities characteristic of familial relations. By ordering the myth into the form of an orchestra score, he is able to read the synchronic relations of the myth.[110] Thus he places the elements of the myth in four vertical columns, each of which include several relations belonging to the same bundle, which all share a common feature. Column 1 has as its common feature the overrating of blood relations, while Column 2 is its inversion; the underrating of blood relations. Examples of the former are: Oedipus marries his mother Jocasta, Antigone buries her brother Polyneices despite prohibition. Examples of the latter are: Oedipus kills his father Laius, Eteocles kills his brother Polyneices.

The third column has as its mythic theme the denial of the autochthonous origins of mankind (personkind); the fourth, the persistence of the belief in autochthonous origins of mankind (personkind). The common feature, the slaying of monsters, of the third column is indicated by these ideas: Cadmus kills the dragon; Oedipus kills the Sphinx. The fourth is made up of elements representing difficulties in walking, standing, and walking upright; Labdicus (Laius's father) means "lame"; Laius (Oedipus's father) means "left-sided"; Oedipus means "swollen foot." By reading from left to right column after column including the vertical arrangement of each column, new themes appear.

The juxtaposition of columns 1 and 2 of the synchronic bundles confronts the difficulties and the contradictions implicit in the family feelings of love/hate and care/indifference. As column 1 portrays the overrating of blood relations enacted through the desecration of sacred boundaries, column 2 presents their devaluing through acts of murder, fratricide, and patricide. The polarities carried in these two columns dramatize the pain and difficulties of attachment.

Columns 3 and 4 interpreted by Lévi-Strauss present themes elaborating theories of birth. The slaying of the monsters or the chtonian beings suggest a challenge to the theory that one springs from the earth. Column 4 presents the persistence of this theory; people born from the earth have difficulty walking and standing.[111] I believe the structural relationship between these last two columns reveals the bewilderment and pain attendant on mental birth as well as physical birth. Column 3 refers to the monsters Lévi-Strauss identifies as the agents challenging autochthony. The battle with the dragon and the Sphinx may also signify the struggle to acknowledge and experience mental birth. In addition, monsters appear when the infants begin to sense the failure of the environment to provide them with a sufficient sense of support and to fantasize ("magicking away") their awareness of their weakness and mortality. Thus they themselves become attacking monsters engaged in a battle with other monsters. This is an instance of prey/predator images.

In the fourth column, the male line of Oedipus's family is signified by the peculiarity of the members' names, as discussed. The painful or irregular bodily functions may be interpreted as wounds incurred in the battle with the monsters to achieve mental birth.[112] The act of killing the dragon or the Sphinx stands for the struggle to give up the comfort of the belief in self-creation, the autochthonous theory of origin. Thus, the creatures may also signify the parents as enemies to the quest and/or as aspects of the self dreading the awareness of need in the context of emotional relatedness.

Lévi-Strauss explains that "the function of the four columns is to demonstrate that the inability to connect two kinds of relationships is overcome (or rather, replaced) by the assertion that contradictory relationships are identical inasmuch as they are both self-contradictory in a similar way."[113] He adds that the Oedipus myth is constructed to mediate polarities and provide approaches to the mysteries of experience. He shares with Bion the notion that the Oedipus myth is a tool for learning about one's origins, birth, family relationships, and place in the universe in that the myth functions to guide the individual through the significant contradictions within mental life, such as love and hate, life and death, presented in the universe in the opposition between plants, life, and care on the one hand; animals, death, and indifference on the other.

Lévi-Strauss understands another function of myth to be the template of mental operations that have already taken place and are taking place within the speaker and listener. The themes of the myth are not only communicated, but reexperienced emotionally and cognitively, particularly for each new generation within the group. Thus, within the sharing of a myth—the telling of it, the elaborating of it—the individual goes through the experience of learning about these important polarities and emotional constellations.

In all these ways, myths are an aspect of and act as part of the container-contained function of the mind which receives the infant's or child's messages, signifies them or codes them, provides empathy and interpretation to the infant, whose mental functioning is not yet mature enough to work over his experience in these ways.

The capacity for the toleration of difference and the pain of integration is an important function of the parental cultural mind. It seems clear, however, that the perpetuation of binary oppositions of sex, age, race, and class are those which designate one of the pair inferior or abject.[114] The Oedipus myth can be seen as faulty or defective as it is structured on the denial of the container-contained relationship and therefore cursed with tragic growth and development as the outward form of the inward bias and difficulty in tolerating differences, ultimately, separation and death.

It seems to me that these cultural oppositions are built not only out of the infantile splitting and binary oppositional structures but out of autistic maneuvers. Frances Tustin's work on autism (1981)[115] has deepened knowledge of the container/contained transactions. Mrs. Tustin describes the nascent self as experiencing largely in terms of critical sensations known through their distinctions and oppositional qualities. Hard and soft are the two archetypal sensations. The integration of hard and soft respectively—nasty, powerful, unyielding, tough, frustrating, firm versus helpless, vulnerable, little, available, comforting—is an important aspect of the infant's growth and of the tolerance of the "not-me."

In what Tustin designates as a normal autosensuality, the infant feels knitted to mother and sheltered in a sensory cocoon of at-one-ment. Premature disruption of the sensory illusion of adhesive attachment is felt to leave a serious, ghastly hole, or wound. In this way, the cluster of sensations of mouth-tongue-nipple as a structure for the illusion of a postnatal umbilicus if hastily nipped off, creates a psychic catastrophe, the black hole of nothingness through which the sense of self falls hopelessly and eternally. Tustin conceives of these early sensation-dominated experiences as the forerunners to symbiotic relatedness and transitional phenomena and therefore as the beginning of emotional signification.

Living through the archaic excited states of autosensuality assists the critical integration of contrasting sensations. Failed integration leads to bias and delusion. Hard, unpleasant, tortured sensations are pushed into the "not-me" sphere while soft, comfortable, flowing sensations are considered "me" experiences. Integration assists development and creates a bridge to the "not-me" experience, and the self is felt to be resilient rather than victimized. Hard and soft are also understood to be both on the outside, softening the enemy and preventing the need for a shell. As a connection is woven out of these critical sensations, the stage is set for transitional play in the sphere of the intermediate and the possibility of symbolizing experience is nurtured (Winnicott, 1981).

It seems to me that a bridge can also be made between cultural configurations and these notions. Bion's and Tustin's ideas allow the formation of the hypothesis that attitudes toward infants and children are to mental life as they are to the choices of a society in which power and militarism are preferred to the welfare of infants and children. The process of assisting the infant or child to give meaning to his or her experience is part of the intersubjective field which unfolds between parents and children; as the parent's mind has the mature capacity to signify and symbolize, allowing meaning to gather in the space of individuation where one object may stand for another (metaphor),[116] or is linked with another through displacement (metonymy). Under these conditions and given the baby's responsiveness, mental or psychological, significance begins to grow through the elements of communication between the parent and the child. In the lively field of two subjectivities exchanging experience, symbols and signs proliferate, carrying meaning from all levels of mental life.

Alfred Silver's work on the psychoanalytic semiotic extends Bion's theory of the birth of meaning through the mating of a preconception with its realization→→ negative realization→concept (thought).[117] Furthermore, Silver provides us with a dimensional model of the formation of semiotics and symbols which transforms and combines elements from both the conscious and the unconscious. Silver has drawn on C. S. Peirce's work on the formation of signs and language and is able to conceptualize the emergence of concepts as forming structures which are triadic. The structure is triadic because of the interpretant, or thinker, who, while part of the structure, creates the meaningful and biased connections between object and sign. For Peirce, Silver, and Bion, the mind of the thinker is the force which gives birth to and determines the nature of the sign. Silver hypothesizes the evolution of a sign as the interpretant relating to an object, experiencing realizations of it, and extending that awareness to the creation of its sign.[118] For example, as the infant meets an aspect of the mother, her sheltering body, or soothing mind, he/she experiences a realization of that encounter. At first, the infant creates in part out of autosensual or narcissistic modes of experiencing what is unevenly perceived to be outside the self.[119] With the chaperone of parental containment, the occult primitive and eternal fill the infant's phantasy signs and provide a safe cocoon for the infant to keep unmediated demands of external forces at bay.

Alfred Silver, exploring the phenomenology of the formation of signs, draws on Peirce's notions of Firstness, Secondness, and Thirdness. In a state of Firstness, the signs created are like icons, hardly different from the object itself, and known almost only in their physicality. In Secondness, the signs are indexical, and while still experienced as physical objects rather than abstractions or representations, some differentiation has been achieved. Objects in Firstness and Secondness are experienced by the interpretant in a somewhat undifferentiated state, without a definite meaning or a clear sense of inside or outside. At this level of the mind, mental processes seem propelled by omnipotence and magic, but it is also at this level that the deep and preconceptual bias of the individual shapes the object for the subject, as well as informing the sign of its task. Silver suggests that the symbol is formed from an intermingling of internal and external forces. From inside the symbol former comes the creative force that involves some knowledge of the primal object in the form of a presupposition or a preconception.[120] Silver states that a sign cannot create or discover the object which it represents, rather, it is fitted by the symbol former to point to and represent the object which the symbol former already knows as a presupposition. The primacy of the preconception follows Kant's notion of the noumena. At the same time, a percept is formed of external data based on iconical or analogical likeness and the fit of something observed and compared to the primal object. Silver also points out that these primitive signs give richness and depth to later symbols, which are more flexible and representational, or to put it differently, Thirdness requires the sensual richness of infantile mental life.

While these two categories of signs are not at all discrete, the individual's contribution, particularly at the level of the unconscious, is made up of his or her unique idiosyncratic coding of deep mental forces related to self-expression and survival. This is not to say that the unconscious is not influenced or transformed by cultural forces; the issue is one of degree.[121] Culturally determined codes, both verbal and nonverbal, are more predominantly influenced by shared values containing elements of unconscious motivations which have been transformed in accordance with the demands of conscious logic and the community's felt needs or as the French feminist writers suggest, the social symbolic order banishes the unconscious meanings.

Silver, following Peirce's idea of Thirdness, conceptualizes it as an agency of understanding which gives meaning and significance to the relationship between objects (mother or father) and baby object and sign. The interpretant as third not only observes the sign-object relationship, he/she is in an active, creative relationship with both as part of the triad.[122] The capacity to maintain the perspective of Thirdness arises out of the preverbal dialogue of projective identification.[123] The infant sends his/her emotionally laden messages out to mother's or father's mind to be interpreted and made human. The parental ability to catch the ballistics of the infant's raw communications with empathy and toleration tones the infant's capacities to gather meaning and search for significance or self-knowledge.[124] Even so, the infant's experiences—primitive, occult, and transcendental—in its origins provide the material for the heightened characters of myth. The infant's search for meaning and signification of unnamed powerfully felt experience from inside and outside creates the characters or personas and dramas of myth.[125] Without the available container, the mythic characters and their adventures become eerie, bizarre, and meaningless, and finally disintegrated or mutilated, as in some versions of the Oedipus myth which I will discuss.

The infant signifies his/her objects from the seemingly self-centered or insular vertex (autistic or narcissistic, respectively)[126] largely because his/her need of the illusion of this world view is adaptive in the early days.[127] Tearing the shield of early skin-to-skin attachment leaves the infant in a catastrophic state in which a world filled with sensory assault rushes in at a time when the infant-subject is not buffered from sensory experience and cannot process its implications. Cradled in primary at-one-ment, or the reciprocity envelope, the infant is able to safely perceive some separateness from others and discriminate the features and voice of mother at three weeks of age.[128] The infant's dependence on the emotional reality of continuing at-one-ment allows the organization of percepts and preconceptions of his/her relationship to the primary object into visual or preverbal signs.[129] Without the assurance of attachment, ongoing being is seriously compromised.

The primitive semiotics of infancy can be understood as mental baby teeth, a scaffolding that complements Campbell's notions of larger mythic structures in that they hold the contents of the mind and interpret and guide the individual in his/her odyssey to self-knowledge and a place in his/her group and in the universe. Since the early structures must provide a sense of safety and bonding, they are created out of images of self and selfobject.[130] The latter is a picture of the mother as attached to the self, and providing for the self the necessary functions of survival. Thus, the selfobject experience is precisely what is missing in Freud's and Sophocles' map of the Oedipus myth. The selfobject experience is also the ground support for the infant's growth. It is the container function in its ultimate form, in that it is the surround that shelters the infant's emergence into mental life. In this context the self object is the background subject-object of primary identification, the legacy of one's parental origins, concretely their bodies and spiritually their love, care, and creativity.[131]

James Grotstein has posited a visual metaphor of the infant's mythic signs of the selfobject relationship or relation to the background subject/object of primary identification in its various phases. As a first image in the stage of autism or normal autosensuality, Grotstein suggests that the interpretant/object/sign relationship is a symbolization of the infant's experience of feeling fused to the mother's body while at the same time perceiving her as a separate object. The image is that of Siamese twins; the infant sits on the mother's lap, joined at the body with two heads, the mother's behind her baby's body, bolstering the baby's experience.[132] The visual expression of the relationship implies not only separateness/non-separateness, fantasy (phantasy)/reality, me/not me, but the needed satisfaction of the illusion of at-one-ment as well. Out of this complex experience, the infant begins to represent and signify the relationship out of both its presence and its absence. However, since the infant can only begin to generalize patterns of experience, and since he/she thinks largely with the senses, these earlier signs are not as yet complex structures capable of expressing the spirit of the relationship or of transforming the experience of spirit and being. They are more characteristic of fusion and identification, and in this way as such, more iconical or indexical.[133]

At the level of symbiosis proper, in which the infant is more able to appreciate the presence of the other, Grotstein continues the metaphor of a pictorial sign of the baby sitting on the mother's lap looking at her face, an image connoting mutuality and respect as well as skin-to-skin intimacy. Another function of the face-to-face relationship is that of mirroring; the mother validates and reflects the infant's uniqueness and grandiose showing off or sense of power.[134] Another stance in which the infant is able to draw on mother or father's power by idealizing him or her is pictured by Grotstein as a papoose relationship, with the baby looking up the rear of the parent's head.

At the level of separation, individuation, and rapprochement, the infant/object relationship can be pictured as a side-by-side relationship, with the infant's and mother's heads facing the same direction, connoting separate mental life, although including a sense of protection through intimacy.

In this theory the dyad is not actually separated from the triad, and thus by adding the father to the pictures, we can see many possible functions of the myth of the Oedipus complex. The triadic structure is often read as the traditional Oedipus complex, with the child holding onto its mother and pushing away the father as the intruder. All the above symbiotic signs may also include a father backing the mother, in other words a lap behind the lap. But also the progress from various degrees of Siamese connectedness into separate mental experience may also be understood as various postures in regard to father. At first, in normal autosensuality, the father might be experienced intrusively, as awareness, challenging the infant's belief in his/her role as creator of the universe and/or the father may represent the guide through it. Later, in normal symbiosis, the father or third element may be conceptualized as the competitor for mother's lap or breast, a being with many encircling arms, or the reverse—a source of additional strength. These first two early stages portray the mythic drama in part object images.[135] The later figure, the father of separation and individuation, may be symbolized as a more integrated person, either a chaperone into the outside world or an interloper/competitor for the mother's whole body and genitals.

As the infant moves from solipsism to socialism, his/her signs change quality and shape. At the beginning they are concrete in character, made from the sensual experiences which are part of the baby's adaptive cocoon. The sensuousness of the parent-infant relationship provides a substitute for the lost placenta/umbilicus relationship. As Tustin has suggested, to the infant, the patterns of rhythm and sensation associated with sucking seem to be the breast, which is experienced in terms of those innate dispositions which are programmed to emerge at this time.[136] Tustin goes on: "Bodily rhythms and vibrations experienced in contact with the mother seem to be the mother. These flecks of sensations constitute the infant's sense of being, not yet clearly differentiated from what is outside the self, or the 'not-me'."

In normal development the infant grows strong enough to tolerate a space between him/herself and the other and to individuate sufficiently to acknowledge the not-me, that which is not attached and not controlled by the self. From the infant's point of view, if the infant can maintain the illusion of the Siamese twin relationship, that is, separateness and non-separatness, he/she can begin to fashion symbols or signs of his/her twin. The first triads are tactile and sensual icons or indexes, and they would necessarily be long and thin, as the infant thinker imagines mother to be part of him/herself, thereby shortening the line between them while pushing away the sign of the interaction. Silver discusses the Oedipus myth as mapping the formation of triadic structures of this kind.[137] Father represents the third in the sense of the not-me which comes between the baby and his/her Siamese twin. Thus, the line between Laius and Jocasta is lengthened considerably while the line between Oedipus and Jocasta is shortened. The manner in which the infant is introduced to various experiences influences the formation of the concepts of Secondness and Thirdness[138] and influences the capacity to move toward open and abstract triadic signs. The containing function of the parental object is crucial here in detoxifying the baby's frightening experience and supporting his/her appetite for knowledge and growth, and also as the representative of cultural values, the parent selecting and filtering what will be encouraged and what will be aborted.

The symbolic structures formed out of the individual's experience with primary objects are the building blocks for larger mythic structures, and like the large myths as analyzed by Lévi-Strauss, these smaller units are structured synchronically as well as diachronically in that they signify historical themes as well as eternal themes which return as preconceptions not only for each generation but at each stage of the individual's life cycle. The themes of familial relatedness return again and again in the Oedipus myth. The cultural values and problems operate in narrative, nonreversible time, and are bound to specifics of the time and place. Thus it can be imagined that each triad works horizontally and vertically and transforms both the eternal and the historical while each works alternatively as the container for the other. The eternal and biological makes sense out of present-day experience, and present-day experience allows for the surfacing of the primary process material, as Freud suggested in his theory of the day residue. Thus the myths of the pre-Hellenic mother goddess culture reflect the eternal mother-child relationship, with respect for the fertility of pregnancy and nursing as well as societal attitudes toward motherhood and contemporary theories of nature.

Harriet Beecher Stowe, Louisa May Alcott, and Mary Cassatt were educated and reared in a culture which invited individuality and tentatively glimpsed the implications of equality and self-discovery. Yet, the codes, values, and myths of their societal and familial culture were filled with profound naiveté and ambivalence in regard to the issues of inner emotional life. Both exhilaration and dread rose from permission to meet with one's self and with the inner forces released by the erosion of old authoritarian structures and the hierarchical model of governmnent, church, and family. The realization of the Oedipal myth or the myth of familial relations that they found in their culture was structured so that women's existence was truncated, her forcefulness buried under "masculine" culture. Since the very signs and images of their thoughts were structured by the bias of this version of the Oedipus myth, the creative process that Stowe, Alcott, and Cassatt undertook is formidable. The signifiers of women required exploration and reintegration. The signification of infants and children waited to be discovered, and the signs for men to be integrated with those of infancy.

Harriet Beecher Stowe, Louisa May Alcott, and Mary Cassatt convey to us, their audience, the struggle to emerge out from the confines of the signifiers of the second birth which threatened to shut off the flow of their being and contorted it into circuitous, unnatural channels of sanctimony, purity, and martyrdom. The creative process of their writing and painting is not only a journey into self-discovery but a record of the process of the healing and integration of the realizations of family life. Stowe's work functions to identify the dichotomized elements in the family myth. She finds them to be structured in a polar opposition between freedom and slavery, male and female, child and adult, and prey and predator. Its constituent elements are split apart to the extent that Stowe as an interpreter of her culture was greatly challenged to articulate these oppositions and to create new mythic symbols for the purpose of integrating these disparate experiences. Alcott, inheriting less violent oppositions between the realizations of male/female and parent/child, structured new modes of female being which began to replace martyrdom and enslavement. Her work begins to release female rage, sexuality, and assertiveness from a state of exile, yet remains disavowed, hidden behind middle-class morality. Cassatt, in flight from the ghosts of martyrdom and the angel in the house, worked with European modernist assumptions to explore fresh versions of the familial myth. Cassatt's paintings work toward re-releasing female and maternal potency and portraying the power and significance of the mother-infant bond as well as integrating scattered elements of the Oedipus myth. Her painting "The Boating Party" is a watershed in Western art in that it continues the integration process and begins the task of integrating female and male elements in a context of equality. The analysis of their work that follows is an effort to trace these processes and through them to trace changes in the American culture of the family.

CHAPTER
3

UNCLE TOM'S CABIN
A Myth of Familial Relations

Evangeline

A young Star! which shone
O'er life, too sweet an image for such a glass!
A lovely being, scarcely formed or moulded;
A rose with all its sweetest leaves yet unfolded.

—Harriet Beecher Stowe

Harriet Beecher Stowe's *Uncle Tom's Cabin* is a towering fictional account of the processes of individuation and self-discovery in nineteenth-century America. As a woman raised by an intense self–appointed messiah,[1] Stowe found herself her father's alter ego, defined as limited, imperfect, and weak, her destiny circumscribed by male fantasies of autonomy and freedom. Stowe was also confined inside a symbolic order which critically restricted woman's personality and being. Myths of nineteenth-century middle-class American culture marked women as limited persons designated by God and nature to temper the flux of democracy with womanly virtue and morality.[2] In response to the linguistic designation of womanhood and femaleness, Stowe metamorphosized the position of women and children in a postrevolutionary culture through the metaphor of slavery. Her interpretation of the sociopolitical dimensions of slavery resonated reciprocally with her mythic phantasies of personal relations and spun a tale of oppression and repression. The powerful and magnetic attraction of *Uncle Tom's Cabin* is found in its elucidation of mythic phantasies of mother-child-father relations and the uncovering of different aspects of infancy and of womanhood.

American culture, lacking a long history of feudal aristocratic authoritarian structures, found its mythology centered on family life. Obsessive concern about the proper conduct in family relations has preoccupied Americans from the first generation of Puritan settlers to the present.[3]

Among the haunting issues repeatedly investigated by writers, artists, and reformers have been the nature of male, female, and childhood, as well as suitable relationships between and among family members.[4] A precocious postrevolutionary modernism in America limped through an awkward period in which reactions to the loss of certitude and the undermining of belief in a cosmos based on hierarchy and preordained principles developed into a quasi-religion of moral family life. The knowable universe and certitude were rediscovered in concepts of the body and in the nature of women and children. Stringent and oppressive as the new concepts of family life appeared to be, they carried in them a force of archaic myth, straining to surface as older repressive structures crumbled along with tradition.

While women artists and writers, cast as Madonnas at the center of the religion of home and family, have had an urgent and critical need to signify and articulate their experience, the climate of American moralism evoked responses in male artists as well. Melville, Hawthorne, Whitman, and Eakins turned their powerful voices on what they identified as the vicious, suffocating shallowness of American asceticism and its requirements that human nature be remodeled. They insisted that like Hawthorne's Hester, branded with the shameful crimson A signifying sexuality and original thinking, the artist was an outcast, an orphaned Ishmael.

American women artists, attempting to discover their authentic voices, were pressed to engage the ravages of asceticism inside themselves in the form of muteness and acquiescence. The symbolic order of language, customs, and belief systems coded women as existing only as mother or domestic madonna. Since woman did not exist in the public discourse, women wrote, painted, and participated in political social movements to resuscitate their own existence. In this way they needed to invent new signs and symbols that would recognize them and express their motivations as purposeful human beings.[5] American culture has maintained a preference for myths which define male and female nature and destiny in extreme binary oppositions. These myths bolstered the religion of moral family life and provided freshly established democrats with guides for child rearing and personal relationships. As I will discuss further on, the self-made man and the pure, moral woman are mythic characters who, like Natty Bumppo, Daniel Boone, and Calamity Jane function to pull together meaning in the raw, rapidly changing modernist culture.[6] These myths, created to manage the forces of transformation, invoke at the same time archaic myths based on universal dilemmas. Since the Oedipus myth is uniquely suitable for a culture fascinated and concerned with family life, it may be applied as an organizing structure in the texts and paintings of Harriet Beecher Stowe, Louisa May Alcott, and Mary Cassatt.

Women writers and artists considering the implications of their place in culture, inside the tomb of good womanhood, searched for escape routes. Their first task was to clear their own minds of false impositions and to find and open the door to the prison in which their own thoughts lay buried. Haunted by the possibility of living out their lives as false selves,[7] Margaret Fuller, Edith Wharton, and Mary Cassatt fled the country, never to live in America again. Others remained, but disguised their voices and intentions: Louisa May Alcott assumed pseudonyms for her seething Gothic thrillers; Emily Dickinson hid her fury and her talent behind the posture of an eccentric recluse; Harriet Beecher Stowe used slavery metaphorically to disguise a personal and psychological dilemma. At the core of all their work, however, lay a profound effort to reclaim what the male moralist writers had disavowed.[8]

Within more traditional hierarchical and authoritarian societies, emotional experience is restrained and interpreted by the group mores. As American and other modern Western societies moved into a secular, urban, technological era, the structures and principles which had guaranteed the organization, control, and containment of emotions became more tentative, even obsolete.[9] In the United States, the sequence of Puritan Calvinism, moral Protestantism, and democratic ideology thinly masked the terrors of the experience of living out Utopian dreams of freedom and equality. Difficulty grew from awareness that these new ideals invited the emergence of self-assertiveness, individual aggressivity, and appetites of all kinds in a culture which was also capable of treasuring human life. Since family life was found to be a structure which could bind and control such appetites the faith in enlightened liberal progress was locked *firmly* to family mores, and familial roles and customs were designed not so much for the benefit of the next generation as for protection against the onslaught of emotions and their meanings in the context of modernity. Deeper still, the bourgeois concepts of the Victorian woman and child mirrored Victorian anxiety about the release of deep feelings associated with infantile helplessness and dependency. Victorian cultural requirements for family life included demands for a belief in self-reliance and the practice of self-control, both of which were to restrain emotional turbulence and the discovery of self-experiences.[10] Harriet Beecher Stowe's novel *Uncle Tom's Cabin* is an aesthetic elucidation of these processes and includes her own journey out of limited modes of being, thinking, and symbolizing.

Uncle Tom's Cabin, or Life Among the Lowly was born as a serial in 1850,[11] in the midst of the American Renaissance, between Emerson's *The Representative Men* (1849) and Hawthorne's *The Scarlet Letter* (1851). Other impressive siblings followed with Melville's *Moby-Dick* (1851) and Whitman's *Leaves of Grass* (1855). These writers spun out their own aesthetic critiques of American culture, each of which implied that Protestant and democratic values had become heavily dominated by omnipotence and materialism. Hawthorne and Stowe placed their analysis directly within the context of family relationships, emphasizing the link between public and private ideologies. Stowe emphasized the place of women in culture and revised the status of the moral woman.[12]

Clearly, Stowe touched her readers deeply. *Uncle Tom's Cabin* not only sold at the rate of 10,000 copies a week,[13] but attracted a variety of readers in England, America, and even Russia. Total sales in America and abroad in the year of its publication alone were estimated at 2.5 million copies.[14] One explanation of the profound and wide appeal of *Uncle Tom's Cabin* lies in its function as myth. Stowe's *Uncle Tom's Cabin* offered nineteenth-century readers a mythic template from which to derive explanations of the sense of upheaval deriving from living within a new cultural matrix based on freedom and equality. Readers might projectively resonate with the affective coloring that bound her characters within the vortex of the opposing forces of love and freedom opposed to cruelty and dominance. Stowe's tale expressed her conviction that American postrevolutionary society was seriously unbalanced in its effort to offer each individual a decent chance at the pursuit of happiness. *Uncle Tom's Cabin* portrays a society in which racial, sexual, and generational relations are largely based on the principles of inequality and dominance-submission. Stowe's text suggests that the structures and functions of traditional hierarchical institutions had been replaced by an opposition between the public sphere of society and the private familial one, and between male and female gender identities as associated with these separate spheres. Stowe's novel portrays the family as the incubator for moral restraint, Christian piety, and altruism. The public arena of politics and economics is shown as the spawning ground for unrestrained individualism, capitalist enterprise, cruelty, greed, and the quest for power.

Stowe's powerful portrayal of family life is structured through several layers of meaning. At the level of the surface narrative, like Zola and Dickens, Stowe scrutinized the problems of class relationships in societies in which authoritarian structures were shifting drastically. More specifically, she focused on the power politics of slavery. Stowe was openly and intensely critical of her country's permissive stance on slavery, which she characterized as a desecration of the nation's original ideals.[15] In particular, the Fugitive Slave Law epitomized for her the corruption of the principles of the Declaration of Independence. This law grated on Stowe's conscience and sensibility not only in its brutal deprivation of liberty and self-determination for African-Americans, but specifically in its treatment of black people as property deprived of all their human rights.

Stowe's special concern was the effect of slavery and its laws on American black families. While marriage between American "negroes" was forbidden by the law, the practice of selling children away from their mothers for profit had its sanctions. Eliza Harrison's desperate odyssey to save her son from the jaws of the slave trader dramatizes Stowe's hatred of this paradoxical misuse of the law. George Harrison, father and husband to the hapless pair, is himself a cursed orphan of slavery. The offspring of miscegenation, he is made a pariah and an exile sentenced to live his life outside the efficacy of enlightened institutions and laws. Harrison as an adult with a family of his own has no civil rights including the right to raise his child.[16]

Inside the prison of chattel slavery, George Harrison finds the circumstances of his life so unbearable that he wishes that he and his children had never been born.[17] Harrison voices Stowe's challenge to the outrageous inequities practiced within the structure of slavery.

> My master! And who made him my master. What right has he to me? I'm a man as much as he. I've learned in spite of him; and now what right has he to make a dray horse of me?[18]

From the perspective of a man sold into slavery by his Kentucky gentleman father, George unmasks the deceit of the Declaration of Independence.

> My Country! What country have I, or anyone like me, born of a slave mother? What laws are there for us? We don't make them. We have nothing to do with them; all they do for us is crush us, and keep us down. Haven't I heard your Fourth of July speeches? Don't you tell us all once a year, that governments derive their just powers from the consent of the governed?[19]

Stowe adds her own view of the dangerous hypocrisy of slavery as well. The narrator warns the reader:

> Who ever visits some estate there and witnesses the good humored indulgence of some masters and mistresses and the affectionate loyalty of some slaves, might be tempted to dream the oft-fabled poetic legend of a patriarchal institution, and all that; but over and above the scene there broods a portentous shadow, the shadow of the *law*. So long as the law considers all these human beings, with beating hearts and living affections only as so many things belonging to a master, so long as the failure, or misfortune, or imprudence, or death of the kindest owner may cause them any day to exchange a life of kind protection and indulgence for one of hopeless misery and toil—so long is it impossible to make anything beautiful or desirable in the least regulated administration of slavery.[20]

Stowe's mythic narrative is constructed out of a hydraulics of liberty and self-determination on the one side and oppression and enslavement on the other. As some enjoy the possibilities of freedom, others serve as a counterbalance and are thus defined as incapable of self-determination. Cultural concepts[21] of blacks, females, and children are associated with defectiveness and limitation, and at the extreme of this perspective as less than human. In this context, Stowe's criticism may be interpreted as an effort to deepen and broaden the Declaration of Independence. Her text brings to the surface a latent emotional situation and value system. While some individuals feel themselves to be liberated from authoritarian restrictions, they require alter egos to remain in the past in a mode of dominance and inequality.

The opposition of liberty/slavery suggests that the experience of liberty is not yet possible.

According to Stowe's analysis, much of the equality/inequality, liberty/slavery was structured through the separation of the public and private spheres, or the segregation of the sexes. The powerless includes women, children, and slaves (men and women alike) whose political and social restrictions range from serious denial of their civil rights to their complete abrogation. Eva, Tom, Prue, Mammy, Mrs. Bird, and Cassie are the victims of the system of slavery, and they are also its passionate opponents. Because they are confined to the domestic sphere, however, their dissent finds few channels for political and social reform. As Stowe defines the problem, the public and private spheres of activity are vastly different and severed from one another by an elaborately constructed structural discontinuity.[22]

In Stowe's scheme, white men have taken over all opportunity for liberty and the reins of power and control of the politics and economics of the nation. They continue their male patriarchal customs in the Senate, in the slave market, and on the plantation. Mr. Shelby, Haley, Mr. Bird, St. Clair, and Legree are variations on this typology. Finding the chasm between public and private existence disastrous, Mrs. Stowe warns repeatedly that the men of the public domain of power are dangerous to women, children, and blacks of both sexes. Stowe portrays men as creatures who assign money and power more value than human life, and she argues that their peculiar search for the secular salvation of modern progress stems from greed and violence and a relentless attack on family ties. Marks, a man of cool calculating business sense, elaborates this state of mind:

"If you could get a breed of gals that doesn't care none for their young 'uns, I think it would be the greatest modern improvement I know of."[23]

Stowe's analysis of the sociology of American slavery shows it to be a male enterprise which interferes with the safety and human rights of all women and children. Thus at the level of the surface narrative, white and black women and children, along with black men, are victims of unchecked white male supremacy. In this scheme Eva, the martyred Victorian child heroine, illustrates the critical social danger of inhabiting what Stowe defines as the domestic realm.

Lévi-Strauss's structural analysis of the Oedipus myth built on the bipolar opposition of the appreciation and disregard of family ties provides access into the second mythic level of meaning in *Uncle Tom's Cabin*.[24] A column 2, representative of blood relations underrated, can be constructed as populated by George Shelby, Senator Bird, Haley, Mark, Marie St. Clair, and Legree. Each of these characters in varying degrees ignores and devalues the significance of family relations, particularly the mother-child relationship. These characters undervalue the emotions of compassion and love as well. A column 1, representing blood relations overrated, would then include Mrs. Shelby, Mrs. Bird, Eliza, Eva, Prue, Mammy, Cassie, Augustine St. Clair, and Uncle Tom. Each of these characters in opposition to the first group focuses intensely on family ties. Their emotions are displayed as heightened, sentimental, and tortured.

The polar opposition between family affection and denial of it, as constructed by Stowe, clearly reflects nineteenth-century American cultural tensions in which the myth of home and family, flawlessly ruled by saintly matrons, was idealized as a replacement for traditional organizing structures, yet an infatuation with democratic opportunity, realized in self-government for the elite and nimble, mastery and exploitation of the continent, its people and resources, and the creation of a technological industrial society required the rejection of family feeling. If the characters of column 2 are predominantly male (with the exception of Marie St. Clair, who plays the role of the woman who has embraced male values), column 1 is inhabited by women (with the exception of Tom and Augustine St. Clair, who have the values of women, and like women, are often overwhelmed by the system which undervalues emotional ties).

The cultural opposition symbolized by column 3 represents the continuation of the autochthonic theory of birth and column 4 symbolizes its denial. In Stowe's view, the mythic elaboration of the eternal struggle to achieve individuation and mental birth was twisted to fit the shape of the American myth of the self-made man. The privileges of self-government had seduced men into believing themselves to be like God, thus freeing them from the challenges of emotional awareness. The men of columns 3 and 4, living inside the realm of omniscient fantasy, perceived no check on their self-assertion and rejected all feelings of vulnerability, dependence, and gratitude.

In an attempt to validate their belief in their autochthonous origins, Legree and the other men of columns 3 and 4 deny the experience of childhood. By prohibiting any continuity between adulthood and infancy, they set themselves against physical and mental growth. Chloe explicates the logic of their bias:

"Don't nature herself cry out on 'em? Don't dey tear der suckin baby right off his mother's breast, an sell 'em and der little children as is crying and holding on by her clothes—Don't dey just tear the husband and wife apart when it's just takin' the very life on 'em?—And all the while does they feel one bit—don't they drink and smoke, and take it uncommon easy?[25]

Legree, the extreme case of the self-made man, suffers from a phobia of motherliness. Cassie uses this weakness to undermine his hubris. By posing as a ghost returned from Legree's disavowed past, she becomes the Sphinx, an invention sprung from Legree's poor relation to his mother, and his denial of his experience as an infant and child. In other words,

Legree's undoing comes about through Cassie's penetration of his fiction of his self-creation and divinity.

Another emphasis in Stowe's presentation of the Oedipus configurations of columns 3 and 4 is the restrained position of women. While men play out their self-creation in the form of political and economic power, most of the women are confined and limited. Ophelia, Rachael Halliday, and Cassie fight valiantly to maintain their sanity and ethics against the dominant system, but with the exception of Halliday, a Quaker in a religious oasis, none of the other women characters are vouchsafed much self-determination. At best, they manage small and limited victories. Mrs. Shelby believes it her duty to mitigate the more severe practices of slavery with Christian compassion. She attempts to protect Eliza's child from Haley's demonic claims but fails. Eliza dares the treacherous icy currents of the wide river to keep her son, but is forced to run away without her husband, the child's father. Cassie gains a victory over Legree, but it comes rather late, after the loss of several children, one by her own hand. Her infanticide proceeds not so much from a Medea-like fury as from the conviction that she cannot bear another child to be a cog in the machinery of slavery. Mrs. Bird can only manipulate her senator husband. Topsy survives her horrendous childhood with vigor and resilience, but remains a stepchild in an alien family. For these women, autochthony as independent thought and action is seriously inhibited. Eva's death represents the potential murder of their self-determined thought and action.

Joseph Campbell's notions of the treatment of male and female in universal mythologies allows for further interpretation of the emotional turmoil and polarization of the two sets of columns. Campbell suggests that the setting apart of male and female is one aspect of the desire to set apart the great and disruptive oppositions of life and death, true and false, good and evil, inward and outward, as though they were absolutes in themselves and not merely aspects of the larger entity of life.[26] The journey into the underworld, representing the turning inward of the mind, portrayed in the myths of Odysseus and Tiresias, is often symbolized by the dual presence of the sun and the moon. The simultaneous appearance of the sun and the moon also marks the identification of the individual with the universe and the integration of the principles of eternity and time and male and female seen in Hermes, Aphrodite (Hermaphrodites), and the two serpents of the Caduceus. Thus, Campbell points out that the myths written by men in the patriarchal cosmogenies function to prevent the integration of polarities, through the emphasis on sexual difference. The normal imagery of divine motherhood, for example, disappears behind a father figure. According to Campbell, the retailoring of myths in this way is accomplished through displacement and condensation.

And as it has been throughout all patriarchal mythologies, the function of the female has been systematically devalued not only in a symbolical cosmological sense, but in a personal psychological. Just as her role is cut down, or even out, in myths of the origin of the universe, so also in hero legends. It is in fact amazing to what extent the female figures of epic drama and romance have been reduced to the status of mere objects, or even functioning as a subject, indicating acts of their own, have been depicted as incarnate demons or mere allies of the masculine will.[27]

Such a strategy prevents any possibility of dialogue: The male has cut himself off from all shattering communication from the underworld inhabited by mother goddesses and unpredictable feelings. The more profound meaning of the act of segregation of those elements that make up the complete and whole fabric of life is the dilution of significance: the significance that springs from the realizations that one is both self-determining but also dependent on others; that one is capable of hatred and violence as well as loving feelings toward those persons one needs and cherishes above all others; and that one is beholden for one's life to the creative act of two people coming together.[28]

However, the figure of the domestic madonna requires that the heightened tension between the concepts of "male/female," "public/private" be accounted for in other ways. It is clear that Stowe focuses on the hazardous aspects of these polarizations and highlights the profound difficulties in reconciling and integrating these key mythic elements for signifying familial life. Yet like many of her contemporaries, including her sister Catherine Beecher, Stowe was impressed by the values and responsibilty designated to women. The maternal redeemer was charged with providing moral direction and continuity for the new nation. While the white domestic sphere was mapped onto obsessive instructions for all aspects of domestic conduct, including child rearing and marital relations, its literature revealed a profound interest in the deeper aspects of mothering and child rearing. Each aspect of domestic life and child rearing was scrutinized and rationalized for its capacity to defend against chaos and impurity—lust was equated with disease and madness; yet these focused concerns imply that the American quest for liberty and equality evoked new awareness of the forces of the inner world, of desire and need. The mythic complex of the angel in the house or the domestic madonna gathered up the longing for personal protection, satisfaction, and glory as well as the fears of their disruptive emergence.

In her text, *Uncle Tom's Cabin*, Stowe explores two aspects of the maternal madonna figure; the slave to the fear of secular existence and the personification of the re-emergence of female and maternal potency. What is new and fresh in the novel is the appreciation of the significance of the mother-child bond. Stowe characterizes external society as ignorant and indifferent to the infant's experience. Indeed, in some respects Stowe's assessment is accurate; present-day society struggles against deprivation, cruelty, and perversity inflicted on children. Individual freedom, equality, and self-realization require the protection of thoughtful nurture. A culture in search of self-experience invites the flowering of maternal potency. But that possibility in turn evokes the archaic dread of mother's body[29] as the giver and taker of life and to purify that body or to banish its sensuality from awareness is part of a compromise to allow a revitalizing and a rediscovery of mother's potency or mother-child interactions without meeting primitive experience at full force.

Stowe's novel is one of the important texts of the nineteenth century that explores the nature of psychic ties. The brute conditions of earlier American society allowed little exploration of the nature of mother-child bonds except within the structure of religious responsibility. *Uncle Tom's Cabin* begins this task, albeit metaphorically, and at the same time fiercely protests their destruction. The oppositional tension between the longing for psychic ties and the fear and hatred of those longings is an important historical juncture which pulls readers deeply into the novel's emotional orbit.

The several women characters constrained by the structure and values of capitalist slavery nevertheless create or attempt to protect an intersubjective field[30] in which children can grow; a field in which the child's mental and physical welfare will receive respect and attention and in which empathy for the child's state of mind is ensured through an open and mutual communication system. Aunt Chloe and Rachael Halliday radiate a bountiful spirit of motherliness that makes the intersubjective field possible. Their competence and generous empathy create an emotional ambiance in which children are safe and lively. Chloe's and Uncle Tom's cabin is a symbol of this familial life and growth.

> The cabin of Uncle Tom was a small log building close adjoining to the "house" as the negro *par excellence* designates his master's dwelling. In front it had a neat garden patch where every summer, strawberries, raspberries and a variety of fruits and vegetables flourished under careful tending. The whole front of it was covered by a large scarlet begonia and a native multiflora bush, which in twisting and interlacing, left scarce a vestige of the rough logs to be seen. Here, also, in summer, various brilliant annuals such as marigolds, petunias, and four o'clocks found an indulgent corner in which to unfold their splendors, and were the delight and pride of Aunt Chloe.[31]

Inside the cabin, maternal abundance and power is embodied by Aunt Chloe herself presiding cheerfully over her fragrant kettles and pans, Chloe is the incarnation of an African-American Themis.

> A round black shining face is hers, so glossy as to suggest the idea that she might have been washed over with the white of eggs, like one of her own tea rusks. Her whole plump countenance beams in satisfaction and contentment from under her well-stacked checked turban.[32]

Children find delightful signs of mother's constancy here in Chloe's relaxed, cheerful generosity. George Shelbey, the master's boy, confides his intense preference for Chloe's food and sociability over his family's artificial elegance and formality. Chloe's and Tom's own children, Mose, Peter, and baby, like George, find the inside of the cabin much like a lap, filled with easy reliable acceptance, protection, and delight.

The chapter entitled "An Evening in Uncle Tom's Cabin" provides the reader with the hope for satisfying bonds, those in which life surges reciprocally between subject and object. Similarly, Rachael Halliday's spirit creates a sanctuary not only for fugitive slaves but as a respite from the public arena in which familial bonds are disregarded and destroyed as is the well-being of children. The Harrisons' harrowing escape from Haley and his mob is made possible by the Quaker woman's courage. They cross from hell into freedom only as they cross the threshold of Halliday's home. Halliday herself is the personification of feminine potency. Stowe describes her as:

> 55 or 60—a face round and rosy, a healthful downy softness suggestive of a ripe peach. Her hair, partially silvered by age, was parted smoothly back from a high placid forehead, on which time had written no inscription, except peace on earth, good-will to men, and beneath shone a large pair of clear, honest, large brown eyes; you only needed to look straight into them, to feel that you saw to the bottom of a heart as good and true as ever throbbed in a woman's bosom.[33]

Rachael Halliday's heroic character signifies the evolution of maternal benevolence into a complex and formidable force. Stowe draws on the Quaker abolitionist tradition to find powerful alternatives to the ethics of slavery. Halliday lives by truly egalitarian ethics and her vision of each living creature as equal and an individual part of God's universal love is not only a counterpoint to the social model of tyranny and dominance but anticipates more liberal concepts of political and familial relations. In this context, slavery is a premodern mode of relating more consistent with harsh authoritarian feudal relationships with little comprehension of civil and personal rights.[34] Thus, Halliday's gracious ample table filled with cake and coffee, her solicitude for neighbors and children and infants look forward to egalitarian values with an ideal of loving respect for each individual. Her concern and care fans out into an extended family network that gathers up and claims the lost children and embattled adults from the cruelty of "Democratic" capitalist culture.

Stowe shapes Halliday as a heroine that replaces stereotypic fragmented images of women that appeared in the Western cultural tapestry for millennia; women as evil witches, as dangerous seductresses and as personifications of death itself or as moral exemplars, redeeming madonnas and ghostly martyrs. The splitting apart of functions and characteristics not only distorts the concept of woman but suggests powerfully the mutilation of cultural realizations of woman.[35] Individual women within this distorted sign system find their capacities and characteristics divided and their potential self made unreal. As they are imprisoned within a cultural container which clouds and splinters female being[36] and refuses the reception of authentic female expressiveness, self-discovery becomes hazardous if not impossible.

In *Uncle Tom's Cabin*, Stowe thinks her own thoughts and feelings. Rachael Halliday is the sign of this experience as the writer discovers and shares possibilities for a more dimensional female character. She finds in her a truly mythic womanly power who can look after the children of the nation.

> Bards have written of the cestus of Venus, that turned the heads of all the world in successive generations. We had rather for our own part, have the cestus of Rachael Halliday, that kept heads from being turned and made everything go on harmoniously.[37]

Stowe suggests that under the care and guidance of this new Venus, children and adults may find the conditions for self-respect. George and Eliza Harrison saved from the hounds of the slave hunters also find the backing to rebuild their lives as they enter a society which cherishes human growth. In this concept, the single, joyful mother-child experience found in the novel is placed safely within Halliday's domestic realm. Stowe shares with the reader a cheerful picture of a young Quaker mother who, spared Eliza's turbulent history, peacefully enjoys her robust infant.

> Kissing him heartily, she sat him on the floor to collect his thoughts. Baby seemed quite used to this mode of proceeding, for he put his thumb in his mouth (as if it were quite a thing of course) and seemed soon absorbed in his own reflections while the mother seated herself and taking out a long stocking of mixed blue and white yarn, began to knit with briskness.[38]

Similarly, Uncle Tom's Cabin as a title can be read as a mythic structure which signifies the mother's body, breasts, and mind which provide solace and comfort. Rachael Halliday, Aunt Chloe, and Uncle Tom personify these functions; they and the home or cabin guarantee the child's entitlement. The guarantee also works in opposition to the forces and characters of slavery that deny or destroy it.

As Stowe makes her way through the mythic structures of familial relations, she finds them to be built around oppositions of sex and generation. The resurrection of female heroines and dimensional motherliness gains a new advantage within her assessment. However, the maternal element realized as character and attitude is endangered by the powerful status quo of "male" dominated capitalist culture.[39] From this perspective, Stowe's text reiterates the Oedipus myth as an interpretation of the child's experience of victimization and martyrdom. In the manifest Oedipus myth as it has survived in Western culture, the male child Oedipus is endangered but lives outwardly as a hero.[40] Stowe's realization is of a female version of the myth and although sacrifice and stunted growth continues to dominate the re-alization, it brings forward what had been largely omitted from cultural consciousness, the female odyssey. While the Oedipus myth as a precon-ception carries a core myth or diagram for the growth and development of both male and female children, the realization of female growth has been buried under the structure of the "second birth."[41] Oedipus as a male child is initiated away from his attachment to mother into a world of male constructions. As the initiate, he moves from Thebes to Corinth, from Corinth to Thebes and to Colonus; despite his tragic fate and endanger-ment, he survives to reach self-discovery and reconciliation.[42]

Eva surfaces as an important female character who signals the acknowl-edgment of the female child's presence, her development and experience. As she breaks free of the entombment within Zeus's male culture, her situation becomes clear. Stowe presents the female child as an American Iphigenia cut off at the beginning of life. Her physical death can be seen as a signifier of her exclusion from democratic equality and of her stunted development.

Stowe as a woman writer, re-thinking the situation of women within her society, also begins to break free of the restraints on women's minds and from the stilted journey from home to home and family to family, from father's rule to husband's, denied access to free experience and education. Thus, her text places the sexual oppositions within a new structure. "Male" "female" are no longer signified "male" manifest, "women" latent. Women gain a manifest place but are revealed as struggling painfully for equality. Now it is they who are placed in the position of slaying their monsters and suffering the hazards of mental birth. Men are exposed as continuing to suffer from the demands of self-madeness. In a more primary context, the male Oedipus is also endangered by cultural biases about sexual difference. As concepts of motherhood are truncated in culture through the fear of sexual differences, generational opposition remains problematical and be-comes obvious.[43]

Stowe as an early modernist locates and interprets these mythic arrange-ments in her own culture. At a time of transition, she suggests that the surfacing awareness of the need for psychic ties and the fear of potentially freed emotions had severely constrained women's mental life. Therefore the version of the maternal container elaborated in other cultural artifacts in Stowe's era is rigid and oppressive. In this system the culture imposes restriction on the person who nurtures the infant's mental growth and is the guardian of sanity.[44] Under these conditions, the mother's capacity for reverie is severely strained and the female child is a ghostly martyr. Aunt Chloe and Rachael Halliday are characters who represent the possibility of the re-invigoration of maternal potency. Yet animosity toward these figures inhibits the birth of the new realizations of child nature and family bonds. Thus another element in Stowe's myth of parent-child relations is a prophecy about the possible breakdown of the processes by which meaningfulness takes shape just as they are being discovered. She warns that the contradictions within democratic society are leading to the deadly truncation of mental and physical development in American children. Eva's father, Augustine St. Clair, characterizes the effect of slavery on all children. He states: "Since training children is the staple work of the human race, I should think it something of a consideration that a system does not work well there."[45]

Eva and Topsy, the prototypes for the nation's white and black children, respectively, exemplify many dimensions of child exploitation. Both are denied significant parental functions. Eva's mother, Marie St. Clair, is characterized as a vapid, irritable, detached woman, a version of Southern womanhood reminiscent of Mary Chestnut's thoughtful diary in which she made clear the dangers of portraying the Southern lady.

Out of Marie St. Clair, Stowe fashions a persona not unlike the wicked stepmother of Snow White and Cinderella, not only cruel, selfish, and childish, but needy and relentlessly tyrannical. She places her desires above the safety of those in her care. Augustine St. Clair, while more aware of his child's feelings, is caught hopelessly in the web of slavery and is unable to protect his daughter's wishes and values against various sources of oppression. By constructing Eva's mother in this mold, Stowe is able to portray generational conflict between mother and daughter as well as the noxious effect of inequality on familial relationships. The opposition between Eva and her mother takes place around Eva's commitment to Christian love and egalitarianism. Eva is deeply opposed to her mother's harsh treatment of the family slaves, and much of this tension centers around Mammy. Marie St. Clair finds Mammy's attachment to her husband and children troublesome. She interprets the black woman's grief as symptomatic of her selfishness and rationalizes the enforced separation of Mammy from her children as necessary since they are dirty, troublesome creatures who would interfere with her own needs. Eva offers herself to care for her mother in place of Mammy, who is burdened to the breaking point, but Marie St. Clair is unapproachable. She finds her daughter peculiar and even mystifying and observes to Ophelia, "Eva somehow always seems to put herself on an equality with every creature who comes near her. It's a strange thing about the child. I never have been able to break her of it."[46] Marie St. Clair's endorsement of the values of dominance places her in the column that undervalues family ties. And like Haley and Loker, the slave traders, she personifies opposition to the mother-child relationship and its emotional bonding. In this sense, she is associated with earlier attitudes, before the recognition of these issues. Eva, then, must carry the responsibility of democratic modes of relating with equality and liberty for each human being and the implication of these values for parent-child relations.

Thus, Eva must go beyond her mother's perspective. Her function as messiah extends beyond the discovery of the ideas of her own generation; Eva must act as a leader and a teacher, roles which cause her to sacrifice her own childhood growth in a number of ways. Eva, without parental guidance and interpretation, develops a hermeneutics of her own, which she shares with Tom.

Stowe contrasts the invalid Marie St. Clair and her pious daughter with another unusual woman-girl couple. Topsy and Miss Ophelia are brought together by Augustine St. Clair, who intuits the benefits that each will derive from their coming together. Miss Ophelia is the epitome of the good New England woman: moral, responsible, and highly organized. Probably modeled on Harriet's sister Catherine Beecher, Miss Ophelia is a good New England woman in the sense that her character is structured and dominated by an overactive conscience. Both Harriet and Catherine Beecher fought male cultural values as they found them in the person of their father, Lyman Beecher, who zealously and fiercely attempted to bring patriarchal Calvinism into the nineteenth century. They had been severely bruised and deeply touched by Lyman Beecher's adherence to the Calvinist doctrine of original sin. Although they rebelled, they endured long bouts of doubt, isolation, and despair.[47] Miss Ophelia's character is the etching of that process bereft of the shadings of the Beecher sisters' rebelliousness. Ruled by the iron grip of New England moral piety, Miss Ophelia found her calling and her destiny in the zealous opposition to the wrongs of her world.[48] A complex, inflated conscientiousness fed every stream of her attitudes and all of her acts so that each of her days was lived in a battle between good and evil. Her sturdy crusades ranged from the reorganization of her brother's Southern slothful home and kitchen to a fierce resistance to the excesses of slavery. Ophelia's politics brought New England abolitionism into the center of Marie St. Clair's pro-slavery domain, contrasting sharply the Southern and the Northern archetypal homemakers.

Topsy, the orphan child of slavery, is placed in the care of this upstanding woman. As with Marie and Eva, the contrast and tensions between the generations emerge at their interface. But Topsy is a counterbalance, not only to her mistress's New England temperament, but to Eva as well. In contrast to these white, genteel women, Topsy is a little savage, untameable. Stowe paints a vivid picture of the little African:

> She was remarkably one of the blackest of her race; and the round, shining eyes glittering as glass beads, moved with her quick and restless glances over everything in the room, her mouth half-open in astonishment at the wonders of the new master's parlor, displayed a white and brilliant set of teeth. Her wooly hair was braided in sundry little tails, which stuck out in every direction. The expression in her face was an odd mixture of shrewdness and cunning, over which was oddly drawn, like a kind of veil, an expression of the most doleful gravity and solemnity.[49]

Topsy not only possesses a keen instinct for survival, but carries an irrepressible spirit. The mirror image of Eva's gentle spirituality, Topsy is obstreperous and saucy. The picture of the prankster, she sings, dances, tells lies, and is full of tricks. Miss Ophelia is repulsed and perturbed by Topsy's heathenish ways, but unlike Marie St. Clair, she allows herself to be taught by her younger charge. In response to Topsy's half-naked and dirty appearance, Miss Ophelia launches into civilizing her heathen protégé, but discovers in herself instead painful concerns for this child's well-being. Discovering that Topsy's back and shoulders are covered with the welts and calloused spots, ineffaceable marks of the system under which she had been nursed so far, Miss Ophelia's heart became pitiful before her. Gradually, Topsy softens Miss Ophelia's rigid moral outlook, and she is able to understand the real conditions of slavery.

On the other hand, Topsy had never before experienced parental maternal concern. She had so long ago lost the comfort of her mother's care that she imagined herself to have sprung into being autochthonously. In response to Ophelia's methodological inquiry about her background, Topsy replies: "Never was born. Never no father, no mother, no nuthin. I was raised by a speculator with lots of others. I suspect I just growed. Don't think nobody ever made me."[50]

Throughout much of the relationship, the African orphan and the New England spinster are a painful mismatch. Miss Ophelia opposes and oppresses Topsy's unascetic temperament. Topsy challenges all of Miss Ophelia's beliefs. As Miss Ophelia tries to impose her New England values on Topsy's heathenish ways, the little eight-year-old finds her a cold teacher. Ophelia's traditional New England concepts of child rearing carries the stamp of Lyman Beecher. Her program included: "To teach them to mind when they were spoken to; to teach them the catechism, sewing and reading, and to whip them if they have told lies."[51] But Topsy's experiences have carried her worlds beyond the constraint of Miss Ophelia's moral training. St. Clair reminds his sister that something else will have to touch Topsy's heart. "I've seen this child whipped with a poker, knocked down with a shovel or the tongs, whichever came handiest; and seeing that she is used to that style of operation, I think your whippings will have to be pretty energetic to make an impression."[52]

Through the juncture of the black slave child and the white northern woman, Stowe brings together two conflicting attitudes toward children: the older, Calvinist notion that children were wild creatures and, as the carriers of original sin, creatures to be subdued, and an emerging concept of children as vulnerable and endowed with human inalienable rights. This new concept requires the complementary notion of parents as protective shepherds for their children throughout the developmental years. Miss Ophelia stops at the edge of cultural change and puzzles over what can be done with Topsy. She is confronted with the extreme offspring of a dominant-submissive mode of relating within slavery. But even more, she is carried to the precipice of the realization that coercion in religion as well as slavery is the same phenomenon. St. Clair explains, "The horrid cruelties and outrages that once in awhile found their way into the paper—where did they come from? In many cases, it is a gradual hardening process on both sides, the owner growing more and more cruel as the servant more and more callous. Whipping and abuses are like laudanum—you have to double the dose as the sensibilities decline."[53] Many notions are challenged here, political, social, and psychological. But at the heart of the challenge is the notion that oppression, control, and dominance are modes of political social relating and of child rearing.

Topsy reminds us of the horror of child abuse. Also, as an impish clown who refuses to be squashed, she suggests an alter ego of the gentle Eva and a little sister to the rebellious Cassie. These black women signify the spirited resistance and rebellion that was seething inside Stowe's imagination. Clearly, Stowe wrote out of her individual experience as the Victorian daughter of a fierce, zealous, religious figure.[54] Moving beyond her personal memoir, Stowe constructed a myth which mirrors failed or injured female growth based on a transformation in sacrifice. In place of an expanding mind, Stowe posits deadly closure and mental stasis. Physical growth is terminated as well. Babies dying of grief or neglect are left untended by slave mothers whose care is demanded elsewhere. The result is infanticide and the suicide of despairing slave mothers. But the central element of her myth is child sacrifice, particularly that of girls.

Little Eva is the female Oedipus of the myth. Iike her male predecessor, she is marked for tragedy. The element of child sacrifice until recently has been overlooked in the Oedipal configuration.[55] Oedipus is characterized as a lad cursed to break sacred law. But Sophocles' play also makes clear that Oedipus was cursed before his birth, by his parents' decision to send him to die on Mount Cytheron as a response to the oracle's decree that their son will grow up to murder his father and marry his mother. The sacrifice of Oedipus may be interpreted, then, as a consequence of his parents' attempt to avoid tragedy. But their judgment itself results in some sense from the difficulty they have in tolerating the child in themselves, to their real child, and accepting the infantile in culture. Each generation of parents meeting a re-presentation of its own infantile and childhood experiences is caught between acknowledging these forces and disavowing them.

Stowe's female Oedipal myth is grounded in similar conflicting themes. Many concerned nineteenth-century writers, in opposition to Calvinist harshness and feudal authority, began to insist on the rights of children to protection and unfettered growth.[56] But at the same time the transition from inequality to equality shaped the new child-rearing philosophy into a quest for moral purity, which required intense scrutiny of all aspects of behavior. New motifs replaced those of human depravity (original sin and possession by the devil) and the belief in the worthlessness of the poor or unsaved. Sexual feelings represented by masturbation and immoral character represented by the lie surfaced as the new version of original sin. George Washington's guilty relationship to his father's felled cherry tree reflects these themes.[57] Lying and masturbation signified more directly the dreaded presence of deep forces within the mind. One of the links in this post-Calvinist mythology was the connection between turbulent emotions and desires in children and the fall of the infant democratic society. Attitudes toward children's rights to self-discovery and authentic growth remained ambiguous throughout the nineteenth century. Since Stowe's myth of development portrays American children as enslaved by the adult generation's aversion to their fresh discovery of inner life and child nature, the freedom guaranteed by the Declaration and the Constitution is revealed to be fragile. Rather, black and white children alike were to be modeled to fit into a rigid cultural, social, and economic mold. Democracy invited self-discovery and freedom but dread of uncertainty and the unknown was counterbalanced by the politics of slavery and concepts of inferiority. As authority as it had been known was dismantled or levelled, inner psychic reality emerged from deep repression and ignorance, provoking great anxieties. New certitude was also to be found in economic enterprises and exploitation of the nation's working people and of American resources. In the latter context children were to be sacrificed to the god of modern secular progress, which demands self-control, the denial of dependency and vulnerability, and the worship of dominance and steely indifference.[58] Paradoxically, women were to manufacture hard, self-made, rugged individualists while maintaining an Iphigenian fleshy softness appropriate to sacrifice.

Harriet Beecher Stowe had immediate experience with the myth of female martyrdom. Her mother Roxanne and her maternal aunt, Mary Hubbard, both taken by tuberculosis, were mythified as saintly, gentle, good women, opposed to the world of slavery and commerce. Although she lost her mother when she was three or four, Stowe attributed great power to her: "Mother was one of those strong, restful, yet lively sympathetic natures in whom all around her seemed to find comfort and response, and although our mother's bodily presence thus disappeared from our circle, I think her memory and example had more influence in molding her family in deterring them from evil and exciting to good than the live presence of many mothers." Later she explained that the passages in *Uncle Tom's Cabin* in which Augustine St. Clair describes his mother's influence were a simple reproduction of her mother's influence, "as it has always been felt in my family."[59] The fictional version spoken by St. Clair pushes the mythic dimensions to the limit. He describes her in that light: "My mother, she was divine. She probably was of mortal birth, but as far as I could ever observe, there was no trace of human weakness or error about her. She was the direct embodiment and personification of the New Testament."[60] Stowe/St. Clair makes the point, however, that while the mythic mother needed to be morally strong in opposition to the hardness of the market place, her soft goodness placed her in jeopardy. "It will never be known till the last account what sensitive natures like hers have felt, cast utterly helpless into what seems to them an abyss of injustice and cruelty. It has been an age of long sorrow of such natures, in such a hell-begotten world as ours."[61]

In Stowe's portrayal of Victorian sexual arrangements, mothers and daughters are in varying degrees of danger. Perhaps on a deeper level, they may be aspects of the same person. Mrs. St. Clair, Mrs. Bird, Eliza, and Cassie are the prototypes of mutilated motherhood that Stowe pressed to understand and rearrange through the act of writing *Uncle Tom's Cabin*. She herself suffered from severe depression and other ailments which may well have been psychosomatic.[62] While writing *Uncle Tom's Cabin*, she declared herself liberated, and her health improved immensely.

Eva and Topsy and the other children of the novel may be read as various portraits of Stowe's childhood self. If the description of Eva's illness and death is a criticism of democratic, capitalist culture, the motif of the martyred maiden is a palimpsest for self-discovery. Eva dies, not Harriet. The seductive attraction to ascetic self-repression and even mutilation is overcome in an artistic exorcism. She has aroused herself from the trance of self-alienation.[63]

Eva, as the child character of the myth, is embedded within the adult mother/wife/writer. The former is the aspect of women that has not evolved and is always in the process of being sacrificed or dying. From another vertex the mother can be seen as encapsulated within the child, a child-mother, a portrait of a future truncation. The two are one, mother and daughter fusing in a precariously weighted balance between sleep and wakefulness, entrapment and growth.[64] Stowe's presentation of familial relationship includes the inner experience of the development of images of self and objects, and of the process of individuation at the beginning of mental experience as they exist in the deep levels of the mind.[65] In Eva's case, her individuation never takes place at all as it is co-opted by her culture.

At a deeper level of her mythic structure, *Uncle Tom's Cabin*, Stowe works with several triadic structures which are transformations of the infant's sign of his/her familial relationships.[66] Stowe, in marked contrast to Mary Cassatt, as we shall see, is unable to represent any of the early signs in a truly symbolic mode. Her triadic signs replicate not so much the early signs of infancy, but rather an arrested version of them. They dramatize an abnormal and autistic symbiotic mode of mental processes and relationships. The subject is caught in what seems to be a predetermined web of the "other's" domination standing in the place of reciprocal bonding. The subject, not experiencing the safety of attachment and the freedom to emerge gradually into the domain of the not-me[67] with its challenges to his/her narcissistic/autistic capsule, fortifies him/herself deeper behind its recesses. The normal thoughts, images, and signs of autosensuality and symbiosis, while dominantly created out of subjective or undifferentiated experience, are not static, nor walled off from percepts and communications found in the area of the "not-me." At the most basic levels in mental life, the infant creates shapes with his/her body or body products. The shape-making propensity comes out of the infant's desire to seek order out of the randomness of the flux of sensation which constitutes the infant's early sense of being.[68] They are also early expressions of the infant's reach into the complex world of the other and his/her attempt to participate in that world.

Stowe's presentation of semiotic shapes at the level of autism and symbiosis and part-objects interactions are closed and filled with sensory-dominated elements of experience which is enslaved, static, and walled off. In Stowe's mythic structures, women and children are caught in the pathological autistic structures of the culture. Stowe is working through an unintegrated culture in which women were signified as soft, entombed in the domestic sphere, and men as "liberated" in the outside sphere. "Not-me" could be found in either aspect. Stowe portrays social and psychological situations in which communication and interpretation are overwhelmed by hard modes of supporting the self which are in fact autistic—the use of the hard to seal away or even destroy the vulnerability of childhood and femaleness and to emphasize powerful control over the "not-me." Autistic maneuvers uncover the roots of the hypothesis that attitudes toward infants and children are to mental life as they are to the choices of a society in which power and militarism are preferred to the welfare of infants, children, and their mothers.

As mythic structures transform and are transformations of inherent and individual experience, the archetypal sensations of hard and soft paint the preconceptual unborn thoughts. Drawing on these qualities, the synchronic moves and transforms according to the fullness of the integration of hard and soft. Stowe's narrative represents a synchronic mode made static and obdurate by the hard "me" enslavement of the elements of psychic life. Stowe's slave owners maneuver to cover the black hole of modernist individuation with an impenetrable shell.

Eva and Topsy, the child subjects of the manifest triadic structures, having poor or nonexistent relationships with their mothers, are deprived of physical and mental safety. The same holds true for the children of Mammy, Prue, Cassie, and Lucy, who find themselves deprived of the conditions necessary for growth and development. Stowe is portraying an infant and adult version of a particular infant situation. Mother is ill, powerless, or apathetic, hence the baby is emotionally and physically unsafe and unbonded. Stowe is working here with signs shaped significantly by cultural forces.[69] The cultural interpretant or container bears down on the sign to produce a representation in which white women are hindered from protecting their children's emotional development and black women are powerless to protect their children's lives.[70]

The little sign-maker is trapped in a situation in which mental growth is mutilated or aborted. Deprived of the functions of a mental partner who soothes, supports, and interprets, the infant thinker or interpretant experiences his/her synchronic preconceptual elements or preprojective overflow[71] as hardening and remaining unintegrated. Without the maternal receiver, the psychosensual elements of early thought agglomerate and harden into a shell. The "not-me" is associated with the shell and is dominated and enslaved, and not allowed the freedom necessary for change and growth. Thus, not only do the subject's signs become obdurate, but his or her development remains stagnant as well. He/she is imprisoned behind the walls of static mental life as a sacrifice to the culture's ignorance or dread of infantile experience.

Eva and Tom share at least two rich and unambiguous relationships within the parent-child triad. In one of these, Tom is like a mother to the child. At first meeting, Tom acts as a "maternal" protector; when Eva loses her balance and topples into the Mississippi (the main artery for slave commerce), Tom capably pulls her out of the water. Since Tom's act is powerless to save the little princess, however, Stowe presents us with another impotent mother as Eva and Tom are bound together in an inevitable martyrdom.

Eva's father, Augustine St. Clair, shares some of Tom's functions in this constellation. Augustine St. Clair is more mother than father and more of a parent than Marie St. Clair. His character is soft, gentle, and compassionate; hers is hard, apathetic, and unfeeling. The more delicate and sensitive of a pair of twin brothers, he has, like his daughter, inherited the special sacrificial character of a divine mother. In childhood he was known as remarkable for a marked sensitivity of character, more akin to the softness of women than the ordinary hardness of his own sex. "Time, however, overgrew the softness with the rough bark of manhood, and but few knew how living and fresh it still lay at the core."[72] Like Tom, Augustine St. Clair adores Eva and ministers to her gently, especially in her illness. But not only is he prevented from reforming the societal ills that undermine Eva's health and sanity; he also dies standing up to male brutality, much like a sacrificial female lamb. Stowe allies him firmly with the female principle: "So he lay for a few minutes. They saw that the mighty hand was upon him. Just before the spirit departed, he opened his eyes as a sudden light as of joy and recognition and said 'Mother' and then was gone."[73] Tom's death is similar. He remarks on his deathbed: "Jesus can make a dying bed feel soft as downy pillows are." For Eva-Stowe, the mother-child triadic sign includes a martyred subject relating to a maternal object, also martyred, the sign of which is Christ.

As Eva's character reveals, the mother-child sign is one which offers little possibility for growth. At first glance, Eva seems a normal, developing child of five or six, "darting with energetic curiosity all over the ship. " Tom noticed that she was one of those busy, tripping little creatures who could no more be contained in one place than a sunbeam or a summer breeze. But it soon becomes clear to Tom and the others who know Eva that she is more than an ordinary child. Stowe portrays her as a beautiful child who had already shed the chubbiness of childhood, foreshadowing her special destiny. Her presence radiates something unusual, characteristic of some mythic, allegorical being. The shape of her head and turn of her neck and bust suggest a gentle nobility, and the long brown hair that floated like a cloud around it, the deep spiritual gravity of her violet blue eyes, shaded by fringes of golden brown, all marked her off from ordinary children and commanded attention from all those who were deeply touched by her presence. Stowe remarks, "A thousand times a day, rough voices blessed her and smiles of unwonted softness stole over hard faces. To Tom she seemed like an angel that stepped out of the New Testament."[74]

The figure of Tom as a maternal protector who loves and understands children suggests a way out of martyrdom. His cabin with Chloe is a bountiful haven for children in which love, good food, and empathy provide the essential elements for survival and growth. Much like a mammy, Tom raises two generations of Shelby boys and continues the tradition as a loving nurse to Eva, but inevitably Tom cannot protect his children from the bias and structures of slavery. Out of this character Stowe creates not only a powerful identification between women and blacks as slaves and martyrs, but out of his maleness, she begins tentatively to build an alliance between some men and women as the disenfranchised and martyred. The Tom-Eva sign is set against the values of the slave market, and of Calvinist militancy.

It seems to me that Stowe created an Eva-Tom sign as an oppositional structure to her Edwardsian father Lyman Beecher's Edwardsian Presbyterian emphasis on damnation and the tradition of Calvinism out of which he had made a cruel agony of the crisis of salvation. Harriet and Catherine Beecher had suffered deeply from their father's constant scrutiny of their religious certitude.[75] Harriet's adolescence was seared by her sister's fierce battles with Lyman over her dead fiancé's religious destiny. When Lyman and the minister of Harriet's fourteenth year found the young girl's religious commitment wanting, it filled her with severe doubt and even drove her to suicidal wishes.

> I began this summer in more suffering than I have ever before felt. I wish I could die young and let the rememberance of me and my faults perish in the grave. You don't know how perfectly wretched I often feel, so useless, so weak, so destitute of energy. Mama often tells me that I am a strange, inconsistent being. Sometimes I could not sleep, and have groaned and cried until midnight, while in the daytime I tried to feel cheerful, and succeeded so well that Papa would reprove me for laughing too much.[76]

Although much of the unevenness in temperament expressed by the pubescent Harriet Beecher is characteristic of these years, her depression and maudlin wish to die alternated throughout her life with rebellious feelings against Edwardsian exactitude. Both Catherine and Harriet spent considerable effort warding off the impinging autocratic god that they found lodged in their father and his colleagues and in their own minds.

Harriet Beecher found much comfort from early years in writing. At the age of ten, she had written a prize essay, an effort at discovering her own religious values, called "Can the Immortality of the Soul be Proved by the Light of Nature?" After her struggles with Lyman and the Reverend Hawes of Hartford, Harriet Beecher wrote a play entitled "Cleon," in which the character Nero expressed her vision of male dominance and cruelty. Against this prototype she opposed the gospel of love which emphasized Jesus as a sheltering maternal figure who protected his children from the wrathful glare of the Calvinist god. In a later novel, *Dread*, written in 1856, after *Uncle Tom's Cabin*, Stowe expressed more directly the themes of rebellion and liberation, and when she finished *Dread*, she remarked that she now walked in liberty and was done with languishing.[77] While drawing the portrait of a brave, fierce rebel, Dread, imagined as the son of Denmark Vesey, and also modeled on Nat Turner, she satirized and humiliated the clergy, particularly on the issue of their hypocrisy about slavery. One minister, a Dr. Packthread, bears a remarkable resemblance to the conniving, impinging Lyman Beecher of her haunted imagination.

> In his boyhood and youth, the man had had a trick of smiling and laughing without considering why; the grace of prudence, however, had corrected all this. He never did either in these days without understanding precisely what he was about. He knew precisely all the gradations of smile which were useful for accomplishing different purposes; the solemn smile, the smile of inquiry, the smile of affirmation, the smile of suggesting, the smile of incredulity, and the smile of innocent incredulity, which encouraged the simple-hearted narrator to go on unfolding himself to the brother, who sat quietly behind his face as a spider does behind his web, waiting till his unsuspecting friend had tangled himself up in cautious, impulsive, and of course contradictory meshes of statement which were in some future hour tightened around the incautious captive while as much blood was sucked as the good of the cause could handle.[78]

Tom, then, springs from the longing for compassion, integrity, and for reconciliation. The identification Eva-Tom integrates the gospel of love and the efficacy of Christ. It offers the quality of softness in opposition to a fierce Calvinist, capitalist male ethic. However, the Eva-Tom sign as unintegrated softness is the sign of martyrdom.

Eva's sign of herself relating to a mother or a family is Christ, as messiah and as sacrifice. Iike the crucified Christ, Eva sickens and dies, because she cannot bear the atrocities of slavery. Stories of suffering and injustice touch her heart so painfully that she withdraws more and more from everyday reality. Her eyes look increasingly heavenward, and she confides to Tom that soon she will live with the angels. Stowe has given her a serious dose of consumption, a disease rampant in the nineteenth century, and one which claimed Stowe's mother and maternal aunt. Though child mortality rates improved steadily, many families lost a child before it reached the age of five; Mrs. Bird's little cupboard filled with her dead child's things is a reminder of this. Stowe had lost her own child, Charlie, to cholera in 1848 and characterized the connection between Charlie's death and the writing of *Uncle Tom's Cabin* as follows: "It was at his dying bed and at his grave that I learned what a poor slave mother may feel." Later she wrote to her second Charles: "I well remember the winter that you were a baby and I was writing *Uncle Tom's Cabin*. My heart was bursting with anguish excited by the cruelty and injustice our nation was showing to the slaves, and praying to God to let me do a little and cause my cry to be heard. I remember leaning over you as you lay beside me, and I thought of the mothers whose babies were torn from them."[79]

In *Uncle Tom's Cabin*, Mrs. Stowe expressed her feelings about her own children, slave children, and American children in general. She draws on the reservoir of her experiences with her own sons to portray painful ruptures in the mother-child relationship as she experienced them as a mother and as a female child who will never grow up, and in a sense does not really want to grow up, but sees her fulfillment in heaven. Stowe's explanation of Eva's destiny and purpose is one of her most sentimental passages.

> Has there ever been a child like Eva? Yes, there has been. But the names are always engraved on little grave stones, and their sweet smiles, their heavenly eyes, their singular words and ways are among the buried treasures of yearning hearts. It is as if heaven had a special band of angels whose office it was to sojourn here and endear to them the wayward human heart. When you see that deep spiritual light in the eye, when the little soul reveals itself in words more sincere and wiser than the ordinary words of children, hope not to attain that child, for the seal of heaven is on it, and the light of immortality looks out from its eyes. Eva, so Eva, fair star of thy dwelling, thou art passing away.[80]

In this passage, Eva becomes a woman who has been put to sleep or confined in the manner of Sleeping Beauty, Snow White, Rapunzel, or Cinderella, and shares their qualities of weakness and softness. In hordes and tribes, such a person may be left behind for the good of the group.[81] In the "male" world of *Uncle Tom's Cabin*, compassion and tenderness, the implication of enslavement and restriction, are disavowed and killed off. They reappear in the Victorian notion of women and children, oppositional signifiers to self-made indifference—of vulnerability and martyrdom. As repository for those conflicts, the martyr must die to save the group from coming in contact with these ideas, which may then be abandoned, like the outcast. In writing about child/female sacrifice, Stowe resists the treacherous seductiveness of self-pity. She calls attention to her resistance, as she calls attention to political slavery.

At the level of the infant's sign of mother and self, Eva's character and situation suggest a baby/mother interaction or dialogue in which the container mother must stifle and abort her infant's expressiveness, perhaps as has been her own,[82] particularly in regard to female will and aggressiveness.[83] Other nineteenth-century American documents testify that mothers were to devote themselves earnestly to raising good future citizens, capable of living under the conditions of liberty and equality. As part of this, they were to instill enormous self-control over feelings. Passions and feelings were defined mainly as dangerous powers capable of bringing on insanity and depravity (anarchy). Harriet Beecher Stowe's sister, Catherine Beecher, wrote volumes in which the fear of emotional chaos was to be somehow managed through minutely arranged programs for cleanliness and order in matters of personal decorum and domestic life.[84]

According to the bias of these writers, democratic society required that mother's container function be selective and repressive. And since within this model of Victorian child rearing, mother herself likely had not enjoyed access to emotional consolation and thus to her own infant-child self, she would be pushed toward the replacement of emotional reciprocity, leading to the translation of experience into meaning, with a rejection or distortion of the infant's communication. Under these conditions the infant wonders whether he or she has destroyed mother or sacrificed her. If the refusal of the acceptance of meaning is massive, a greedy, devouring anti-meaning persona develops, destroying the capacity to alphabetize the data of experience. Society shows us this persona in religious and political zealotry. At worst, the relationship between mother and child becomes a battleground where elements of expressiveness are hurtled like ballistics at higher and higher velocities, fragmenting all the capacity for thinking;[85] at the least the mother and child relationship is disturbed and personal expressiveness in the form of phantasies or dreams or innate preconceptions are aborted or stillborn, a sacrifice to a society that disavows primitive feelings. Eva's death is the death of her mind, her individuality, and of her authentic self, the fate that Stowe sought to outrun by writing Uncle Tom's Cabin.

But Christ is more than sacrifice; Christ is also a messiah. Eva takes on this function as well. The messiah is a crucified container into which society jams all that is problematical and unthought. The messiah then knows only too painfully what has been split off and disavowed by the group. The messiah may genuinely have a solution or new idea that can move the group along,[86] but the group may also wish the figure to save them from thinking and psychic pain.[87] Some aspects of messianic cultism originate in the infant's need to be safely taken care of by a wise, ideal, god-like parent. Under difficult circumstances, that impulse may degenerate into a wish to remain asleep and unborn, and is accompanied by a hatred for the messiah, who reminds the group of disruptive emotions.

Eva is the young prophet and evangelist in her group who offers the gospel of Christ in opposition to the bias and cruelty of the system of slavery. Because of her special insight, she must give up her own place as a child and the right to be taught in order to become teacher to her own parents. She must teach them about the fairness and compassion of Christ's love, and remind them that He understood true equality, loved each person equally, and was father to each and every one of his creatures. Eva teaches the black people as well, bringing Christ to their lives, and attempting to provide them with protection from the danger of their worldly situation. Eva preaches to her black friends from the pulpit of her deathbed. "Listen to what I have to say. I want to speak to you about your souls. Many of you, I'm afraid, are very careless; you are thinking only about this world. I want you to remember that there is a beautiful world where Jesus is, and I am going there, and you can go there too. But if you want to go there, you must not live idle, careless, thoughtless lives. You must be Christians." Remembering sadly that her black friends are not allowed to read, she exhorts them to believe in Christ and to find access to the Bible however possible.[88]

Eva as a messiah who brings new ideas is greatly burdened with the thoughts that her society and family disavow: she comes to believe that she must offer her life to redeem her society. Eva shares her conviction with Tom that she must follow Christ's path. "When I saw those poor creatures on the boat, you know, when you came up, I saw that some had lost their mothers and some their husbands, and some mothers cried for their children. And when I heard about poor Prue and other times, I felt that I would be glad to die if my dying would stop all this misery. I would die for them, Tom, if I could."[89] Eva confides her sense of mission to her father, hoping to influence him to end slavery: "When I am dead, Papa, you will think of me and do it for my sake. I would do it, if I could." Since the group will not listen to Eva, she is sacrificed for her new idea. While Stowe escaped the solution of martyrdom for herself, she still admired its code of ethics and felt safer making a direct attack on the other kind of slavery. However, her mythic template makes clear the danger to women and children enlisted as sacrificial messiah figures.

Another aspect of the meaning of the Christ figure is a respect for children and a belief in the power of their innocence and purity to lead their elders out of sin. At the level of the infant's sign, the infant is portrayed as a messiah of joy, a symbol of the parents' pride and hopes for the future. *Uncle Tom's Cabin* reflects the nineteenth-century interest in children as free selves or heirs to the struggle for human rights, liberty, and equality, while at the same time noting the sacrifice made necessary by the inability of the parental generation to experience the experience of freedom and to think about its consequences. Symptomatic of this difficulty, Stowe presents the sign of the American three-person relationship in *Uncle Tom's Cabin*, mother/baby/father, the latter as a devil figure.

As with the two-person structure, Stowe cannot find a way of presenting an intact, thriving family. The dominant father typology represented by Legree is an anti-father and an anti-Christ. Men in the novel fall into three categories: cool and demonic slavedrivers, fellow travelers (those who participate in slavery as gentlemen, but find it distasteful), and the impotent opposition. Among the characteristics of the first group (which is made up of Legree, Sam, Quimbo, Hailey, Loker, and Marks) are a cruel brutality and a muscular contempt for weakness. Its representatives, like Legree, live outside the family and society. Loker, for example, is a hardened Daniel Boone type, modeled on the frontiersman. Stowe describes him as "a muscular man, full six feet in height and broad in proportion, dressed in a coat of buffalo skin, made with the hair turned outward, which gave him a shaggy and fierce appearance, perfectly in keeping with the whole air of his physiognomy." She continues, "Every lineament expressive of brutal, unhesitating violence was in a state of the highest possible development."[90] Loker foreshadows Legree as Stowe introduces him: "From the moment that Tom saw him approaching he felt an immediate and revolting horror of him; he was evidently, though short, of gigantic strength, his round bullet head, large light-grey eyes with shaggy, sandy eyebrows and stiff, wiry sunburned hair and his large coarse mouth was distended with tobacco, the juice of which from time to time he ejected from him with great decision and explosive force, made him appear wild and coarse."[91] Dwelling exclusively in the domain of the self-made man, Loker and his sidekicks, Marks and Haley, abhor signs which remind them of their disavowed unconscious feelings about their infantile helplessness and human need for mothering. For the sake of capitalism and progress, Marks wants the nation to breed breeders who feel no attachment to their young.[92] Haley comments, "Since children are a great deal of trouble, one would think the mothers would be glad to rid themselves of the burden, yet the more troublesome they are and the more good for nothing, the tighter they stick to 'em."[93]

As the men talk about efficiency and profit in the business of slavery, they make a concerted attack on family ties, specifically black family ties. However, Stowe presents a network of contagion in which both black and white family relationships are affected and infected by the customs of slavery. Loker voices what could be taken as the apotheosis of the self-made principle: "When I buys a gal and if she's got a young one to be sold, I just walks up and puts my fist to her face and says, 'Look here, Nell, if you can give me one word out of your head I'll smash your face in. This yere young 'un is mine and not yours, and you've got no kind of business with it.' "[94]

Legree, a painful caricature of fatherhood, who Kronus-like destroys those who are in his keeping, has created a nightmarish anti-family. His kingdom at the end of the Red River is a place of darkness and decay, reminiscent of Poe's House of Usher. The surrounding vegetation and the house reflect the eerie malevolence of Legree's slave society: "The road which led there was wild, forsaken; now winding through dreary pine barrens, where the wind whispered mournfully, and now over log causeways, through long cypress swamps, the doleful trees rising out of the slimy, spongy ground hung with long wreaths of funereal, black moss."[95] The house itself also reflected Legree's inner state of mind: "It was purchased at a bargain, solely as an implement for money-making. It had that ragged, forlorn appearance of serious neglect which led to utter decay."[96]

Tom's journey south is a dreadfully dangerous descent and a falling away from civilized moderation. The wholesome influence of parental love is entirely excluded under the rule of its regent. In particular there is no maternal principle to soften the nature and quality of human affairs. Stowe presents a hellish vision of a family, or small society, in which all the dangers of self-madeness congregate and multiply. She offers a savage looking-glass world of reversal and distortion. The emotional connections between people are colored by brutality, fear and hopelessness. Sambo and Quimbo are siblings who tyrannize each other and their own people. Mothers mourn their children who have been lost to forced neglect or infanticide;[97] children grieve for their mothers or fathers. Emmaline is sold away from her mother in the same auction that brings Tom to Legree. Mothers and sisters are degraded as concubines; Cassie and Emmaline are brought to the plantation to satisfy Legree's sexual need.

At the level of mythic narrative, these arrangements attest to a failure to gain knowledge within the group. The myths of the Tower of Babel and the Oedipus myth dramatize the dilemma of ignorance and stupidity. The people of Babel have lost the means of communication. Oedipus must find the answer to the riddle in order to free Thebes from the plague. However, the impediment to the learning from experience is found at a deeper level as well. With the blessing of parental reverie, the very gathering of meaning forms a triadic structure composed of self, object, and sign, the structure of which is held together by the forces of emotional relatedness. Within the mother/child sign thoughts about the self's experiences as an individual evolve. As the infant manages this growth, he or she begins to see him or herself as one of three. Within that sign, thoughts about the self in relationship to the culture evolve.

Imagine the baby at the vertex of a triad, looking up the line (side) at the object which is now the parents in relationship to each other. If Eva represents the baby and the St. Clairs are her parents, the cultural poison of slavery and cruelty has infected mother's nurturing function and father's protective cleansing function as well. They have deteriorated. Legree as a paternal principle has subsumed men like St. Clair under his demonic power. If Eva is the baby of slave society and Legree the devilish father of that society, then who is the mother? Mother in the novel is represented by several people. Stowe has had to devise a cultural mother in several parts, although Rachael Halliday suggests the reinvigoration and wholeness of maternal functions. In the novel there is yet no character that is a match for Legree. Parcelled out amongst the many black and white women characters are diverse capacities and skills, but they do not come together in an integrated, formidable way. Perhaps Stowe means to echo the cultural tendency to split apart women's capacities and to disown them. The relationship between the two parents is one in which the father cruelly dominates the mother. Intercourse between them is presented as cruel and sadistic.

Within the stage of autism, Legree the father represents the intrusive, outside world presented cruelly and dangerously. In the stage of symbiosis Legree is the father who enslaves and steals the breast and lap for his own needs and purposes.[98] In the stage of separation/individuation, Legree is the father who not only dominates and enslaves the mother but imprisons her in a martyr's role and makes her his sexual slave. The girl child looking forward to her future life will envision a similar path marked out for her.

Legree, then, is a subjective father figure who appears when parental reciprocity and containment are prevented from functioning. At the extreme he is the personification of−K, the eerie reassemblage of the mind's contents after infantile catastrophe,[99] an explosion of the mind, resulting from the increasing intensity of unaccepted infantile untranslated emotion. Legree is the apostle of anti-meaning when meaning is not tolerable, and his domain becomes one of attacks on emotional linking because linkages are the threads weaving together a meaning that has become unbearable.[100] Negation and reversal are characteristic of his realm because they too cancel out meaning. Love becomes hate or perversity, helplessness becomes grotesque weakness, and parental care is transformed into slave driving. Given the rules of this kind of mental functioning, the child quickly makes an enemy of reality as it gains awareness of itself and others; it blames the father for having had to have been born and having had to struggle with responsible mental life.

Under these conditions the shape of the infant's semiotic may become more and more distorted. Within the signifying triadic structure, the distance between the self and the image of the parental object collapses if the infant opts to finesse separateness by disappearing into the parental image. At the same time the infant expands the distance between the parental image and its sign to rid his/her mind of the awareness of the relationships taking place partially in a sphere outside his/her imagination.[101]

Furthermore, the infant's intense need of mother (which normally with empathy is expressed as some kind of possessiveness and reticence to allow Mommy her own life) under these conditions explodes into enslavement as a dominant mode of relating. The object, i.e., the enslaved, victimized black woman with her other babies, is created out of the hapless, troubled infant's intense projective transformations,[102] but also out of the cultural and parental infant inside the adult. A sign of the slavedriver/daddy Legree is similarly fabricated out of baby's uncontained feelings about mommy. But whether the baby resides in the culture, in the adult or in the real baby is not always clear.[103] All of this works in two directions: from forces outside the child's mind, his/her environment and culture and his/her parents' projections toward him/her; and his/her projective transformations. Legree, then, is the name of the entity which forms out of all these emotional vicissitudes.

Cassie and Tom are two partial images of mother within the three-person relationship. Tom has been touched by Eva and, as her apostle, opposes Christian love and compassion to Legree's infernal factory ethics. When Tom begins to doubt that God has followed him into the hell where he has been taken, Eva appears to him reading the Bible, refreshing and renewing his faith, so that he feels Christ to be at his side.[104] Since Tom and Eva function as alter egos here, Tom quite logically assumes her role as the agent of Christian principles.[105] Like Eva, he sees the truth in the sea of lies, and like her, he offers sacrifice and resistance: opposing the ethics of Legree's infernal factory system, he becomes its victim and is murdered by Legree.

Cassie is Legree's enemy as well, but she manages to carry out alternatives to martyrdom and victimization. Whereas Stowe idealizes Eva and Tom for their elegant self-sacrifice, she admires Cassie for her courageous and rebellious nature, basing her on the model of Hawthorne's Hester, a powerful woman of independent mind who aids those harmed by society. Stowe creates her as Eva's alter ego, a heroine of vigor and earthiness, and gives her the corporality and passion she denied to Eva. As imagined by Stowe, Cassie is a handsome, tall figure with a fine head, firmly chiseled features, and dark expressive eyes, which although filled with despair and suffering also shelter the fire of pride and rebellion.[106]

Stowe brings Tom and Cassie together perhaps to contrast two views of the hero. Cassie and Tom begin to debate the meaning of their existence when Cassie comes to Tom to nurse and advise him after his vicious encounter with Legree's cruelty. Worn down by betrayal and the loss of her children, Cassie reveals that she has no belief system but bitterness and violence. She warns Tom that his allegiance to Christ and his refusal to hide his antipathy to Legree and his values and customs will bring on the wrath of Satan. Tom courageously remains loyal to the Christianity he shared with Eva, despite the painful loss of his family and hopeless situation. He opposes Cassie's nihilism, as he opposes Legree's tyranny, with an unswerving belief in Christ's love. He insists that his soul belongs only to God, and that to surrender it to the ethics of slavery would break his compact with Christ. Tom is able to interpret his ordeal as meaningful in the manner of Christ's earthly trials.[107]

Stowe's invention of the sign, Uncle Tom, is complex and has several functions. Within the family sign, Tom's courageous resistance to Legree signifies the maternal force opposed to the indifference and cruelty of the "paternal" power. The binary opposition male/female works here in favor of the tolerance for vulnerability, anguish, and the relinquishing of control over these experiences. The title, *Uncle Tom's Cabin,* and the chapter "An

Evening in Uncle Tom's Cabin" are the signifiers for the re-integration of maternal functions and the release of the maternal goddess from her long imprisonment within "male" culture. Uncle Tom is the sign of the maternal principle, and in the mode of Mammy, Chloe, and Rachael Halliday, stands for the love and protection of infants and children; they themselves being the signifiers of mental growth and development. The design of Tom as a black man acting as a mother in opposition to the father of the marketplace gathers up many of Stowe's themes. On the one side, Tom is martyred like a woman by the hard, phallic elements of the culture. On the other, as a male who loves and protects children and embraces a god of love over the god of self-madeness and who has known the experience of enslavement, he looks forward to the integration of male and female, independent/dependent, hard/soft.

Cassie as well looks forward to integration, but from a different vertex. Although she is moved by Tom's passive resistance and is restrained by him from committing murder, Cassie is a woman who draws on maternal strength. Her resistance to Legree's power departs radically from the principles of the domestic madonna. Emmaline's persistent obedience to maternal moral teaching inspires Cassie's virulent opposition. Cassie challenges Emmaline's innocence: "Mother told you? What use is it for mothers to say anything? You are all bought up and paid for, and your soul belongs to whoever gets you. That's the way it goes, Emmaline."[108] In Cassie, Stowe invents a mother who will not be locked away. In the garret, where another slave woman had been entombed and tortured, Cassie finds a splendid device to take revenge on Legree for herself and her children sold into slavery. Cassie knows Legree's emotional history, and enters into it in a way that drives Legree mad and enables her to find her way out of the plantation, carrying Emmaline with her and fortuitously finding her daughter and granddaughter in Canada. Tom contributes to Legree's decline by juxtaposing unswerving faith in Christ to Legree's sadism; he is nevertheless the maternal Christ who dies. Cassie becomes a happy, lively mother, who lives to enjoy and interact with her family. She is one side of Stowe in disguise, black and in another country.

Legree's demise is largely engineered through Cassie's impersonation of a figure from within his personal myth. Stowe reveals to the reader that Legree's familial history is both surprising and problematical. As infant and child, Legree was nurtured by a pious, unselfish replica of a domestic madonna. But like the larger cultural myths of men and women, Legree's family was bifurcated by extreme, exaggerated signs of male and female. Mild and sacrificing as his mother was, his father was hard and ill-tempered, "a sire on whom that gentle woman had wasted a world of undervalued love."[109] Legree, pulled this way and that, settled on his father's path. Boisterous, unruly, and tyrannical, he despised all his mother's counsel, and would have none of her reproofs; and at an early age broke from her to seek his fortunes at sea.[110]

Legree as the subject, or interpretant, of a mother-child sign is trapped within the force of extreme opposition. His mother's martyred forgiveness reaches out to him from the grave through her gift of a golden lock of her long, curling hair, which curses him, and haunts him as the disavowed force of grotesque softness. Even after death, the madonna's sacrifice drives itself into every thought in his mind.

> There is a dread, unhallowed necromancy of evil, that turns things sweetest and holiest to phantoms of horror and of fright. That pale, loving mother, her dying prayers, her forgiving love, wrought in that demonic heart of sin only as a damning sentence, bringing with it a fearful looking for judgment and fiery indignation. Legree burned the hair and burned the letter, and when he saw them hissing and crackling in the flame, only shuddered as he thought of everlasting fires.[111]

Stowe constructs a personality in torment, persecuted by a maternal conscience and by the culture's radical splitting apart of oppositional elements. When Cassie incarnates the ghost of the woman in the attic, the two phantoms mingle in Legree's imagination, painfully resurrecting buried characters within his personality. As Legree crumbles, Cassie is liberated. This woman of vigor is a phoenix, metamorphosizing into a woman of the future.

Outlining the making of a devil, the other uncle of the sacrificial figure, Stowe conveys her understanding that just as a culture or society places its unacknowledged messiah thoughts and meaning into the image of a figure and then sacrifices that figure, who is crucified by the weight of those feelings, so too can a group destructively split off and disavow the contents of its mind in such a way that the hostile evacuations transform the Christ container into the devil.[112] Seen in this way, Legree's mercenary cruelty and opposition to family ties reflect distortions of the emotions between family members that the culture has disavowed, and therefore changed into their opposite. Legree is the child who hates his mother; he is the father who hates his children; he is the caretaker who values business over human lives. But what he has disowned comes back to him in an inimical fashion: the ghosts of mother and child and the related emotions of vulnerability and longing which insist on taking their place within his mind. In this way, Legree represents the culture's malaise, haunted by its victims, both people and values.

Although describing this process, Stowe is not yet out of it. Men are still devils for her, the root of all that is troubling her; women and girl children are idealized and ennobled by their sacrificial suffering. Cassie is the exception, the hope: she is aware, and she has a vigorous mind. She is the figure who symbolizes the women's suffrage and abolitionist movements. But by sending her to Canada, Stowe suggests that the meaning of her character and its potential is not yet safe to acknowledge.

CHAPTER

4

LITTLE WOMEN
A Study in Adolescence and Alter Egos

I think my natural ambition is for the lurid style.
I indulge in gorgeous fantasies and wished
that I dared inscribe them upon my pages
and set them before the public. How should
I dare to interfere with the proper greyness
of old Concord and my favorite characters!
Suppose they went to cavorting at their own
sweet will to the infinite horror of dear Mr.
Emerson. To have had Mr. Emerson for an
intellectual god all one's life is to be invested
with the chain armor of propriety. And what
would my own good father think of me...if
I set folks to doing the things that I have a
longing to see my people do. No, my dear,
I shall always be a wretched victim to the
respectable traditions of Concord.

—Louisa May Alcott

Louisa May Alcott's *Little Women,* published a quarter of a century after
Uncle Tom's Cabin, like Stowe's novel became an instant best seller, remaining
enormously popular in many countries over several generations. The novel
continued the task of functioning as a myth which speaks deeply and mysti-
cally to its readers, interpreting the inner dimensions of family life. The
text touches on the enigma of women's place in democratic America and
the nature of woman's personality. Alcott expressed her hopes for women's
independence of mind and of her heroine's potential to become a serious
artist.

Since childhood years, Alcott had been much encouraged by her Tran-
scendentalist father, Bronson Alcott, to express much of her inner feelings
in letters and diaries, for he believed that spiritual truth might be obtained
by the scrutiny of the inner self. At age thirty-three, Louisa had written
her first novel, and as she approached forty, her literary efforts brought

her enormous success. In 1870 the sales of *Little Women* had topped 80,000 copies; *An Old-Fashioned Girl*, 45,000; and *Little Men* was selling 1,000 copies a day. That year she earned $12,000, and another year $20,000, making her the highest paid American author at that time.[1]

The women of *Little Women* dramatized critical cultural transitions and conflicts as they were being worked out in the sphere of male/female parent/child relations. Jo March is a much beloved American heroine whose odyssey fascinates in its failure. Much like a butterfly whose wings cannot quite metamorphosize, she struggles to soar beyond cloying sentimental moralism. A female Prometheus, her quest flounders, more an ill-timed gesture than a blasphemous one.

Jo's tentative resistance to the extremes of the marble immortality of the domestic icon prepares the way for new concepts of girls and women and carries the weight of cultural transition. Jo, her mother, and her sisters remain partially engulfed in the myth of pure, good womanhood. No longer endangered as victims and slaves, they find themselves instead inhibited by a softer but cloying cocoon of moralism and idealization. Yet, the March women are allowed to awaken from the Stygean dew of female impotence.

The emergence of the prepubertal and adolescent March girls signifies a marked departure from the concept of girlhood personified by Eva St. Clair. The March women, particularly Jo, are attempting a second birth for women—out of martyrdom and into a more lively and dimensional mentality for women and children. They perform and are allowed access to the rituals and scenes of ordinary female growth and development. Their adolescent dreams, their hope for adult competence, their participation in vigorous activities—dancing, boating, skating—and the pleasures of friendly male companionship all suggest the emergence of adolescence and the demise of the martyred maiden. Jo and Amy's interest in creative work, writing and painting, respectively, parallels social groups and reform movements of the century in which women resisted various forms of restriction and isolation.[2]

Stowe's myth of family relations has little if any evidence of normal child development. Infants and children are trapped within the priorities of a "male" culture emphasizing adult aggressivity. Female development is particularly endangered by the "lust" of male tyrants. Eva dies before the onset of puberty, killing off any possibility of powerful sexuality and rebellious individuality. Her death represents their sacrifice.

As a myth of female existence, *Little Women* departs from the equation of culture with male mental life and projects. Its main characters are women, and their concerns, fears, and emotions determine the force and direction of the narrative. Strong paternal figures are absent, and deprived of their power to shape destiny. Their influence and activities, symbolized by the Civil War, are kept at a distance, as is the war itself. Reversing the dominant perspective that centers on *man and his culture*, Alcott bases her legend of familial relations within a female-centered society. The March family odyssey is one of female development and a structure within which the emergence of a female self can flower.[3]

In *Uncle Tom's Cabin*, Stowe presents the intense antipathy between hard autistic maneuvers and the vulnerability associated with mother/child experiences. The novel presents a dichotomy between an inner self denied any armor of hard aggression and a personality structure which is etched in hard cruelty. American Calvinist psychology allows only the typology of the very hard or the very soft.

In *Little Women*, some twenty years later, Alcott continues to work out family relations in a postrevolutionary modernizing culture. She presents the possibilities of a female self, authentic and lively, but as yet gingerly, hesitantly, wary of the explosiveness of female individual will and of the painful nakedness of a self hatching into an undetermined universe.[4] One problem that Alcott faced (and other women as well) was the distortion of the lens out of which they looked to the new possibilities. They look through the lens of moral encasement. Melville and Hawthorne had already scrutinized the male lens shaped by the male quest for self-aggrandizement. Alcott's characters come at the experience from the position of the good woman. Thus they are not entirely free to experience the exhilaration and terrors of self discovery. Assuming the role of pilgrims, their development is taken up by the achievement of moral rectitude. Marmy defines the little pilgrims' journey in this way:

> We are never too old for this, my dear, because it is a play we are playing all the time, one way or another. Our burdens are here, our road is before us, and the longing for goodness and happiness is the guide that leads us through many troubles and mistakes to the peace which is a true celestial city. Now, my Little Pilgrims, suppose you begin again, not in play, but in earnest.[5]

At the same time, Jo is allowed to demonstrate other elements of female development: autonomy and willfullness. *Little Women* is an incubator in which female ambition may grow. Jo's ambition is to do something very splendid.

> What it was she had no idea, but left it for a time to tell her; and meanwhile found her affliction in the fact that she couldn't read, run, and ride as much as she liked. A quick temper, sharp tongue, and restless spirit were always getting her into scrapes.[6]

The context for the innovation of *Little Women* was the transformation of Calvinist piety into more liberal strains[7] of religious vision.

As *Little Women*'s author was raised not in the glare of the Calvinist father but in the heavy altruism of transcendentalism, in her mind the mythic pattern of the Madonna and child redeemer took on new dimensions. Her father, Bronson Alcott, along with Emerson and Thoreau, constructed a new understanding of ethics and human nature out of the notion of the goodness and perfection of the universe, to which they added a new notion of human character. Thus, an atmosphere of intense idealization and a sense of mystical missionary zeal provided the background for Alcott's family tales.

Louisa May Alcott's infancy, childhood, and adolescence coincided with her father's passionate attempts to realize an identity as educational messiah and prophet.[8] Bronson Alcott, born in New England in 1799, reached adulthood in the Jacksonian age of democratic equality and was one of several figures of his generation to become intoxicated by the possibilities of personal godliness.[9] Just as politics or economics were for some men the spectacular means by which they realized individual will, Transcendentalism was Alcott's instrument for overcoming such pessimism as was left in the wake of the receding Calvinist God. As suggested by Quentin Anderson in his excellent study entitled *The Imperialist Self*, the postrevolutionary secularizing culture stimulated and nurtured in some individuals a gigantic sense of self, or outrageous narcissism.[10] Men (this reponse did not apply to women) not only felt that they were to do God's work but understood their own will and powers as coincident with the entire world. The boundaries of their being were imagined to extend to the farthest reaches of the universe.[11] The limitations posed by the secular assault of modern science on the faith in omnipotent egalitarianism might be confounded by reaching for more wealth and power or, in Bronson Alcott's case, by Transcendentalism, a philosophic stance which allowed him to fantasize his incorporation of the universe which he would then re-create. Following Emerson, Alcott found in Transcendentalism the means to be one with the universe or to re-create it in his own self-image as perfect and devoid of evil. For Alcott, Moby Dick and Chillingsworth were figures of the Calvinist anxious imagination. Moving from the notion of original sin to its polar opposite—the belief in the goodness and perfectibility of human nature, Alcott believed that he could produce a Utopian society by evoking and nurturing the divine potential in humanity.[12] As children in their innocence and freshness were closer to the divine and spiritual, Alcott proposed to make childhood the centerpiece for his Utopian reform.[13]

Emerson, admiring Alcott's notion that access to ultimate spirituality might be achieved through the innocence of children, explained the new messiah. "Infancy is the perpetual messiah, which comes into the arms of fallen men, and pleads with them to return to paradise."[14] As Alcott believed the human mind to be a limited part of the infinite mind, he proposed to locate salvation and assurances of a manageable well-ordered society in child study, education, and the reform of child rearing. He argued that parents and teachers were no longer to force-feed their offspring the values that their own generation held important. Since the divine already existed in children, Alcott believed that the educational process should be a drawing out, not a pouring in.[15] Freed from the task of wrestling with innate depravity, parents and teachers could encourage imaginative playfulness and active communication between themselves and their young charges. Sympathy, encouragement, and loving guidance were to replace strict discipline and harsh physical punishment.[16] Alcott explained that if children were difficult, it was because parents failed to fulfill their developmental needs. He insisted that vulgarity and impulsivity and impurity of association were the products of a dim and degraded ideal. The infant came into the world with only the associations of celestial forms. If impure actions or gross sentiments emerged, it was not owing to innate impurity or inborn depravity but to the emblems and words by which the child has been addressed. Alcott pressed his case further.

> Life, external, is the nurse and feeder of the internal life. It nurses the spirit and purity and cherishes its innocence, and all its issues will bespeak its virginity.[17]

Here, Alcott approaches a theory of bonding and attachment in which the emotional reciprocity between parents and children generates the nature and coloring of familial relationships and shapes the form of the child's potential character.[18]

Alcott's child-rearing philosophy challenged the old Calvinist fear and hatred of childish will. He took the opposite view, suggesting that will was not an enemy to proper child development but its ally. Under Calvinism, individual will had been linked tightly to sinful hubris and had had to be broken, but Alcott, in a stunning leap into modern notions of child nature and child rearing argued that infantile will might act as a barrier to injustice and tyranny against small creatures. He suggested that the belief that will was an enemy to good character simply provided parents with a rationalization for their harsh discipline and indiscriminate authoritarian attitudes. Alcott argued for self government. The child must be treated as a *free self-guiding, self-controlling human being.* He must be allowed to feel that he is under his own guidance and that all external guidance is an injustice which is done to his nature unless his own will is intelligently submissive to it. He must be free that he may be truly virtuous, for without freedom virtue would die on the vine.[19]

Yet like many people of his generation and interests, Alcott still worried about the overflow of human feelings. He designated the problematical area of human expressiveness as the passions.[20] In his *The Child's First Year,* he poured out his anxious concerns. Infancy as the period of animal activity and the immaturity of the intellect was ruled by passions, appetites and sensuality.[21] Alcott wavered between the two extremes of brutal oppression of the child's emerging will and a proto-modern accommodation to primitive mental life and its expression through sensuality and raw emotions.[22] Alcott's route through these contradictions in himself and in his group was to find both a defense of individual will and its use as an instrument for control of the passions. Educated will would yield a conscience, not to be used for harsh repression but for the tasks of self-scrutiny and reasonable self-control leading to the attainment of spirituality and divine potential. A mature conscience promoted enlightened self-government, and tempered individual expression. Alcott's compromise allowed the newly emerging self, hatching out of feudal institutions, an inner authority as protection against wild excess. His theory approaches a modern concept that the child's ability both to be expressive and to control his or her feelings stimulates the growth of the self without evoking the fear and anger of inner and outer parents.

Furthermore, Alcott's pleas to parents and teachers to take the responsibility of providing a pure, suitable environment worthy of the evocation of the divine potential in children,[23] built a barrier or defense against the violence and hatred perpetrated on children. Alcott's theories made a place for infants and children as vulnerable, dependent beings, part of a network of loving, protective ties. Thus, Alcott's position was against the excesses of child abuse.

Yet neither he nor the younger writer Alcott were able to comfortably bring together childishness and passion. Both found protection from emotional turbulence in psychological morality. Self-control over appetites and desires provided a "soft" capsule to contain or circumscribe the self's experience.[24] Minute, excessive directions and scrutiny of infants' and children's feelings and behavior replaced the old scaffolding of the hard shell of emotional slavery.[25] *Little Women* carries on Bronson Alcott's strategies in which obsessive morality becomes a paradoxical means for loosening the oppression of the lively elements of psychic life as well as protection of inner selves. From inside the structure of the moral cocoon, the women of *Little Women* stir and press to emerge as selves who attempt to experience their own thoughts and feelings, which they regard as serious and primary. However, the walls of the cocoon structure provide a skin of protection in a somewhat unyielding fashion to the extent that the self's effort at metamorphosis is endangered, as are the elements of desire and will.

The psychic skin needed for the cushioning of the hatching individual self is hardened within Calvinistic child-rearing ideology. Stowe understands these early protective maneuvers, and she traces their nightmare manifestations and the typology of the gods of self-madeness in their effort to cover soft, fleshy selves within the armor of hard, dominating control and the murder and torture of soft baby selves linked with the restriction and domination of women. The Alcotts attempt to soften control and to courageously midwife thin-skinned selves by implementing the moral cocoon—not only as a shelter but as an internal boundary for the segregation of different emotional attitudes.[26] Louisa May Alcott manages to separate the darker, more intense elements of psychic life from the gentle, acceptable ones by creating her woman characters as signs of binary oppositions. At a deeper level, ambition, pure aggressivity, and passion are split off or leached out of *Little Women* almost entirely. The absence of these qualities is paralleled by the exclusion from the narrative of powerful, dominant male figures. These characters and emotions appear in another genre, Alcott's pseudo-Gothic tales, and in two novels, *Moods* and *A Modern Mephistopheles*, in which women are faced with the problems of sexual desire and malevolent male power, as well as the implications of their desire for their own nefarious omnipotence.

Within the domain of *Little Women*, the characters of Jo, Beth, Meg and Amy not only oppose but balance each other, so that self-expression is furthered as well as it is curtailed. The nature of these binary oppositions is dramatized by the juxtaposition of Jo and Beth. Jo has many ambitions and appetites. She wishes to be all that a man can be and to enjoy all the freedom that she envied in men. In contrast, Beth is the woman of selfless moral virtue, the domestic saint who serves the family and cares for the home and asks for nothing in return. Thus, the woman who succumbs, who surrenders her will for some higher good, is juxtaposed with one who, although she has strong will and passion, is not yet allowed to fly out of her cocoon.

The other sisters contrast and reveal tensions between willfullness, vanity, egocentricity, worldly ambition, and degenerate character with the ideal of the woman of pure altruism. The Jo/Meg, Jo/Amy, Amy/Beth oppositions reflect possibilities for young women in adolescence; at the same time, moderating self-expression through the interfacing of oppositional attitudes. If Jo is tomboyish, restless, temperamental, and ambitious and longs to move out beyond the restrictions of ladylike gentility, Beth as a devoted nun of the church of the moral family is the counterbalance to Jo's unconventional ways. Amy is too vain, while Jo is not vain enough. Meg is too conventional. She is attracted to the rewards of marriage and a family. Jo is not conventional enough. She detests women's dress, the customs of making calls, of being ladylike in any way. She detests the rituals of proper middle-class society and rejects marriage as unbearable. Jo is tempestuous, her temper is uncontrollable and problematic. Beth is entirely controlled, seemingly without any outward emotion or will or apparent desire to move beyond the family circle.

Within these polarized oppositions, Beth's fate suggests the infanticide of the concept of female adolescence. Beth's death, while a way to counterbalance, is one end of a spectrum. The other daughters enjoy development and expansion of the self into adult life. But, shadowed by the influence of Beth, they too never leave home. Jo and Beth are opposed, but as aspects of the same person. Each personifies aspects of full womanhood; Jo, more than assertive and creative, suggests the American girl re-thought, looking toward the twentieth century. Beth continues to maintain the gentleness and the compassion of a domestic madonna looking backward toward Eva. The Jo/Beth axis, moving from lively girl→female adolescent to a woman of self-abnegatory renunciation, signifies more than the social parameters of chronological development from tomboy to proper wife and mother. It suggests a very serious argument about the nature and extent of female development, the troubling elements of which are independence of mind and sexuality.

A few years earlier, the fictional and didactic works on child rearing focused on the child's pure nature in a way which required enclosure within the domestic circle. Infants and children of both sexes were to be sheltered from public life, which was defined as contaminated. The fear of the polluted world outside was symbolized in images of pregnancy and nursing— mother and her milk were believed to be contaminated, the latter poisoned by mother's exposure to improper society and particularly those customs and values associated with city life.

Adolescence as a concept and a stage of life slowly became familiar throughout nineteenth-century America. However, it was not until the early twentieth century that G. Stanley Hall formally defined adolescence as a stage in the life cycle.[27] The notion of a period in the life cycle devoted to leaving childhood and preparing for adulthood had required a deepening appreciation of the implications of democratic/Protestant individuation. Religion and social theory increasingly made a place for individual mental life. This in turn stimulated an open quest for the self. Children were gradually understood to have a differentiated self.[28] The development of a more secular, urban, and technological culture meant that the children's world, social values, work life, and personal lifestyle increasingly departed from those of the parental generation. Parents had more and more difficulty providing support and guidance for their offspring. They simply had not experienced the same rites of passage.[29]

By and large, before the eighteenth and nineteenth centuries the emotions of rebellion, individuation, and the expansion of the self had not been recognized as associated with a prolonged stage of the life cycle and deep psychic states.[30] Rites of initiation, baptism, and apprenticeship marked the profound departures from one stage of life to another throughout human history.[31] In nineteenth- and twentieth-century America, these outward signs gradually become replaced by the recognition of internal rites of passage in which relationships to the gods of infancy and childhood are engaged in a drama of the relocation of power, responsibility, and of separation itself. As the young individual begins the phase of practicing and rehearsing for adult life,[32] the psychic narrative calls for further distancing from the surround of support of the internal family, and alternatively the expansion of the self. Physiological maturation and the pain of the inward rites re-enact separation anger and other intense volatile states of intensity, sensuality, and exhilaration. As generational distance is increased outwardly along with the softening of cultural attitudes toward infantile mental life, adolescence emerges, released from its potential hidden state, now invited to unfold.[33]

As *Little Women* puts together elements of these adolescent processes, it relies on various transformations of the image of the American girl.[34] As suggested by Stowe's Mary Scudder in *The Minister's Wooing* (1859), the New England girl was to act as a moral bulwark against the riptide of secular appetites and declension into secular lifestyles. However, Scudder is in many ways Eva's alter ego in that her moral teaching flows from a healthy, joyful sense of herself. Mary Scudder's religious convictions are not opposed to development and satisfaction. She teaches without offering her life as weight for her moral argument. Mary Scudder's character grows from the soil of a new idea. Bronson Alcott's Emersonian notions had begun to unearth the elements for new attitudes toward the young. Jo March benefits from the softening of the concept of original sin. However, since moral wariness provided the context for the emergence of female self interest, the transition from altruistic female figures to narcissistic ones was to be slow and tortuous. Henry James engaged in this process as he struggled to free his heroine Isabel Archer in *Portrait of a Lady* from the hold of the American madonna and allowed her her own desires and grief over the frustration of her wishes and will. Thus, the four March girls are part of the evolution of the concept of the American girl from Harriet Beecher Stowe's Eva to Alice Walker's Celie (*The Color Purple*, 1983), who breaks the restraints against black female development and is allowed access to her developing intellectual and emotional life.

In this sense the March girls also represent the female analogues for Huckleberry Finn and Tom Sawyer. While the March girls remain partially within the moral sphere similar to the one that Huck Finn rejects as immoral, they also present themselves as early important figures in the saga of adolescence. At the opening of the book, their ages range from high adolescence to pre-puberty. Meg is 16, Jo 15, Beth 13, and Amy 11. The novel carries them forward into young adulthood and marriage and motherhood for Meg. *Jo's Boys* and *Little Men* continue their development. Each of the young women, except for Beth, has a roster of rebellious complaints, as well as hopes and dreams. Individual quests and grandiose projects for fulfillment are expressed openly. Jo stages her rebellion around the limitations of female character. She dissents from the elder generation's notions about women, characterizing herself as the "man" in the family and enjoying the privileges of boyishness. Meg asks that she abandon her tomboyishness, admonishing her to be a proper young lady and to fulfill the tasks of that role. Jo sees no hope in that role of Little Woman.

> I hate to think that I've got to grow up and be Miss March and wear long gowns and look as prim as a china aster. It's hard enough to be a girl, anyway, when I like boys, games and work, and manners. And I can't get over my disappointment in not being a boy. And it's worse than ever now, from dying to go fight with Papa, and I can only stay at home and knit like a pokey old woman.[35]

Meg defends feminine decorum, but hardly from an ascetic position. She has her own appetites and rebellion. In the chapter "Castles in the Air," Meg reveals her rebellious attitudes.

> I should like a lovely house, full of all sorts of luxurious things; nice food, pretty clothes, handsome furniture, pleasant people. And heaps of money. I am to be mistress of it, and manage as I like, with plenty of servants so I never need work a bit. How I should enjoy it! For I wouldn't be idle, but do good, and make everyone love me dearly.[36]

As the young people create their own castles out of their ambition and ideals, a generational breach appears. Laurie, as a representative of male adolescence, argues for his escape. He wishes to make his own life out from under the control of his grandfather. His grandfather, on the other hand, wishes Laurie to avoid the pitfalls of his father and to follow a safe road. Laurie is a young man with a hatred of subjugation, and he longs to try himself in the wide world. He says,

> After I'd see as much of the world as I'd want to, I'd like to settle in Germany and have just as much music as I chose. I'm to be a famous musician myself, and all creation is to rush to hear me; and I'm never to be bothered about money or business, but enjoy myself and live for what I like.[37]

Amy also openly expresses her personal ambitions and goals in Faustian style. She says:

> I've got lots of wishes; but the pet one is to be an artist and go to Rome and do fine pictures and be the best artist in the whole world.[38]

Jo defines the changing emotional climate for Laurie. She explains that their outing, in which the Castle building is aired, is an emulation of an older game of theirs, that of playing at pilgrims. She tells Laurie that they are no longer pilgrims on their journey to the celestial city. They are now players in the drama of personality, its self-exploration and growth.[39]

Beth is the exception; she remains the moral pilgrim as an unembodied self without passion and desire for personal fulfillment or for this world. The narrator assures us that Beth is no angel, but a very human little girl, "She wept a little weep for not having had her heart's desire" (music lessons and a piano). Yet, the evidence of the novel allows us to see Beth as a signifier of the sacrificial maiden. Her sacrifice is on the altar of an old needed concept, that of the angel or redeemer in the home, with its ideal goodness and purity. The persona of Beth is one possibility on a spectrum of growth↔stasis.[40]

The dynamic opposition of Beth↔Jo takes place on many levels of signification. Within the more public cultural mythic structures, Beth is an old-fashioned girl, the title of another Alcott children's novel, in which the temptations of adolescence are recognized but safely constrained through the power and efficacy of the virtues of a girl of fine moral character.[41] The heroine of this novel, Polly, reflects the bias that a woman must restrain herself from venturing into materialism, ambition, or the egoism and pretension of self-aggrandizement and, of course, potential sexuality.

In *Little Women*, the narrator reflects on Beth's influence on Jo, particularly the lesson learned by her sister through her illness and suffering.

> Jo, being in the darkened room with that sad, suffering little sister always before her eyes, learned to see the beauty and the sweetness of Beth's nature. To feel how deep and tender a place she fulfilled in all hearts and to acknowledge the worth of Beth's unselfish ambition to live for others and make home happy by the exercise on those virtues which all could possess and all should value more than talent, wealth, or beauty.[42]

Within *Little Women*, martyrdom is the blight on the possibilities of adolescence, and at the same time it is valued as a protection against the excesses of generational conflict and the possibilities of sexual explosiveness. Beth also offers comfort and stability in the face of cultural and social change. A new woman, personified by Jo, hints at hopes and ambitions for entry into the public sphere, and suggests a potential loss of the icon of peace and continuity. Beth's place is at home. Home and family claim her mortal self while her body becomes slowly refined away to allow for the immortal spirit to shine through. The family appetite for sacrifice dissolves her embodiment. Beth is the personification, then, of the sacrificial maiden, her personality seriously dismembered.

> 'I don't know how to express myself, and shouldn't try to anyone but you, because I can't speak out except to my old Jo. I only mean to say that I have a feeling that it never was intended that I should live long. I'm not like the rest of you. I never made any plans about what I'd do when I grew up; I never thought of being married as you all did. I couldn't seem to imagine myself anything but stupid little Beth, trotting about at home, of no use anywhere but here. I never wanted to go away, and the hard part now is the leaving you all. I'm not afraid, but it seems as if I should be homesick for you, even in Heaven.[43]

Beth's ascetic character, stripped of desire and will, reflects more than antagonism toward female sexuality, creativity, and individuation. She is the personification of self-control. In another sense, she is Jo's alter-ego as conscience, a conscience which acts for cultural bias and for the forces of internal conservatism. The confidences expressed and shared in the chapter "Castles in the Air" reiterate the growth↔stasis relationship. On one side is creativity and exploration; on the other, moral certitude, or to put it another way, the "Castles in the Air" dialogue juxtaposes the pilgrim's progress with the progress of creative exploration. Laurie's interest in music and Amy's passion for painting make the polarization clear in terms of a Beth/growth opposition. Jo takes the middle position. She explains that she does not yet have the key to her castles in the air, and throughout the novel, she seems rather ambivalent about her writing and unclear as to whether or not it is a legitimate activity. This ambivalence reflects the Beth side of her. The Beth self is burdened with the psychic relics of the past and present to the extent that it becomes the graveyard of new ideas about female development and adolescence. Unlike Mary Shelley or the Brontës, March-Alcott had more difficulty writing in a way that encouraged a gathering of her whole personality.[44]

Jo's failure of nerve to commit to her writing proves the difficulty of her overcoming her Beth self. The moral vision or the moral solution places the individual within a confined view so that the frightening specter of emotional turbulence is mitigated. The cocoon woven out of moral platitudes and dogmatic certitude cushions the psyche from the shocks of change, separation, and the unknown which are integral to emotional growth and lively mental experience. But, at the same time, this particular method of finding shelter mutilates aspects of the self and their thoughts and feelings. The creative process, on the other hand, attempts the entry into the center of the storm of emotional life. The various possible creative solutions achieve the formation and understanding of meaning which leads to self-knowledge.[45]

Jo's attraction to writing reflects a deep longing for the experience that is on the other side of genteel womanhood. The narrator suggests that she feels something calling her from inside, pressing her toward the unknown.

> Jo's ambition was to do something very splendid; what it was she had no idea, but left it for a time to tell her; and meanwhile, found her greatest affliction in the fact that she couldn't read, run and ride as much as she liked.[46]

Jo confides in Mr. Laurence that she feels a sympathy with his grandson's yearning for freedom, a freedom that will take him outside the family and its proscriptions. She says, "I often think I should like to get away, especially since my hair was cut; so if you ever miss us, you may advertise for two boys and look among the ships bound for India."[47]

Jo wants to leave home in a number of ways, but as she suggests, inner and outer obstacles make the journey uncertain. The idea that a young woman might enjoy her own odyssey into self-exploration and expression is severely jeopardized in Jo's mind. It is clear that creativity and the standards of morality are antithetical. Jo's aspirations to become a serious artist are firmly linked to the idea that she would have to behave as a young man.

In Hester, Hawthorne had already explored some of these same issues. Hester can be seen as an artist whose palette is her mind, and whose paints are her original thoughts and feelings. Her gorgeous scarlet letter embroidered splendidly in gold gathers together all the implications of her devotion to originality and the discovery of fresh approaches to her situation as a woman, in relationship to herself, to her family, society, and God. Hawthorne's model for Hester Prynne is Anne Hutchinson, and he finds in her as well the sign of the American cultural conflict between moral culture and self-exploration. The Puritan distrust of aesthetic exploration parallels the elders' distrust and hatred of Hutchinson's probing antinomianism: undoubtedly because antinomianism encourages the unmediated encounter of the individual with his/her subjective experience or the state of one's soul in religious terms, and thereby threatens the "patriarchal" hierarchical hold of the church over its congregation.

Hawthorne is tracking shifts in American culture as to the means of control of inner states. Prynne's act of sexual indiscretion suggests the evolution of American value systems from piety to moralism,[48] which peaks in the nineteenth century's obsession with moral propriety. Bronson Alcott's plea for gentle child nurture attempts to free children from these kinds of hard beliefs. Hawthorne places his Hester Prynne within a mythic structure which opposes her originality of mind. In this way, she explains more than a woman's dilemma, but perhaps Hawthorne's dilemma as a male artist. The writer, poet, and artist of either sex has had no home within either the Puritan or the moralist culture. The aesthetic explorer reaches into states of mind and images that threaten to engulf and topple the messianic zeal of the self-serious Puritans and the belief system of the ideal of the madonna and child of the nineteenth century; both pose themselves as oppositional forces to what they designated as threatening forces stemming from the human mind.

Jo's longing for a career as a writer and the realization of her adolescent dreams to escape the domestic persona of wife and mother are seriously curtailed by Jo's conscience.[49] The young writer maintains a curious relationship to her writing throughout the novel until finally she has abandoned it almost entirely. Throughout *Little Women* Jo seems ashamed of her writing, calling it "scribbling" or even "trash." While she turns out a novel (probably modeled on Louisa May Alcott's *Moods* which, because of its frank discussion of sexual desire and the possibility of divorce, was poorly received), Jo remains strangely detached from her offspring. Her passivity in regard to her novel, allowing others to criticize and challenge it, allows us to see her ambivalence. She assumes the position of a novice who loses control of her work, perhaps because she has no central voice. As the mature wife and mother of the end of *Little Women* and of *Jo's Boys* and *Little Men* Jo March Baer heads a children's school with her husband. The educational policies of Plumfield are progressive and creative in that it is a school whose program is centered around the cultivating of personal development. But in this domain, Jo reigns as the incarnation of the moral mother, the artist self having been overcome as the rebellious adolescent girl has been firmly tamed.

The tasks of adolescence and those of the artist are not dissimilar. In adolescence the subject's inner reality is broken down in its existing form and recreated in new structures. The structures of the mind which hold emotions, thoughts, signs, and symbols are no longer useful in their present form. As the gods of yesteryear, the internal parental figures must be encountered to yield up their power and wisdom. Support, soothing, regulation, interpretation, authority, and wisdom must now be gradually taken into the self's orbit of initiation and responsibility. Though the sense of being held in a support system continues, the surrounding parents recede into the background space of the mind.[50] These shifts take place within a violent and impassioned re-enactment of the dramas of infancy. Once again, the ecstasy of merger shuts out the terrors of abandonment. Once more, possessiveness dominates. The belief in magical powers and desire for bodily delights sets off fiery emotions and rhythms that accompany the birth of the self; now laboring through long spasms and states of engulfing blissful union, now in exhilarated awareness and terrible excitement accompanied by interminable battles to break free of the old parental gods, who seethe at dethronement and strike out with cruel revenge as long ago the infant self had when dethroned from autochthonous grandeur. The umbilical connections are severed and placenta poison brews dispelled as the heady exhilaration of freedom becomes possible. Now, new bodily power and competence becomes potential and is fused with the terror of incompetence and paranoia. Repeatedly, these dramas are played out. Over and over, the inner rituals are enacted. Initiation rites from which the young subject strains to emerge, are negotiated, having taken love and strength into the self to become a self.[51]

The creative act is also played out in the high dramas of internal life. It too reaches into the archaic characters and focuses not so much on a phase of development and the passage from childhood dependence to adult independence, but a lifelong process of self-exploration, self-knowledge, and self-creation. Creative structures from primitive signs to complex symbol systems gather the stuff of potential meaning from many wells of experience from deep within the body and the mind; the sensory and preconceptual, and from external sources perceptual and cognitive. As with the inner rituals of adolescence, creative states give birth to new states of mind and new structures. As old ones are torn down or discarded, emotions set free escalate out of control; self states of exhilaration and terror flowing out of the power of creativity and self-expression sweep the self along a torrent toward the unknown. Yet conversely out of the wellsprings of memories ghosts emerge painfully dancing on the graves of old familial imagoes exhorting to be transformed or threatening to undermine the new structures, the new pathways for thinking and the new thoughts themselves.

Successful adolescence and creativity both bring on and repeat painful and wrenching rituals as the self emerges out of autism and symbiosis, exploding into the glaring light and sound of unenslaved, unstatic, synchronic mental life, that is to say, individuality in the context of many subjectivities. The creative process itself symbolizes death and rebirth, submergence back into the mother's body or the depths of the mind, and rebirth with new meaning.

Both adolescent development and the creative process require the subject's capacity to live in a state of mind that acknowledges space and time and is not exclusively sensuous. As discussed in chapter 2, the first early signs or proto-symbols are created out of the maternal presence. That is, the experience of interfacing sensually with the primary object. In the early weeks of infancy, meaning is created out of these sensuous experiences as mental life functions at the level of the body. Eventually, the little sign-maker is able to give up the exclusively sensual mode of making meaning. Silver describes this change as the development from the level of icons to the level of abstraction.[52] Bion characterizes this change in symbolizing and thinking as the achievement of the toleration of the "no breast," the ability to imagine or signify the object of experience in its sensory absence. Thus, the achievement of internal mental space is the prerequisite for the emergence of the self and of its capacity to signify. Mental space is the stage on which these processes take place.[53]

Adolescence brings to bear on the general task of separation and individuation further maturation of the capacities of the body and of the mind as well. With the enactment of the inner rituals, the internal space expands, including the capacity to signify in the third dimension with deepening dimensionality.[54] The acceptance of the discipline of time and space increases and complements the growing cognitive capacities.[55] Thus "I's" capacity to become more distanced from inner mythic systems of the self and the family and to create revolutionary challenges to these value systems places the emerging young individual in a precarious position. No longer immersed within the family myth, he or she is not only torn out of the system (out of his or her niche), but as the messiah of new values and implicitly the critic of the old ones, becomes potentially an object of hatred.[56] The family requires a messiah for deliverance from mental stasis, but at the same time, the family may also require a messiah who will die (give up their life) in order for the family value system to be protected from the emotional challenge of new ideas. Eva St. Clair fulfills this function for slave society, and the Jo/Beth interface can also be seen in this way.

Jo is the avant-garde figure who attempts to break the bonds of the family myth in which daughters are enshrined and made into icons of peace and harmony. On other end of the spectrum, Beth replaces Eva as the Christ figure who is sacrificed to the need for stasis and ignorance. Beth also balances the account. As new values are developed out of the different concepts of women and children, the gods of morality require appeasement. Beth's death suggests the death of a typology, the end of a line of maidens too good for this world, while Jo's character implies mental freedom, but at the risk of madness. In the 60s, before the March family books were written, Alcott explored areas outside family morality. The main characters were young women who balanced their emotions precariously between forceful revenge and madness. Alcott split her consciousness between the accepted sentimental notion of girlhood as it appeared in the March novels, and an alternative, a turbulent femme fatale placed in pseudo-Gothic tales.[57]

The Gothic genre lends itself well to Alcott's intentions, with its interest in evil decay and secret and mysterious forces. Leslie Fiedler[58] suggests that the Gothic style reflects an important vision of postrevolutionary society:

> The guilt which underlies the Gothic and motivates its plots is the guilt of the revolutionary, haunted by the paternal which he/she has been striving to destroy, and the fear that possesses the Gothic and motivates its tone is the fear that in destroying the old evil ideas of church and state— the West has opened its way for the eruption of darkness; for insanity and the disintegration of the self.[59]

Fiedler argues persuasively that the carving out of an individual consciousness means the cutting of the umbilicus of communal ties. The figure of the Gothic maiden in flight and her pursuer, Fiedler suggests, are two halves of one person which represents the uprooted soul of the artist who has lost his/her moral home. Fiedler adds the last horror of disintegrating separation expressed in the Gothic. He says:

> Beneath the haunted castles lies the dungeon keep; the womb from whose darkness the ego [self] first emerged, the tomb to which it knows it must return at last. Beneath the crumbling shell of paternal authority lies the maternal darkness imagined by the Gothic writers as a prison, a torture chamber.[60]

Fiedler's understanding of the Gothic genre suggests an analogy with the internal rites and rituals of adolescence. He suggests a process like that of the breaking up of the old internal community and mythic structures and the madness of that experience.

The heroines in Alcott's Gothic tales are safely removed from the New England present and are found in England, France, or in a lush Cuban countryside. Out of the grasp of New England mores, these women are able to explode into sensuality and aggressivity. Despite the tone of the March novels, Louisa May Alcott had revealed somewhat directly her longing to escape New England propriety:

> I think my natural ambition is for the lurid style. I indulge in gorgeous fantasies and wished that I dared inscribe them upon my pages and set them before the public. How should I dare to interfere with the proper

greyness of old Concord and my favorite characters! Suppose they went
to cavorting at their own sweet will to the infinite horror of dear Mr.
Emerson. To have had Mr. Emerson for an intellectual god all one's life
is to be invested with the chain armor of propriety. And what would my
own good father think of me . . . if I set folks to doing the things that I
have a longing to see my people do. No, my dear, I shall always be a
wretched victim to the respectable traditions of Concord.[61]

While Louisa was not able to act according to her own desires, Jean Muir,
Pauline Valery, and Virginie Varens did cavort at their own sweet will.
These women characters as personifications of the force of the internal
ritual enact a dark reversal of the optimistic myth of the moral redeemer.
In the myths built into the Gothic thrillers, exile, murder, manipulation,
revenge, and suicide replace the gentle, controlled interaction of *Little
Women*.

The one incident of murderous feelings, jealousy, and hatred that appears in the novel is handled quite differently. In the chapter "Jo Meets
Appolyon," Jo and Amy clash violently over Amy's destruction of Jo's manuscript. Jo's moral persona is disrupted by feelings of violent revenge against
Amy's jealous attack. Out together, on an ice-skating outing, Jo deserts
Amy. When her younger sister falls behind and slips through the ice Jo is
so overcome with hatred she is indifferent to her safety. Amy's adventure
with the ice ends without tragedy, and Jo rejects the outburst of uncontrollable feelings without exploration. Like her mother before her, she
disassociates herself from such feelings. In the mother and daughter dialogue that follows, awareness of female aggressivity surfaces, but repression
wins the day. Jo anguishes that her dreadful temper is incurable and unruly.
Her mother's response implies that for women, self-censorship is a lifelong
struggle:

> "Watch and pray, dear; never get tired of trying; and never think it im-
> possible to conquer your fault . . . I've been trying to cure it for 40 years
> and have only succeeded in controlling it. I'm angry nearly every day of
> my life, Jo; but I've learned not to show it; and I still hope to learn not
> to feel it though it may take me another 40 years not to do so."[62]

The narrator supports the view that patience, humility, and control are
qualities which should be developed to overcome tempestuous feelings in
young women. Within *Little Women*, Jo tips in the direction of self-control.
In the thrillers, on the other hand, Pauline, Jean, and Virginie as alter egos
of the self-sacrificing, virtuous woman are at the radical end of the spectrum, of the cultural Eve/Mary polarity.[63] More extreme than the dark
ladies portrayed by Hawthorne's Zenobia and Hester and Melville's Isabel,
they explore sensuality and the lust for power to the edge and beyond to
insanity and criminality. In keeping with the Gothic interest in the parameters of evil and the individual's Faustian quest, Alcott's heroines experi-

ment with omnipotent control and power over others. In *A Modern Mephistopheles*, Alcott created a male Faust who evoked another aspect in the respectable Gladys.

> Her identity was doubled; one Gladys moved and spoke as she was told, a pale, dim figure of no interest to anyone; the other was alive in every fiber, thrilled with intense desire for something and bent on finding it, though distant oceans and boundless realms of air were passed to gain it.[64]

In this novel, it is the male who brings out and enjoys the darker passions and powers while Gladys eventually relinquishes that aspect of herself and realizes herself as the good woman opposed to the Mephistopheles character.

In the Gothic stories *Behind a Mask, Plots and Counterplots,* and *Pauline's Passion,* no male agent is required for the realization of dark, mysterious powers. These women take on Faustian power for themselves. Like Satan's emissaries, they appear as if from nowhere, insinuating themselves into the very heart of familial society. They present themselves as orphans, who having suffered some family disaster are vulnerable and in need of protection and shelter. On another level, their detachment from any family ties suggest idiosyncratic and mysterious origins. In addition, their peculiar situation outside of family responsibility and the training of moral constraint has served to nurture sophisticated independence and the power to charm and dazzle.

Alcott designs her femme fatales as artists of a certain kind, who make art out of their personalities, conjuring up many selves to enact their wiles and tricks of sorcery. Jean Muir is a consummate actress who presents herself to the Coventry family as a young, genteel, and accomplished but properly modest governess. In fact, her background remains rather sordid. Her father deserted the family and went off with another woman. While some of the Coventry family, particularly Gerald and Lucia, sense something disturbing about Jean, her too compelling charms disarm the family and eventually even Gerald becomes drawn into her spell.

Jean is a sculptor who sculpts herself into forms that will trap and dominate her victims. She shapes masks and personas out of her imagination and out of her flesh. In a tableau of Eastern exoticism, Jean enthralls the Coventry entourage with a sultry portrayal of power and sensuality:

> Bending over a swarthy darkly bit of man was a woman robed with barbaric splendor. One hand turned back the embroidered sleeve and the arm, which held a scimitar—her purple mantle swept down from snowy shoulders; filets of gold bound her hair.[65]

Jean had metamorphosized into another self of dark and volatile temperament.

> She had darkened her skin, thrown such an intensity of expression into her eyes that they darkened and dilated. Hatred, the deepest and bitterest, was written on her sternly beautiful face. Courage glowed in her glance. Power spoke in the nervous grip of a slender hand.[66]

In another scene, Jean brings Gerald under her spell by wearing the mask of the sweet, helpless, but sensually full maiden. Gerald is moved as he has never been before.

> Now, as he knelt there, with a soft arm about him, a slender waist yielding against his touch, and a maiden heart throbbing against his cheek, for the first time of his life he felt the indescribable spell of womanhood.[67]

Lucia and Gerald are set against each other by another of Jean's dangerous selves. To a confidant she reveals the complexity of her playwrighting and acting:

> The cousin was lovely but detestable with her pride, her coldness, and her very visible adoration of Messieur, well let her worship him like an inanimate idol as he is. I hated them both, of course. And in return for their insolence shall torment her with jealousy and teach him how to want a woman by making his heart ache.[68]

In Jean Muir, Alcott fashions the dark lady of her imagination. Hawthorne and Melville had already given life to theirs, while Alcott's Jean and Virginie grow out of the fantasies of a woman writer.[69] Jean's furious hunger for revenge and power is enacted within the family circle, the scene of a woman's imprisonment. Jean contrives to wreck the Coventry family, then marry the senior Coventry and become heir to their land and money, displacing the rightful sons. She plays the role usually commandeered by males; she breaks hearts, conquers others, and makes victims out of the male characters. She is the creator of her own destiny.

Virginie Varens in *Plots and Counterplots* is also a consummate actress, but more complex and insidious than Jean Muir. Virginie is the exotic, sensual mirror image of the teenagers of *Little Women*. In costume for a performance at a Paris theater, she is the consummate image of the alter ego.

> A sylph she seemed, costumed in fleecy white and gold; the star that glittered on her forehead was less brilliant than her eyes, the flowers that filled her graceful arms were outrivalled by the blooming face that smiled above them.[70]

Virginie adopts many masks. She shares with Jean a hatred for conventional family life and, particularly, affectionate ties which elude her power to charm. Virginie moves her maniacal plots and counterplots to triumph over the Douglas family, but her mayhem is especially focused on Earl Douglas, the male heir. Like Jean, the destructive projects of the evil femme fatale are played out through many selves: now she is an exquisite European dancer; now an orphaned victim; now a princess; then a passionate lover; a beautiful, kind, sympathetic widow; now a ghost; a scheming murderer; a gypsy, who loves carnivals; a sympathetic friend. Virginie has such power to transform herself that at one point she seems to be several people at once.

However, Virginie's deceits involve life and death matters. She has the power to invoke murder and suicide in others, through powers and roles which are shifted internally and enacted outwardly. Victor Varens (Arguelles) kills Alan Douglas, Earl's twinlike cousin over love of Virginie. She uses and betrays Victor to the point of madness and suicidal feelings. Victor's death comes in a duel defending Virginie; his obsession with her ended at last. Diana Stewart drowns herself in a dark, deep pool, a scene not unlike that of Zenobia's suicide. Like an insidious fifth columnist, Virginie whispers to Diana of Earl's treacherous betrayal. She shows her her own child, allowing Diana to assume that it is Earl's by another woman. Diana, enthralled by Virginie's powerful charismatic spell, breaks down or is lured to her death. Earl believes that Virginie's responsibility is more than propaganda. He confronts her:

> "Diana's death lies at your door as much as if your hand stabbed her with the same dagger that took Alan's life. It may yet be proved that you beguiled her to that pool, for you were seen there, going to remove all traces of her as you sprang away with an agility that first suggested to me Virginie's presence."[71]

Earl's effort to discover the identity of the murderer of Alan and Diana leads him through the labyrinth of Virginie's plots and counterplots. He is led through the many quicksilver shifts of her moods and masks, and while attracted to the siren, even moved by her powerful beauty and grace, he finds the center of each aspect of her personality to be empty, the deeper currents out of reach. Earl confronts Virginie with her duplicity:

> "But while you have laid your plots carefully, as you have erased all traces of your former self and skillfully as you have played your new part, the truth has come to light."[72]

The truth revealed is that there is no Virginie Varens, only a kaleidoscope of counterfeit selves, shifting and exorting in their attempt at nefarious success. Alcott is presenting a personality with many contradictory masks or selves. Women not allowed to be themselves assumed many personas.

Pauline, Jean, and Virginie live in the looking-glass world of female development. The mythic narratives of these Gothic tales rediscover female potency by entering the netherworld of the alter ego. The alter ego, or double, as Alcott creates her is a structure for all that had been split away from the good female character. Alcott takes up the aggressivity, self-involvement, and sensuous sexuality that the good woman/girl is to overcome or control, really not allowed to develop. Alcott is working not only with the spectrum of possibilities Beth↔Jo, Jo↔Virginie; she is working in a dialectical process to overcome the rigid binary oppositions between maleness and femaleness and between the good/bad Eve/Mary woman archetype. By exploring the potential tomboyness of Jo and even the negative parameters of the very bad Virginie prototype, Alcott is attempting a reconciliation between the members of the opposition parties.

As she probes the other side of female potential, the Eve or dark lady persona, she finds female potency and aggressivity in their negative form. As Alcott presents these women as evil, Faustian Eves, she echoes the culture's fascination with the other side of obedience and morality which involve freedom and license. In regard to the issues of women's proper characters and sphere of influence, Alcott faces the mirror image of the domestic madonna Mary. On the one hand, these femme fatales seen through the lens of moral rigidity are like wild, caged children threatening to break out. On the other, they present the possibility of the more balanced concept of womankind.

Both the dreaded and the more balanced elements of the alter ego are abundantly present in other nineteenth-century literature: Marlowe's *Doctor Faustus*, Dostoevski's *The Double*, Melville's *Pierre* display the authors' interests in inner dialogues and their awareness of inner selves with different personality types and agendas. The entrance of the double or alter ego onto the cultural stage was made possible by the evolution of a self culture. As Bronson Alcott's concerns make clear, postrevolutionary culture allows the concept of an individual self, really demands it. It requires inquiries into the nature of that self, its psychology and potential. What had been designated previously to either supernatural powers (gods and goddesses) or to earthly authorities (given their status through property or by divine right) now is taken back into the self. The self becomes the locus of force and determination. This process does not take place all at once; it takes several hundred years for these changes to evolve.

This probe leads to the awareness of personifications of different levels of different kinds of mental functioning within the same individual. Much of this cultural trend explodes in Freud's work, in which he discovers the dialogue of inner selves. In *On Narcissism* and *Mourning and Melancholia*,[73] Freud describes the evolution of the double. He calls these doubles or inner selves the ego ideal, the superego, the id, and the ego. Contemporary psychoanalytic theory adds another approach to the formation of the alterego or double. The legacy of the deep preverbal communications of the container/contained transactions are the persona of dreams and myths. The gargoyle, the dragon, and the witch structure disastrous experiences. Christ, the madonna, fertility gods and goddesses elaborate hopeful, satisfying bonding experiences. Each is a partial realization of the archetype of the self. Each is structured out of the mind's capacity to code experience by separating data into binary oppositions. The infant mind in particular organizes experiences by more extreme splitting. The splitting takes place in the infant thinker in order to have experiences reworked by parental reverie, and to place feelings and experiences into categories so as to make them assimilable,[74] and it is these infantile structures that give imaginative richness and passion to cultural symbolic structures.

The formation of alter egos as subpersonalities, each with their own conscious, unconscious, and inner world, functions to hold the mirror image or the antithesis of the self that is not consciously known. As the tension between the various selves holds apart that which cannot yet be integrated, the alter egos and subselves think and experience through a limited dimensionality.[75] Dimensionality is achieved through internal dialogues or hermeneutics of internal selves to internal objects, or self-self conversations, etc. In the absence of an empathetic parent receiver/container, the normal splits of early mental life become discrete fiefdoms incapable of dialoging. Grotstein's notion of the subject/object of primary identification is apposite in this regard. As an overall backing, shepherding container, it provides the solid ground for the growth of a pervasive sense of *I* that promotes the toleration of the forces of passionate differences as well as their integration. Conversely, the less containment is available, the personality falls into more or less fragmented identities with strongly oppositional clashes. The double, or the alter ego, is more turbulent and dichotomous under these conditions: a conscience may evolve into a savage critic or an ego ideal into a relentlessly exacting perfectionist; or a twin may become murderously hostile to one's everyday self, monstrously antisocial.

Alcott's alter egos grow under these conditions. A similar evolution can be seen in the work of Charlotte Brontë. Sandra Gilbert and Susan Gubar have suggested in *The Madwoman in the Attic: Women Writers and the Nineteenth Century Literary Imagination* that Jane Eyre's double is Bertha.[76] In "A Dialogue of Self and Soul: Jane Eyre," they suggest that Jane's ordeal in the red room makes clear the presence of rebellion and madness in an alter ego. Bertha Mason Rochester represents the full potential of denied potency and aggressivity. Bertha's anti-social, anti-marriage, anti-male, anti-submissive attitudes are Jane's. As she rips the wedding veil to shreds, Gilbert and Gubar suggest that Bertha is Jane's truest and darkest double.

She is the angry aspect of the orphaned child, the ferocious secret self that Jane had been trying to repress ever since her days at Gateshead.[77]

The double's sinister, dark nature and monstrous quality grow from the horror of exile.

Virginie Varens is the Bertha to Jo March's Jane. But, the fact that they are found not only in two different works but in two different genres, and given two "different" authors (Louisa May Alcott and A. M. Bernard) suggest the powerful and deep fault lines in American culture. Eve/Virginie is profoundly split off from Beth/Jo in the same way that the male/female spheres are signified as antagonistic and antithetical entities in Stowe. Virginia's and Jean's cruelty and heartlessness appear as part of a strategy to rectify the imbalance between hardness and softness associated with male/female child/adult. They commandeer the role of predator, making men their prey. Feminine charms of soft allure are hardened into weapons to vanquish and humiliate men who normally are impenetrable in their power, in their armor, arrogance, and grandiosity.[78]

Earl Douglas and Gerald Coventry are humiliated and endangered in ways that fictional women characters usually are. Earl is helpless against Virginie's poison. He loses both his cousin and his sweetheart to her machinations. Gerald loses his usual cool certitude. These women reverse the hard/soft, victim/aggressor relationship when they implement their power and cruelty. While they have not reached into the arena of politics, they are able to gain their ends and profoundly change the destiny of entire families.

Jo↔Jean/Virginie moving from left to right reveals the development of the female predator and of hard shells not unlike those of the men in *Uncle Tom's Cabin*. Their hard characters are built out of predatory and vengeful feelings. Yet, as in the processes of adolescence, Virginie and Jean explore a new stance in order to separate themselves from the past, from old overwhelming identifications and old idealizations and the terrors of childish powerlessness. Out of the adolescent's inner rituals and exortations, the old powers of the inner world are regrouped and new inner selves are achieved and emerge. The shifting facets of Jean's and Virginie's characters reveal something of this process as they appear in one persona after another. Some of these selves have qualities of gentleness and vulnerability, as for example, Virginie's mother self, who is deeply grieved by the death of her little son, and her genuine feelings for Earl. Similarly, Jean is a fine teacher to her little charge and a capable nurse. They both present many possibilities of a female archetype—the nurse, the wife, the mother, the artist, and the mysterious femme fatale.

The panorama of potential selves suggests the breaking of the constricting mold and the begining of freedom of choice, but also the deep inner processes of transformation as well. Frances Tustin illuminates the etiology of the early self in a way that may throw light on these early processes of adolescence. In normal development, the self is gathered from the integration of basic sensations into a viable entity as it comes to comprise hardness as well as softness, roughness as well as smoothness, hotness as well as coldness.[79] Tustin adds that these contraries are differentiated but com-present. They become part of the "me-ness" of "me." This is a step the autistic child who hides behind the hard shell has not been able to make. Encapsulation insulates the little subject from hard, rough, cold experiences and pushes the unpleasant sensations into the nasty, contemptible "not-me." With integration, new sensations are created from hardness and soft-ness. From hardness and softness comes the experience of resilience and firmness. For example, soft, receptive mouth and hard, thrusting nipple work together to create a forerunner of a sense of self. The soft self sur-rounded by the hard shell, the hard nasty "not-me," is the prototype of the victim. The predator is the all hard.

Alcott's femme fatales immerse themselves in the hard in order to break out of the cultural dichotomy seen in the signs of male hardness and female softness. The twins or masks that Jean and Virginie exhibit are attempts at integration of basic states of being. However, the Gothic heroines are outsiders who have no place within conventional society. Furthermore, they are orphans whom fate has treated very badly. Jean's father abandoned and disowned her, while Virginie at eighteen is adrift without any ally but her own capacity to attract and enthrall men. The stories themselves are without respectable family credentials. Alcott, like her fictional alter-ego twin Jo, wrote her thrillers pseudonymously or anonymously. Both authors dub them "necessity stories." Although these tales went against moral stan-dards, they bailed out their respective families from a flood of financial worries. However, the metaphor of female exile within the structure of the forbidden genre is more to the point. Alcott needed to expand herself and her creative explorations into the sphere of the split off or forbidden. But since neither she nor her young woman characters had familial or cultural empathy and support for these efforts, the dark, tempestuous characters and feelings could not be well integrated into the sunny, optimistic sphere of the moral novels. Jo and Alcott are very much ashamed of their non-moralistic efforts. They fear that the need for money is not sufficient to rationalize the writing of the thrillers. Alcott has Jo say:

> "They are trash, and will soon be worse trash if I go on, for each is more sensational than the last. I've gone on blindly, hurting myself and other people for the sake of money."[80]

The rebellious, challenging elements are ignored, and the femme fatales as alteregos and structures of integration for female aggressivity and po-tency are to remain hidden and somewhat feared.

The meaning of Hester, Zenobia, and Margaret Fuller (Zenobia's pro-totype or model) as strong, passionate, individual female selves is unwel-come in the mainstream culture or the symbolic order. They suicide or are murdered or exiled. As the creative work recreates states of minds (self states), the process threatens to present all the selves and their many feelings, dialogues, and conflicts. Alcott managed to divide her selves and keep them in separate worlds. In this way, she prevented the explosive potential changes stemming from their intersection. The arrival of new ideas about female potency is slowed down as well. The moral view and the Gothic view, separated as they are in her work, leaves each with a myopic vision. The binocular view would come out of a reconciliation between the Beth/ Jo Jo/Virginie selves. The binocular view integral to the reconciliation of the Beth↔Jo, Jo↔Virginie selves is still in the exploratory stage.

In *Little Women*, Jo "overcomes" a great deal of her artist, angry, individuated self. The gentle, moral narrator explains that Jo learned to place family and gentle love before ambition and creative interest. Beth, as the sign of female acquiescence, teaches Jo to repress her possible egocentricity and mania of self-exploration. Beth's death, as well as her nature, brings Jo to the acceptable mature stance. Jo's elegy to her sister explicates this theme:

> Beth, our pardon daily loseth
> Something of its bitter pain
> And while learning this hard lesson,
> My great loss becomes my gain.
> For the touch of grief will render
> Wild nature more serene,
> Give to life new aspirations
> And new trust in the unseen.
> Henceforth safe across the river,
> I shall see forevermore
> A beloved household spirit
> Waiting for me on the shore.
> Hope and faith born of my sorrow,
> Guardian angels shall become
> And the sister gone before me
> By the hand shall lead me home.[81]

Beth, as angel teacher of the gospel of love,[82] guides Jo toward proper maturity. She says:

> "You must take my place, Jo, to be everything to Mother and Father when I'm gone. They will turn to you—don't fail them, and if it's hard work alone, remember that I don't forget you, and that you'll be happier in doing that than writing splendid books or seeing all the world; for love is the only thing that we can carry with us when we go, and it makes the end go easy."[83]

Jo leans toward her Beth self after her sister's death. The Beth↔Jo and Jo↔Virginie spectrum veers heavily toward the limitation and mutilation of the Beth character and type. Jo actually becomes Beth:

Other helps had Jo, humble, wholesome duties and delights, that would not be denied their part in serving her, and which she slowly learned to see and value. Brooms and dishcloths never could be as distasteful as they once had been, for Beth had presided over those; as she used them Jo found herself humming the songs Beth used to hum, imitating Beth's orderly ways and giving the little touches here and there that kept everything fresh and cozy, which was the first step towards making home happy, though she didn't know it.[84]

Unselfish domesticity is juxtaposed against adolescent self-exploration and the creative process, both of which call up forces from the deep inner world. Within *Little Women*, the self of adolescent self-exploration suffers mutilation.

Thus, Beth, Jo, and Virginie are signs of female existence in its limited and potential forms. The sacrifice of female individuality continues in the death of the Beth alter ego, yet Jo, Meg, and Amy suggest some of the willfullness and rebelliousness of adolescence, and Jean and Virginie as well signify and contain extreme forms of rebelliousness and animosity toward conventional cultural patterns, particularly those enacted by men. Earl's unmasking of Virginie's devious selves compromises the triumph of female power. She suicides rather than submit to genteel imprisonment under Earl's rule. But as a signifier, Virginie discovers and expresses female rebellion, and in this way, like Jean and Pauline, is the antidote to sacrifice, and will later be integrated more completely and richly into American culture by Edith Wharton, Mary Cassatt, and later Alice Walker.

The Gothic heroines, having escaped moral confinement, are not deprived of their sensuality and sexuality. But since they are at war with male authority and society, they are not to enjoy the fulfillment of a male/female liaison. Perhaps their function as signs is exclusively to overcome the limitation of the madonna–angel extreme archetype. Alcott wrote these Gothic stories in the 1860s before the March novels, and while they were disavowed and certainly unbalanced in themselves, the characters of Jean and Virginie may have offered Jo some of her spunky resistance to the Beth sign. However, Jo's ambition to write in any genre is seriously compromised. She almost entirely abandons her artistic curiosity in favor of settling down in the role of wife and mother and as the headmistress of Plumfield, a school for orphaned lads that she and Professor Baer head up together. But the Beth/Virginie dialectic yields Jo a resilience that allows activity and creativity, albeit within the moral sphere. She becomes a more social and active version of Marmy at the end of *Little Women*.

Jo smiled at her Fritz from the head of a long table lined on either side with rows of happy young faces, which all turned to her with affectionate eyes, confiding words, and grateful hearts full of love for Mother Baer.[85]

She continues the role of educative reformer in *Jo's Boys* and *Little Men*. Her relationship with her male wards in the later March novels is consistent with the girls' relationship in *Little Women* to Laurie. Jo provides her students, as she had Laurie, with redemption by saving him from his wild and foolish desires. Amy finishes the task. Laurie gives up his dream to be a musician and comes home and settles down to business and a family. The boys of Plumfield are tamed and domesticated and trained to resist the temptations of the "male world." In this context it is possible to suggest that Jo's interest in boys not only carried on her wish to be a boy herself, with all the advantages that that role offered, but allowed her to bring women's superior values to the world of males.

In *Little Men* and *Jo's Boys*, Alcott gave full vent to her interest in boys. She drew many detailed portraits of boys of all ages, but the most full-blown were of rough city vagrants who, lacking a mother's restraining guidance, had turbulent lives which ended badly. Like the femmes fatales, these lads moved outside the moral domestic realm; and although the author revealed her fascination with their separation from conventional family life, it was difficult for her to allow them to follow this path.

Jo spoke from this position in *Little Men*. She reminisced sympathetically about her own wishes as a young person to "bolt and have liberty." But she also reflected that it was the love of her mother that kept her at home.[86] In *Jo's Boys*, as many of Jo's lads grew up and left home, reducing her influence to a disintegrating umbilicus, she worried that they would fall into a bad lifestyle and come to a bad end.[87] In this last novel, Jo had developed a more pronounced fear of the male world of ambition and appetites. She feared for her own sons, despite what she labeled their superior moral education. Jo explained:

> "I can't spare either of you. My boys get into trouble unless I keep them close to home, and I've no right to hold the others, but I won't let you out of my sight, or something will happen."[88]

The boys of Plumfield, as her sons, are to renounce personal quests and grandiosity.

At the same time an integration process is taking place, the femme fatales have taken some of the horror out of the mythic male. Furthermore, Jo, Meg, and Amy for the most part live in a female-centered society. Father is away for most of the novel, and his presence is mild and accommodating enough to allow women characters to experiment with center stage. Laurie represents a friendly male presence, manageable in its equality, and his neighborly proximity introduces the friendly commingling of the sexes. Teen crushes, sexual attractions and flirtations seem normal and acceptable. Even Beth enjoys the companionship of the Laurence family as she crosses the line from her separate domestic female realm into their house, and into the world of men. She finds pleasure and enjoyment in Mr. Laurence's interest in her, although a shadow falls on this relationship as well, as Beth reminds Mr. Laurence of his little granddaughter who died in childhood. Similarly, Beth has an interest in Laurie, and is comfortable with him. Alcott even hints at the flaring of a sexual interest, although Beth's illness cuts off her development.

Clearly, Beth's move out of complete sexual segregation is not permanent and efficacious. The other children interface with males of their own generation often in a pleasant and non-endangering mode. Alcott, by focusing on peer relationships, is avoiding the dark spectre of the paternal imago or the male who dominates the public sphere, i.e., the other of the binary oppositions, that of male/female. Yet, out of the alter-ego's dialogue begins a dialectic which, while not yet achieving a complete synthesis of these disparate and contradictory elements, is building the basis for the integration of good/bad, male/female, hard/soft. Thus, perhaps if there is a softening of the male or paternal imago as women are allowed to be more predatory and aggressive and less confined in their soft victim posture, the male imago becomes more balanced as well. These integrations are part of the normal development integral to mental growth and the emergence of the self. Analogously, the various forms of adolescence that Alcott is creating and presenting allow for a cultural concept of separation and individuation and the hatching of a more mature self into adulthood as a cultural concept.

CHAPTER

5

MARY CASSATT

"Your breasts are as fragrant as wine; their whiteness whiter than milk and lilies, their scent
lovelier than flowers and balsam wood."

—Anonymous

Mary Cassatt left America for Europe determined not to be another sacrifice on the altar of good womanhood. As a child she had traveled to Europe with her family and had a glimpse of other cultures and lifestyles. In 1855, at the age of eleven, she was taken to the Universale Exposition, where her imagination was fired by the work of Ingres and Delacroix. As an American adolescent, Cassatt struggled to find an environment in which her expressive self might be born and raised. Determined to be an artist, she enrolled at the Philadelphia Art Academy, but finding it inadequate, she defied family and social conventions and set out for Europe. Cassatt settled in Paris in 1873 after several shorter stays in other European cities, particularly Parma, where she studied Correggio and Parmigianino for their portrayals of robust infants.

Cassatt followed in the path of many American artists who took refuge in Europe, a culture which cherished its artists. Ambitious and serious, she found the role of a bourgeois daughter of an American entrepreneur father a deadly trap. Stowe and Alcott in their representations of a treacherous alter ego of the maiden who was too good for this world gave alternatives of themselves in Eva and Beth; Cassatt did not, but a possible model for Cassatt's mutant self is Lily Barth of Wharton's *House of Mirth*, a Victorian butterfly pinned under glass. However, it seems more true that Cassatt's vision seems to flow from a more vibrant sense of women's interior lives, and the blight of mutilated womanhood casts few shadows on her oeuvre. Women are portrayed as involved in their daily lives, their portraits filled with self-respect and lively interest. Motherhood as a calling of significance emerges largely uninjured by religious and moral restraints.

When Cassatt settled in Paris in the early 1870s, she found an artistic home within the avant-garde group of the Impressionists. Stowe and Alcott and their male contemporaries like Eakins and Whitman worked as isolated rebels against the American antipathy to art and the cultural addiction to moral certitude. America not only offered them no encouragement for their innovations in form and content, but the rawness of the culture and the American aversion to artful experiments deprived them of colleagues. The American artist was singed by the pain of exclusion and scorn, or he/she became an expatriate. As Cassatt settled in Paris, she found support in the work of others. Courbet, Monet, and Degas were already working out important issues and techniques that concerned Cassatt deeply.

The Impressionists, or the Independents, as she preferred to call them, were one of several such groups in Europe in the nineteenth and twentieth centuries that sought to develop the aesthetic means by which to describe and express modern culture and experience. Degas, Monet, and Renoir, for example, were not only in rebellion against the Academy, but were questioning older notions of the purposes of painting. Influenced by liberal, democratic, secular ideas, they no longer believed that their task was to establish a fixed correspondence between the syntax of language or the notational system of art and an ideally structured universe.[1] Experiencing themselves as released into the activities of self-creation and self-discovery, the structure and processes of their own perceptions became the content of their work. As the Impressionists escaped from the tyranny of mirroring the one true reality, they moved out of the bias of perspective and the belief in one single exalted view of the object.[2] The old notion that the painting was organized to focus the viewer's attention toward the one important place on the canvas (the place where God had ruled) had been integrally grounded in traditional religious and political authoritarian belief systems that now were being fractured by the impact of urban industrial and secularizing forces. Thus, the Impressionists sought to extend the Realist impulse in a different way, and discover the world of objects shorn of history, myth, and allegory and to find them through pure perception itself. The rebellion against the object of theoretical knowledge allowed them the freedom to explore the world of objects known through immediate sensory experience.[3] Their revolutionary stance encouraged a new appreciation of personal psychology as a central force and influence in their work.

Like Stowe and Alcott before her, Mary Cassatt sought to rethink the bias and perspective of the history and mythology of American family life. The Impressionists' experiments with perception and new subject matter provided her with new models and inspiration. Degas in particular shared with Cassatt a compatible artistic outlook and provided her with personal encouragement. During the period when Cassatt and Degas became colleagues and friends, Degas was well into a change by which his work had moved away from beliefs based on causality, temporal progress, and the related moral and metapsychological theories[4] to a rendering of reality as process, flux, and simultaneity, that is, as immediate experience. Cassatt's portrayals of personal and family life explored existence in similar ways. She used new techniques to free the imaginative concepts of women and children from the deadly enclosure of American domestic mythology.

Yet the content of her work makes clear that in addition to her interest in avant-garde issues and techniques, she remained involved in American Victorian concerns about women and the family. Indeed, as Munch, Flaubert, and Klimt made clear at the end of the century and into the next, much of Western culture's struggle with modern liberty was encoded through the images of a domestic madonna and her alter ego: the sirens of Klimt, Vlaminck, and later Picasso. Klimt coded the upheaval of his culture in images of a depth psychology of eroticism and madness which he specifically mythifies in the strange, powerful, and erotic figures in "Judith and Holfernes" (1901).[5] The women in "Pallas Athena" (1901) and "The Water Snakes" (1904–07)[6] are breaking loose from cultural restrictions as bizarre archetypes of the deeply feminine. Pallas Athena, an ancient icon of political order and social wisdom, is distorted and characterized as a mockery of the cultural icons of good women and the certitude of traditional values. Her face is a sunken blue mass behind her metallic hair and bronze forehead, while out from under her tunic peers a senseless, jeering clay image, its tongue dangling foolishly in defiance of sanity. Petite Nuda Veritas is transformed into an erotic imp, who mirrors only a blank future to the confused and agonized observer.

Cassatt continues the inquiry into the myths of family life, not so much from a critical or satiric stance, but from the view of a woman thinking from inside that society. If Cassatt brooded over the oppression of women, or the neglect of children, she overcame her outrage by inventing a new family mythology. Within the body of her mother and child works, women and children exist almost entirely apart from men within an isolated domestic sphere. Men and their world, i.e., the world of politics, economics, and urban life, are absent from her palette.

The Impressionists have been criticized for their special views of nineteenth-century French life. Some critics condemn the various paintings of Argenteuil such as Monet's "Boating Party in Argenteuil" (1874) as a sublime, narrow view of the nineteenth-century French countryside, and it is true that "The Boating Party" suggests the difficulty that the Impressionists had in rendering the brutal chaotic transformation of the countryside and the emergence of cities, factories, and slums side by side with the respectable bourgeois parks and dwellings. The male Impressionists by and large edged these new realities out of their canvases perhaps because, as art historian Tim Clark has suggested, they were unable to acknowledge all the disruptions that confronted them.[7] Cassatt was no exception, but I should like to suggest that her focus on the private life of the family was not simply to evade modernist dilemmas, but to build a new foundation out of different ways of organizing and discovering meaning. Thus, Cassatt's "Boating Party" (oil, 1893) comes near the end of a complex scrutiny of bourgeois family life and the effort to develop new personal myths designed to over-come the distortions of the concepts of male, female, child, and their related emotions as she had known them.

Cassatt's paintings are a record of her effort to free herself from the restraints of historical narrative and from bourgeois and Victorian myths. An expatriate living in a new culture that did not entangle her, Cassatt was able to use avant-garde strategy by imagining and projecting a new vision of family life and putting that fresh vision into a new form. But Cassatt was a meticulous realist who drew carefully on the familial reality around her. This combination is the essence of Cassatt's Impressionism and mod-ernism, and within it she allowed her intense personal preferences to take a form drained of romantic illusion. Manet, in his "Dead Christ with Angels" (1864) and "Le Déjeuner sur l'Herbe," had already managed to present significant subjects of universal appeal and concern without the weight of religious and societal bias, presenting death and sexuality as the viewer might actually experience them. Since Manet, Monet, Renoir, and Degas were searching for the immediate truth of sense perception,[8] they were wary of the faulty vision that grows out of accommodation to social mytholo-gy and various forms of idealization. Cassatt was investigating that kind of truth as well. Her portrayals of the mother-child relationship as a significant part of here-and-now experience delivered that relationship from its role as a sterile icon of redemption or fertility.[9]

The evolution of the iconography of the madonna and child reveals diverse theories of the mysteries of continuing life in images of pregnancy, birth, and infant care. Ancient culture interpreted maternal power and creativity as a universal force which creates the universe and all of its life forms.[10] At Çatal Hüyük, forty shrines dating from 6500 B.C. onward yield images of the mother goddess as the focus of cultural life. She is seen in her three aspects: as a young woman, a mother giving birth, and as an old woman. As an aspect of her role of creator of all life, the female goddess was also associated with the beginnings of agriculture.[11] The reign of the mother goddess as a complex and powerful persona formed the center of culture and civilization for many thousands of years. Robert Graves, draw-ing on surviving artifacts and myths, suggests that the whole of neolithic Europe was dominated by the religion of the great goddess, who was re-garded as an immortal, continuous omnipotent figure. In this ancient pe-riod, the great goddess was unchallenged by any other concept of creativity. As fatherhood was not yet discovered, she enjoyed an exclusive reign over the sky and the earth.[12]

Byzantine and medieval icons of Mary and Christ reintroduced aspects of the mother goddess into patriarchal culture.[13] Borrowing from ancient myths and Greek Orthodox religion, the later Christian icons coded the potency of the mother-child relationship in flat, formal blocks of color meant to capture the essence of an idealized motherhood. The maternal icons of European Christianity portrayed the mother goddess's potency transformed from the creative power of fertility to that of divine redemption. Her dormition and assumption linked the female procreative capacities to salvation. Mary's immortality and unnatural pregnancy transcend the bleakness of ordinary human destiny, and at the same time soften the exclusive patriarchal aspects of Christianity and Western culture. Like Christ himself, Mary intercedes for humanity, providing divine protection and forgiveness.[14]

As the Renaissance unfolds, the work of such artists as Raphael and Bellini display secular themes breaking through the religious facade. Mother attends to a real baby, eyes meet eyes in sweet passionate gazes, and nestling, cuddling, and nursing replaced rigid concrete forms and poses.[15] Leo Steinberg suggests in his splendid work, *The Sexuality of Christ and Modern Oblivion*, that the Renaissance portrayals of the madonna and child, despite their religious trappings, are inextricably linked with dawning notions of secular existence. Steinberg explains that many Renaissance paintings emphasize Christ's private parts in order to elucidate the idea of the incarnation. The debate about the divinity of Christ evolved into a fascination with God's descent into manhood. In keeping with Renaissance notions of nature and science and the value of human existence, Renaissance faith gathered around Christ's humanation. A late fifteenth-century sermon characterizes this change: "What man praises most especially in God are his works and deeds. Of these, the first was the act of creation, but his second great deed was his becoming flesh and dwelling on the earth."[16] God had descended to shepherd secular humanity and redeem it from the dilemma of sin and vulnerability within earthly existence. The godhead had vested itself in the infirmity of the flesh. The incarnation in the virgin womb made God present in the here and now "in an armful of baby flesh."[17] The powerful awareness of the human condition is found in the figure of a baby in the care of his mother. The drama of human survival is worked out in countless paintings of the Christ child and madonna. Procreation and kinship gains importance through the emphasis on the infant's penis; displayed, investigated, held, or cuddled, the little Christ's phallus signifies the themes of survival and mortality.

Similarly, portrayals of mothers' breasts continue the elaboration of the themes of the incarnation. In several of the paintings, the infant turns from the nipple to the viewer as if to suggest, "I, like you, am dependent on mother's breast for survival."[18] In these paintings, which Steinberg categorizes as the "signal at the breast," images of the infant with mother carry the weight of new realizations of human existence and the hope for survival.[19] While religious morality and idealization continue to color the Renaissance madonna and child paintings, they look ahead to the modernist rendezvous with unmediated human family life with all its pains and pleasures.

One of the great embodiments of the incarnation is Leonardo da Vinci's "Madonna and Child with Saint Anne," in which Christ is portrayed as a flesh-and-blood infant, close to his mother's body, and in emotional rapport with her. Behind the figure of the mother Mary, not clearly separated from her, appears the figure of Saint Anne, who doubles the maternal background and holding environment. Mother Mary, in secular fashion, bends to pick up her little boy, who in turn holds a little lamb, the little lamb of love.

Freud, in his study of *Leonardo da Vinci and the Memory of His Childhood* (1910)[20] approaches the painting and the London Cartoon as a secular psychological expression of the body ego. He suggests from the perspective of his libido theory of development the projection and transformation of narcissistic oral and sexual fantasies onto the canvas. For Freud, the two women entwined as they are portray the condensation of the two mothers of Leonardo's infancy and childhood, his mother and his father's wife. Freud discusses the enigmatic smile of Mary and Saint Anne, which in the fashion of the Mona Lisa offers a promise of intimacy while suggesting simultaneously a mysterious disappearance into self-concern. Freud links these dualities to Leonardo's loss of his mother at the time he was taken into his father's household and made the child of his stepmother.

Much of Freud's discussion of Leonardo's mother and child takes place around the image of the vulture found in the shape and folds of Mary's skirt and in Leonardo's associations. Freud interprets the bird shape as a condensation and displacement of da Vinci's infantile memories and wishes associated with sucking at the breast, his longing for his missing father, and the need of a nipple-phallus. Freud continues his analysis of the shape as symbolizing the mother as an example of a species impregnated not by a man but by the wind. The Egyptian goddess Mut cast in the likeness of the vulture suggests, in Freud's reading, both the mother of the virgin birth and a woman who has not been castrated. Freud uses the tail of the shape for evidence of these fantasies. He adds the possibility of Leonardo's narcissistic identification with his mother, deepening the interpretations of the variations of his libidinal cathexis to his mother and suggesting that the vulture has qualities of Leonardo's own personality. Freud finds impressive evidence for this interpretation in Leonardo's own memoirs:

> It seems that I was always destined to be deeply concerned with vultures; for I recall as one of my earliest memories that while I was in my cradle, a vulture came down to me and opened my mouth with his tail and struck me many times with its tail against my lips.[21]

It seems clear that Freud has found an example of his notion of a screen memory, which according to his theory is a synchronic structure woven out of the condensations and displacements of inner life. The screen memory brings together layers of reality with dream, history with fantasy, desire with limitation, and the diachronic with the synchronic. In this way, we can view the painting and Freud's interpretation of it as mythic structures of the incarnation of madonna and child. Da Vinci chisels out the flesh-and-blood mother and child from the context of religious iconography. Using the vocabulary of the libido and the drives, Freud carves out the realm of the inner world, filled with the bonds of need and desire. Today, we need only add the importance of the vicissitudes of dependency. In this context, the strange shape may be seen as a linking organ, a womb, a placenta, an umbilicus, a penis, or a breast. The two women are suggestive of an emotional history of mothering as well as the amplitude of the two breasts. As in Cassatt's work, the father is not yet thoroughly united with the family.[22]

Cassatt and her modernist colleagues' commitment to the portrayal of immediate personal experience reveals a shift in nineteenth-century culture. In the same era as Nietzsche, Freud, and the Expressionists Kafka and Dostoevski, the avant-garde artists came face to face with complex layers of consciousness and the value of internal life. The Impressionists' respect for perception and the appreciation of private, immediate vision in some ways is analogous to Freud's theory of the origins of the manifest dream symbol. The French artists and the psychoanalyst believed that the subject's interaction with external forms was vastly influenced by the mind of the viewer. Although impressive theoretical differences exist between psychoanalysis and Impressionism, each dramatically rejects the emphasis on given external forms and values and substitutes an appreciation of shifting processes and relative experience. Later the Cubists and Surrealists in painting; Joyce, Proust, and Virginia Woolf in literature; and Eugene O'Neill in drama carry on the approach which not only sees artistic symbols as filled with internal life, but as free from the enslavement to a given external reality.

Thus, the Impressionists' commitment to a vision of the senses is one important stream of new ideas leading to an emphasis on process over form and a new reciprocal partnership between content and form. Susanne Langer, in her work *Feeling and Form*[23] theorizes the existence of living form which, as I interpret her notion, suggests not only form merged with feeling, but form arising out of the elements of inner life, of the emotional power of fantasy (phantasy) and dream. Langer describes the artistic symbol as a significant form which not only carries feelings by signifying the meaning of the subject's inner reality or connection to the object, but presents this meaning in a new form that illuminates new meanings.[24] Langer defines the artistic symbol as a highly articulated, sensuous object which by virtue of its dynamic structure can express the forms of vital experience in a way that discursive language is unfitted to do.[25] The dynamic expressiveness of the significant form functions through the juxtaposition of all the possible relationships between its constituent elements with vital experience. The qualities distilled from body rhythms, sensual and emotional forces, and primary fantasy (phantasy) images flow into and around a center of vital being which then generates abstracted and coded forms of color, shape, sound and movement. The audience viewer-reader slips partially from history and conscious knowledge into the vortex of forces and forms. In viewing a painting, for example, the participant enters into the world of illusion and of the semblance of space. The canvas, animated by the articulated, coded elements of feeling and form, pulls the viewer into its field while inviting the observer to contribute to that vital vortex from his/her inner life.

The genesis of living form is approached from another perspective by Jane Ellen Harrison as a distillation of ritual enactment. The dithyramb, the song of birth, emerges as a narrative that tells of the voyages of the self and of birth into mental awareness of individuation and initiation.[26] The dithyramb begins as a lyric full of excitement and magic which gradually crosses the boundary from the most primitive signs to the symbolic order. In this way *le sémiotique* contributes to art, ritual, and tragedy.[27] Harrison tells us that these ritual songs and dances are always mimetic. The expressive action, the leaps of fear or joy, or of the rhythm of a song are a doing or a redoing by which inner forces and feelings are given shape and meaning. She suggests that culture grows from this mimetic process, which signifies inner experience. The experience itself is squandered, whereas the symbolic process provides tangible forms and the means for communication.[28]

Harrison supposes that the need for protection of the enfeebled, immature human offspring shapes the forms of ritual enactment. Hardening and purification processes through the baptism of water and fire are to guarantee magical strength. The dangers of weakness and helplessness are purged by extending the logic of the baptism and initiation rites to the dimensions of culture itself. Since the imposition of the paternal law, culture is made "male" as the rites of second birth at infancy and initiation in puberty separate the infant or child from mother's body. Within the drama of ritual the father god calls aloud, "Come, oh dithyramos, enter this, my male womb."[29] The fact of real birth is submerged in an act of magical intent, which becomes sacred. The intent involves the shift from a matriarchal foundation of culture to a patriarchal one. Harrison identifies the rite of the new birth[30] as the mimetic rites par excellence. In the new birth of the dithyramb and the new birth of the kouros, infancy and adolescence are commandeered by paternal power. In the case of the kouros, the child is taken from its mother. In the case of the dithyramb, the child is actually reborn from the thigh of its father.[31] The intent of the ritual of the birth from the male womb is to rid the child of the weakness of mother's body and to turn him from a woman thing into a man thing.

It seems intriguing to me to read Harrison's analysis of ritual as similar to the concept of living form that Langer has described, but Harrison's discussion of the meaning of particular rituals makes clear that the living symbolic forms of the critical rituals of the life cycle in Western culture are often subverted to bypass the helplessness of infancy. We need add only the infant's experience of prey anxiety, as well as disintegration anxiety and the notion of autistic hardness as maneuvers against such anxieties to follow the contours of this solution. Mary, the madonna of Christianity, is a critical figure in this context. Through her relationship to the son of God, powers of maternal capacities are restored to Western culture and the autistic solution is challenged. Although cast as a secondary character, Mary brings in her many guises the influence of maternal love and care. Marina Warner, in her splendid study of the Virgin Mary, *Alone of All Her Sex*,[32] describes the persona of the madonna as providing the single sign of feminine influence in the male dominated religion. In *The Gnostic Gospels*, Elaine Pagels suggests the refusal of a female godhead at the very origins of Christianity. Pagels demonstrates the image of God as a dyad within heretical texts; God is understood as both a mother and father as a counter-image to the patriarchial one.[33] The notion of a divine mother as part of an original couple is found in several texts in *The Gnostic Gospels*. The teacher and poet Valentinus writes of an indescribable god whose divinity can be imagined as a dyad consisting in one part of "the Ineffable, the Depth, the Primal Father, and in the other of Grace, Silence, the Womb, and Mother of All."[34] Pagels's discussion makes clear that the dominant Christian theology overrules the recognition of the female aspect of God found in the so-called heretical texts. The Virgin Mary restores these elements in altered form.

Warner describes Mary's importance and influence as found exclusively in her motherhood. She explains that "the most consistent theme in the theology of the Virgin's intercession is her motherhood. She is approached as a human mother who brims over with a mother's love." From Byzantine times, she emerges as a maternal figure whose love of mankind is as a mother to her child. Her qualities of mercy, gentleness, loving kindness, indulgence, and forgiveness are all derived from maternal affection. All men are her children through Christ, her son. However, this portrait of the madonna splits off the dark, fearful, awesome image of the archaic mother. Maternal presence and power is reintroduced into Western culture but are revealed only in their milder, benign aspects.

Furthermore, the presentation of the madonna as singularly benign hides another aspect of the relationship to the mother's body. The myth of the Virgin's impregnation by the Word represses mother's sexuality, particularly her participation in the act of copulation. The primal scene is censored out of existence and the alternation of female gods with male ones becomes more understandable. The infant and child contributed to culture the fear of the knowledge of the reality of procreation which excludes the infant from playing a role in his/her own creation. Analogously, the denial of sexual difference is coded into cultural values through the equation of the word with breath. In turn, breath is associated with the anal sphincter over the glottal. Anal pregnancy or penetration by an anal penis reveals a confusion of anus and vagina, which signals denial of sexual difference.[35]

Another transformation of the madonna is present in Protestant theology, which defied Mary's maternal potency by amputating the mother from the son. Her reappearance and transformation into the domestic madonna suggest the painful harshness of the experience of exclusive paternal rule. Also, as Stowe and Alcott have conveyed to us, the final stages of the exile of the maternal goddess and the repression of the maternal birth were self-conscious and tortuous but finally illuminating and signaled the potential for a sexually potent couple based on the coming together and toleration of sexual difference.

Cassatt's works reinvigorate living form and emphasize its roots and its connection to the mother's body and to father's as well. Her living form is embedded in the sensory life of the baby, and speaks the language of the eyes, ears and skin.[36] Cassatt's pictures function as pictorial analogues which reach into and combine elements of unconscious structures with rational cognitive ones.[37] Much like the dream work, pictorial analogues fulfill a mediating function between sensory experience and the disembodied forces underlying the objects and the events of that experience. Thus, they perform the task of making meaning by bringing together sensory data and generic concepts into one unified cognitive statement. In this way, pictorial analogues function like the psychosomatic breast. Bion posits that the infant needs love as well as milk and that the relationship between the infant and mother needs to provide both. The human infant is capable of drawing love from the breast and taking it in. Love nurtures emotional growth and meaning alongside the milk, which nurtures physical growth. In pictorial language, the sensual and the conceptual are represented and developed in parallel forms.[38]

In Cassatt's many oils, pastels, and drypoints, mother and baby or mother and her children live through the simple daily life of child rearing. As suggested, the gradual appearance of an incarnated mother and child had been caught up in the countless renderings of the Virgin Mary and her son.[39] Cassatt's portrayals, an offspring of this development, explore the immediate experience taking place within the family, much as Freud had done in his investigation of da Vinci's "Saint Anne and Two Others" in order to peel away the Christian and Victorian mythologies of madonna and child.

As her predecessor Stowe had, Cassatt investigated the mother-child dyad as a critical experience for the child's mental and physical growth. Cassatt's imagination seems to free the mental elements from mental slavery and from the constraints of morality. In "Mother About to Wash a Sleepy Child" (oil, 1880), "Emmy and Her Child" (oil, 1889), and "Baby's First Caress" (pastel, 1891), she explores the many facets of bonding and reciprocity.[40] On the level of social meaning, Cassatt depicts her couples in France at the turn of the century; well-dressed, well-cared-for bourgeois women who have the time, means, and enthusiasm to care for their children. The contrast with the depiction of these scenes of child care in *Uncle Tom's Cabin* is hauntingly clear. The settings are for the most part private and delightful interiors in which family life takes place undisturbed. While mother tranquilly and devotedly attends to her child, the forces of politics, class strife, and urban change do not make an appearance on the canvas. Almost verging into the realm of the ideal, Cassatt nevertheless retains command of her subject matter and develops a modern icon for growth and development. For the moment, her couples seem safe from history, tradition, and biased mythology. These mothers are neither despairing nor saintly, the children protected by the membrane of maternal concern.

These three canvases (among others) bring pure relatedness onto the cultural stage. Out of the living form that she found in Impressionism and other modern styles, Cassatt elegantly and vividly recreates important elements of human development. As the artist, she focuses her subject matter on the attachment phase, in which mother's reliable continuing presence and devotion protects the infant's emerging being and the sense of surround. In the earliest days, mother is an environmental mother[41] who is needed to provide a postnatal shelter, buffer, and membrane for the infant's thin skin and state of unintegration.[42] The paintings also show the necessity for an environment which gradually becomes more specific as mother holds her infant, looks and touches and stimulates his or her skin to stimulate a sense of self and a self of aliveness.[43] Cassatt's mothers always pay close attention to their babies' moods, feelings and communications; they provide the bonding of containment which is used to gather meaning as they hold, detoxify, and translate their infant's undigested distress, converting it into manageable experience.[44] By offering a reliable presence and empathetic interaction, Cassatt's mothers promote the infants' sense of a continuing self and a vitality to individuate and develop his/her own mind.

In all three of these works Cassatt uses soft bright colors and ephemeral brush strokes to evoke the sense of process, growth, and the emotional moment. The mother's dress in "Emmy and her Child" and in "Baby's First Caress," the wallpaper in "Mother About to Wash Her Sleepy Child" shimmer and blur in such a way as to present movement, lack of rigidity, and a complex view of the object. The incompleteness of one of the child's feet in "Emmy and Her Child" and "Baby's First Caress" suggest a promise of development and the open boundaries associated with individual growth.

"Mother About to Wash Her Sleepy Child" (oil, 1880) is Cassatt's first rendering of mother and child in their daily life. Reaching back to the madonnas and chubby infants of Rubens and Parmigianino and Correggio's classic well-modeled infants and children, she presents a baby fully immersed in the body life of infancy.[45] Awkward, dangling legs drape over mother's body. A sleepy expression and full red mouth suggest childish sensuality, as does the child's fit into the crook of mother's arm. The style of the picture reflects Cassatt's interest in Impressionism which she uses to signify the interactive processes between mother and child. The background wallpaper pulses with vibrant forms, the ephemeral white dresses

Mary Cassatt, "The Boating Party." National Gallery of Art, Washington.
Chester Dale Collection

Mary Cassatt, "Mother and Child." National Gallery of Art, Washington.
Chester Dale Collection

Mary Cassatt, "Mother About to Wash Her Sleepy Child" (1880). Los Angles County Museum of Art. Mrs. Fred Hathaway Bixby Bequest

of mother and child mottled with blue, yellow, and pink represent the rhythm of life through reflected and mutually modifying colors.[46]

The content of the picture continues the thematic exploration of the rapport between mother and child. Mother focuses her deep attention on her sleepy offspring as if to empathetically help him or her make the transition from sleep into wakefulness, signifying the leap from phantasy to reality. The infant relies on mother for holding in his or her confused state, while mother responsively but tastefully introduces her little child to civilized custom and the integration of interior experience with the world of others.

"Emmy and Her Child" portrays a quiet moment of reverie and intimacy shared by the bonding pair. Circling arms and caresses give form to the feeling of emotional attachment as mother's body and mood provide the ground and context for the child's physical and mental existence. The little one both enjoys the closeness and voyages bravely into her or his own thoughts. As in "Mother About to Wash Her Sleepy Child," thick strokes and unfinished forms signify process and growth. The meaning of the picture is elaborated by the contrast between the child's well-modeled body and his incomplete foot. Similarly, the placing of a white pitcher into the curve of Emmy's neck reiterates the nestling of the two figures and embodies the container-breast relationship.

The pastel "Baby's First Caress" articulates for us an exquisite moment of rapport and contact. Baby looks deeply into mother's face, finding in their mutual gaze an entire world of meaning. The little fellow relaxes contentedly against mother's body, his form revealed robust and invitingly babyish. The two are in a physical contact that is the ground for their emotional rapport. The infant touches mother's face adoringly as mother holds her infant's foot. All of this is brought together by the shimmering lines and dynamic forms as they convey the emotional interaction of overflowing at-one-ment and what the infant researcher Brazelton has called the reciprocity dance.[47]

Brazelton has observed the mother and infant from earliest days to be engaged in a dance or drama of reciprocity which involves all the modes of sensual and motoric interaction. Winnicott, Brazelton, Stern, and Fletcher, in their thoughtful appraisal of the elements of reciprocity, believe that the infant is a social being from the very beginning who is gathered together and integrated by the mother's holding capacity, but at the same time, they see the infant as a little person whose social skills and capacities are part of his/her endowment by which to elicit from the environment the elements needed for his/her own epigenesis.[48] Within the surround of the holding environment of earliest days, the infant's unintegrated potential self is gathered together and provided with a growing sense of integration and going on being.[49] Out of the rhythm and empathy of the bonding process, the maturation of the central and autonomic nervous systems evolves smoothly.[50] As these systems regulate the infant's capacity to control reactions to incoming stimuli, he or she is protected from an overload of disorganizing data, which in time allows the infant to pay attention to various internal and external stimuli and to begin to give them significance. Out of these experiences, the infant develops confidence in his/her ability to achieve homeostasis and to elicit necessary responses from the environmental caretaker. Each level of achievement encourages new capacities such as the infant's willingness to reach out and endure disruption to achieve new competence.[51] Mother or father gain not only pleasure from the responsiveness of the baby, but are satisfied by the conviction that their reciprocal field is the ground of the infant's epigenesis and fruitful development. The unresponsiveness of the other results in a grievous sense of disappointment and loss on both sides.[52]

Part of the infant's growing sense of safety and viability comes from his/her increasing ability to regulate states of consciousness.[53] The infant's organizational capacities given in the constitution of the individual and nurtured in the reciprocal bonding experience evolve normally into a capacity for state control by which the newborn increasingly differentiates, integrates and modulates states of consciousness (from deep sleep to alert states to intense crying with increasing capacity to maintain a quiet alert state enabling social interaction).[54] The quiet alert state is important in that it is the means by which the infant interacts wisely with its internal and external worlds, avoiding noxious experiences and reaching out for beneficial ones. State control also goes hand in hand with homeostasis, which in turn is an important element in the trust developing from attachment experiences.

During the first year of life, the reciprocity dance develops into a more complex field of intersubjectivity. Fletcher describes the period from two and a half to five months as a period of increasing reciprocal exchange in which the interactions between mother and child are carried on through multimodal sensory discourse in the activities of moving, talking, and looking.[55] Increasingly, a pageant of little pantomimes and dramas are presented in the field of empathetic exchange. Baby exhibits his/her feelings and skills to mother in body gestures, play, and vocal sounds. Mother gives meaning and validity to them through soothing, interpretive, and appropriate response. If mother fails to respond appropriately, the infant's ground for expression gives way.[56] Within the reciprocity envelope, the field of intersubjective, motoric, and sensual responses, the structures of play and communication open out into the symbolic and cultural spheres.[57] As the infant stirs mother and father, the affective images within the parents link up to personal feeling, personal history, and culture. Rabain-Jamin, writing of the infant sound envelope and the organization of parent-infant communication, explores several levels of nonverbal exchange.[58] She explains that the caretaker responds to the baby's sounds through the *sound effect of complicity*. The sound effect may be sensually and effectually evocative, moving gradually to the realm of the symbolic. Rabain-Jamin gives the example of a father responding to the gurgling sounds of a six-week-old infant boy. The father's noises in response take on the character of a wild boar's grunt. The boar has an emblematic value for the father, born in Ardennes. Rabain-Jamin concludes, "Hence, for the father what was initially mere sonority or sounds or body noises still closely linked to libidinal experience comes to meet a chain of significance and takes on allegorical meaning referring to patriarchal origins."[59] The boar as an emblem provides an example of the layering of the subjective field and the infant's internal structures as they move out into cultural mythologies.

Primarily the infant finds him or herself in the responses of the parent. As the infant responds to his/her experience, he/she finds in the mother's or father's attuned response the confirmation and support of their sense of the moment. What is matched here and exchanged is something of the internal feelings of both participants.[60] At a more profound level, the mothering one reflects the viability and significance of the baby's existence. The mother thinks the baby;[61] and the attitudes that are reflected on her face tell the little individual that he/she exists or not and is worthwhile or not. Winnicott describes the finding of the self in the mother's face in this way: "What does the baby see when he or she looks at the mother's face? I am suggesting that ordinarily what the baby sees is him or herself. In other words, the mother is looking at the baby and what she looks like is related to what she sees there."[62] Pauline Kernberg also suggests that the child finds his or her self in the mother's face. In "Self-Awareness and Self-Recognition," she suggests that self-awareness and self-recognition are mirrored in the mirror of mother's face and that the vicissitudes of that process shape the self-image in the physical mirror.[63] Thus, one aspect of the reciprocity dance as it evolves from at-one-ment through transitional space, the space of illusion, to the space of individuation, and from the early signs of sensory motor life to complex individual and cultural language systems is the discovery of the self growing and expanding found or mirrored in mother's face.

In "Baby's First Caress" and "Emmy and Her Child" and the Japanese print, "The Bath," the place of contact located between the two persons' eye-to-eye and body-to-body interface or the overlapping spirit-to-spirit experience illuminates a crucial semiotic chain. The images of the contact replace the spot on the canvas which authoritatively directed the viewer's gaze through the devices of perspective or the expectation of hierarchy. The eye contact in "Baby's First Caress" is Cassatt's puntum, the manifest form or transformation of an unconscious memory fragment. Victor Burgin traces the etiology of the puntum by drawing on Roland Barthes's discussion of the image of the strapped shoe of a woman in James Van der Zee's "Photograph of an American Family." Burgin makes links from deep layers of feeling and memory to the image used or seen at a conscious level. Barthes himself had noticed connections between the strapped shoe and feelings of sympathy and "a kind of tenderness." With this in mind, Burgin expands Barthes's ideas about the chain of meaning. The strapped shoe is a displacement from the necklace of a now deceased aunt. The necklace carries within it aspects of the relationship. Burgin interprets: "We can now see the process of significance at work. The investment of emotional affect (cathexis) in the ankle strap; the metaphorical displacement from the circle around the ankle to the circle around the throat; the metonymical displacement from the woman in the photograph to the maiden aunt, 'whose necklace was now shut up in a box' "; allows us to "arrive at the source of emotion in the themes of death and sexuality played out within a family scenario."[64] Burgin explains the puntum as a visual image which grows out of the subject's myth-making and dream processes. He adds that its origin is found in the real "or the thing in itself" placed within the context of the emotional vicissitudes of the infant's finding and losing the mother's body and presence. Burgin, following on the explorations of Lacan and Kristeva, probes the unspeakable or the unsignifiable[65] as almost found in the image and traces its emotional shadow in molding that image, the image that conjures affectual resonances of the loved one.[66] In these portrayals of mother and child, perhaps Cassatt conjures up the mother of her infancy signified in a puntum. She might include the re-finding and exploration of her infant self, as well. It is in this way that she rediscovers for her culture its lost and forgotten child selves.

In the 1890s, Cassatt exhibited ten brilliant Japanese color prints, of which five were of mothers and children. Cassatt was one of the first of her group to appreciate the implications of Japanese printmaking. She was particularly impressed by the simplicity, boldness of color, and the starkness of the wood block, and she soon adapted the lessons of Hokusai and other Japanese printmakers to her own purpose, which was the abstraction of personal familial experience.[67] In "The Maternal Caress," "The Mother's Kiss," and "In the Bath," Cassatt continues the exploration of the bonding pair. But in these prints, Cassatt has moved from the flux and spontaneity of the earlier period toward an emphasis on the dignity and monumentality of the relationship. She achieves these effects through the use of clear figures and large, simple blocks of colors rather than the short, thick strokes of the 1870s and 1880s.[68] The new technique is well-suited to evoke unsentimental and unemotional realism. In "The Maternal Caress," Cassatt reveals the modernist impulse for searching inward and examining mental life, life underneath appearance and custom. The baby suffers, and mother comforts and soothes. Style and content work together here as the simplicity and flatness of the style enhances the power of the emotions and releases them from social history, custom, and myth. The flatness of the space invites the viewer to think independently and to avoid the seduction of the narrative of the painting.

Cassatt's portrayals of these early episodes of infantile life are critical in that they introduce less idealized and distorted images of mother and child. They function not only as reparative images of painfully disjointed signs of the mother-child relationships as they had been signified in American cultural artifacts, but they present many moments of child care and emotional bonding that are integral to human survival, which had been buried beneath the rites of the second birth. Bion's theory of ideographs, then, seems apposite here. He theorizes that ideographs, that is, unique and personal dream images, function to repair thoughts that have been attacked and disavowed. He applies the same notion to the mind itself, giving as an example the powerful fantasy of attacking and evacuating aspects of the perceptual and mental apparatus that gathers and evaluates data.[69] Cassatt's paintings may be seen to function as ideographs, though of course they are also sophisticated, well-crafted, well-thought out works of art. They also function as new mythologies in that they attempt to integrate emotions which had not been allowed birth in her culture. The pictures act specifically as reparative images by presenting the emotions between mother and child as mutually beneficial and open. Barthes's concept of the puntum and Bion's notion of the ideograph complement each other, and take us inside key images and processes of living forms. Da Vinci's "Saint Anne with Two Others" provides us with an example of the reciprocal relationship between the ideograph and the puntum. The family grouping, grandmother, mother, and child, form a chain of bonding which is an ideograph for Renaissance culture beginning to form realizations of the secular family, and also a puntum of desire and loss of the breast as mother is reiterated in the bird's shape.

Cassatt's presentation of living, open relationships also reflects the ideal of respect for the self-determination and liberty of each individual, built into the political ideology of American and other Western bourgeois cultures. However, these values have been more than difficult to achieve on a personal and social level, not only because of the failure of a conscious belief in democracy and equality that renders the realizations of openness, liberty, and equality stillborn, but also because of the difficulty in experiencing oneself openly. Stowe's fictional representations of relationships reveal them to take place in abnormal, primitive dimensions. As normal at-one-ment and the symbiosis of reciprocity are disrupted, the openness of the two separate subjectivities overlapping and diverging is precluded. Much of the mental experience of *Uncle Tom's Cabin* is represented as taking place in the static concrete space of emotional slavery.[70] Since *Little Women's* moral certitude prevents the lively movement of thoughts and feelings, Alcott felt it necessary to invent violent fantasies for her Gothic heroines for the purposes of freeing them from the cloying coercion of moral idealism. Cassatt's representations of the infant-mother dyad are radical icons that tolerate and embody psychic space in which the reciprocity dance can take place. Her vision expands and benefits from the work of the earlier women.

Cassatt's open-minded perspective about the relationship between mommies and babies carries her not only beyond Victorian stereotypes, but beyond her Modernist colleagues, who either omit this relationship from their new, innovative subject matter, or present it in a charming, decorative style without emotional depth.[71]

Cassatt and Paula Modisohn Becker are exceptional in their effort to incorporate this relationship into their Impressionist vision. Unlike Becker, Cassatt did very few representations of nursing itself. Of the hundreds of Cassatt oils, pastels, drawings, and prints of mothers and children, fewer than ten are of mothers and nursing. One of these, "Mother Nursing Her Baby" (1908),[72] combines nursing with the tactile, sensual intimacy of "Baby's First Caress" (1891). Mother and child are in a concentrated rapport; each studies the other's face; eyes meet eyes, as one of mother's arms encircles the child's body. The other fondles the baby's foot. Baby nurses and strokes mother's face. This portrait of nursing suggests the deepest levels of bonding, the creation of trust and mutuality. Yet Cassatt focused more on other aspects of child rearing. It seems suggestive that Cassatt's interest is in the sensuality of the baby. Her many portraits of bathing and caressing the infant's attractive body abstract the infantile body ego or existence in all its lavish, enjoyable sensuality. In the oil "Reine Lefebvre Holding a Nude Baby" (1902) and the pastel "Sleepy Nicole" (1900),[73] mother holds and cherishes the chubby, delightful, naked body of her child. The baby's nude form, dominating the canvas as it does, suggests the importance of the hands-on experience, which is a critical part of the child's sense of a mental skin and of cohesion. The pastels "Sleepy Thomas Sucking His Thumb" (1893) and "Little Anne Sucking Her Fingers Embraced by Her Mother"[74] portray the enjoyment of skin-to-skin contact and the sensual pleasures of sucking in a way that restores to the viewer the lost experience of infantile body pleasures. The participant is invited to overcome Victorian phobias and to be at home in the body.

Cassatt's treatment of women focuses predominantly on women as competent persons involved in every task of their daily lives. They are portrayed as engaged and independent as they participate in reading, drawing, sewing, and theater-going, to suggest a few activities, and it is this view of women that Cassatt brings to the mother-child portrayals. In this genre, a sense of dignity, competence and intelligence characterizes the children's mother, and while the settings are domestic, the vital involvement of these women suggests the liberation of individuation. Although perhaps alternatively for Cassatt, women's sensuality remains linked with images of women's body parts as enslaved.

Cassatt casts her women in fresh roles and perhaps writes new narratives for them. She not only works to recognize women as full persons but, it seems to me, intuits brilliantly the relationship between modern society, mental life, and the minds of women. As she rejects the old maneuvers which sought to block the awareness of modern randomness by restricting and idealizing mothers and children, she replaces them with an exploration of the processes from which coherence and individuality develop.

Cassatt's pictures provide triadic structures which are the signs of a resilient container-contained relationship, and all of her studies of mother-child interactions are depictions of the processes of the germination of meaning. One of the much-discussed and debated cultural issues of the nineteenth century was the origin and indeed the viability of social cohesion. American Victorians, in the midst of their celebration of the possibilities of democracy and equality, brooded over the fate of their souls and society. American cultural artifacts suggest fears associated with the loss of authority and thus they convey fears of seduction and damnation and, deeper still, the anxieties of non-existence. Hence, the protective maneuvers found in asceticism, self-madeness, and slavery in a so-called democratic culture. These remedies sent Cassatt, Whistler, and Wharton scurrying across the Atlantic. In Europe, similar experiences drove artists to probe the problems of emotional coherence. Munch, Kafka, and Klimt, to name only a few, portrayed fears of explosion and disintegration.[75] As several waves of social and political upheaval undermined any notion of authority, American and European Victorians experienced an upheaval from inside, something which may be identified as emotional turbulence.[76]

I would like to suggest a map of these cultural tensions through an analogous situation in the group inside the individual.[77] The attraction to and dread of freedom may be likened to the experience the infant, child or individual undergoes when new thoughts emerge so powerfully as to almost fragment his/her container. Bion imagines such new thoughts as messiah thoughts which, emerging from the level of deep biological inclinations and from the limitlessness of the vast unconscious, herald new meaning which disturbs the individual's sense of continuity.[78] Eva's ideas that democracy like Christianity might find its values in justice and equality are the messiah thoughts that her group dreads and fears. Alcott's femme fatales are messiah thoughts in themselves, albeit extreme ones. Alcott's Jean and Virginie surface as alter egos to the angel in the house to announce the emergence of women's lust, vindictiveness, and ambition. Alcott's felt necessity to orphan her messiah characters reiterates the group's (in the writer and in the society) dread of volatile ideas particularly without group support. The bias of reactionary ideology is an expression of this dread.

Cassatt's pictures are container mothers for new thought babies. Her pictures shelter and nurture new concepts of cohesion stemming from parent-child containment and reciprocal intersubjectivity. Her new idea is the realization that the potential direction and cohesion of society originates in the infant's mind.

It had been long thought that cohesion, direction, and interpretation came from outside, from God, from the father, such as the papal father, the king, and related traditional principles and institutions which directed and bound social and mental life. In Christian Western culture, disruptive expressiveness has often been branded heresy or evil. The sentiments of the Counter-Reformation or the New England witch trials are instances of extreme antipathy toward new ideas and experience, but over the course of the nineteenth century the designation of sin and heresy became increasingly complex. Tumultuous cultural change, the undermining of the very notion of traditional givens or a single reality out there to be understood by all stimulated many new ideas and freed individual desires and preferences. One response to such uncertainty and flux has often been the invention of new religious or moral certainties and isms—patriotism, racism, or anti-Semitism. Nazism, although related to a complex history of political and economic factors, also filled the vacuum opened by tradition's departure.

Cassatt's presentation of holding, supporting, empathizing, mirroring, translating, caring, and soothing taken together provide the structure for the birth of the mind. Mother (father) as the background for the infant vouchsafes the baby's sanity under circumstances of extreme vulnerability, helplessness, and the emotional turbulence of constant flow and change. Father too is a background object, first promoting the safety and serenity of the mother-child unit and later backing the child as he or she moves into a larger world beyond the family. A crucial aspect of the overall parental container is its creation of the conditions that make thinking and individuality possible. The innovative and healing aspect of Cassatt's messiah thoughts lies in her understanding of the need of an overall container, the background object of primary identification.[79] Furthermore, her notions about bonding and integration, while taking up issues that are not easily integrated into her culture look ahead to the culture of the later twentieth century. If we understand Cassatt's work as a reparative ideograph or pictorial representation of messiah thoughts, we can understand her use of the mother-child relationship. Her pictures are structures of containment for her new idea that mental strength emerges from the depths of familial relationships. In this way Cassatt finds her way out of the myths which she found outdated and invented new family myths, particularly for female children, as will be discussed.

Mothers and daughters had been placed on the center stage of American Victorian culture, but given curious roles shaded by the specialness of weakness, defectiveness, and of exemplary moral goodness and saintliness. The frequency and intensity of the debate over woman's nature implied the presence of unease about the effects of freedom and liberty on the family and on female adults and children in particular. At the same time there was an intense need to secure the stability of the sources of continuity and nurturing. Those concerns shaped the Victorian archetypal female and the meaning of female in society and in myth.[80] The ubiquity of the discourse of these issues also implied that the concept of mother and daughter under conditions of equality was troublesome and needed redefining.[81]

Cassatt's treatment of mothers and daughters makes a strong effort at cleansing her canvas of these painful distortions and saturations,[82] and in the light of fresh perceptions she restores to women and their daughters a more genuine existence associated with emotional reciprocity and independence of mind. Her new visual concepts carry a sense of life that overcomes mental emaciation, replaces it with the vitality and processes that make up the flesh of mental life, and in a lively ambience Cassatt projects a friendly spirit and a positive view of these personal relations.[83] The emotional connections between the two people interacting are open, affectionate, tolerant, and perceptive.[84] It is as if Cassatt has constructed her own personal version of a female Oedipus myth, a version that overcomes the biased emphasis on the male child as men from Greek tradition to psychoanalysis have written it. Although often leaning toward an ideal situation, her myth importantly also departs from the myth as a tale emphasizing generational conflict and child development ending in tragedy and the destruction of parent/child ties. In this way Cassatt's oeuvre sees the reworking of important mythic structures and themes. As Cassatt rethinks the cultural stereotypes of men and women, she uncovers the story of female development. This allows her to find her way out of the old cultural notions of development in which the child is endangered by the faulty mythic solutions of their parents, as Oedipus himself warned us.[85] Thus, Cassatt is able to explore new mythic structures suitable for groups of her generation to re-think different structures of authority and cohesion as they freed themselves from traditional ways of thinking.

As part of these interests, Cassatt did many representations of women as individuals in many stages of the life cycle and often with their daughters. The women and female children in her work have clearly emerged from the constraints of a second birth, martyrdom or the moral role. While they have not yet left the bourgeois interior world nor joined the private to the public sphere, they possess independence of mind, mental vigor and self-respect. Their focused attention on their own thoughts and activities reveals women with intact dimensional personalities. The portrait of the artist's mother, "Reading LeFigaro" (oil, 1873)[86] brings powerfully to the canvas many facets of women's lives. Mrs. Cassatt, seated, reading a newspaper, is thoughtfully involved in her activity. Calm concentration and self-containment suggest not only an active mind at work, but a woman at home with herself. The activity and the paper that is French connote the literacy and education of this woman.

The white dress, painted in lovely, simple white folds, moves away from idealized purity but maintains associations with calm, light and peace. The down-to-earth quality of the woman in her everyday activities is caught in the pince-nez which sits informally on her nose. The significance of the capable hands that hold the newspaper as they had held the artist as a child is doubled in the mirror image which is dominated by one hand.

A slightly later portrait of Cassatt's mother entitled "Mrs. Robert Simpson Cassatt" (oil, 1889)[87] presents another aspect of women's lives. The woman of the painting is seated, staring off into the space away from the canvas, deeply lost in her own thoughts. Although a less vigorous woman now, the work having been painted when the subject was in her early seventies, Mrs. Cassatt's eyes suggest a depth of feeling and reflection about the meaning of her past life and its approaching conclusion. Cassatt shows her dressed in a deep black dress, in contrast to the white one of the earlier portrait. The large expanse of black implies seriousness, not tragic, but formidable. It conveys the black of mourning and of old age, but it also seems to symbolize the dignity of her mother's long, productive life. The portrait signifies the artist's great respect for her mother and for the monumental meaning of the different phases of women's lives.

In her sister Lydia, Cassatt found a beautiful and vibrant alter ego. Two important portraits of Lydia bring to the cultural stage women's sensuality and vitality. In the painting "Lydia in a Loge Wearing a Pearl Necklace" (oil, 1879),[88] Lydia appears in a loge, enjoying the social ambiance, dressed in a fresh pink gown. Lydia's lovely shoulders and décolletage announce her physical presence. At the same time, Cassatt signals that she is not a passive object for the male gaze. Her happy expression and unrestrained enjoyment of the performance makes clear her participation in the world of others. The bright colors of her clothes and of the theater reflects a state of mind which is open and engaged.

"Lydia, Leaning on Her Arm, Seated in a Loge" (pastel, 1889)[89] shimmers and glows with pastel strokes of color. In this piece, Cassatt continues her exploration of a young woman who has emerged into the social world. Leaning forward actively and intently viewing the theatrical performance, Lydia is the subject whose mental activity dominates the painting.[90] The shimmering, glowing colors create an ambience of psychological and social movement. The woman's vital state of mind is abstracted into the dynamic lines of color, and her red-golden reflection in the mirror reiterates the themes of growth and process.

Cassatt explores another alter ego in a contrasting treatment of the loge genre. In "A Woman in Black at the Opera" (oil, 1880)[91] a woman of the world, mysterious and elegant, peers through her opera glasses at the spectacle below. She is dressed entirely in black, in contrast to the luminous colors of Lydia's clothes and setting. The opposition of the loge pictures parallels the opposition between the two Mrs. Cassatt portraits. The polarity of illumination and stability against solemnity and resignation is paralleled by youthful sensuality opposed to independence and sophistication. As the woman views, she is unknowingly viewed by a gentleman in another loge, peering at her through his opera glasses. However, the woman seems self-possessed and in control in a way that suggests to the viewer her ability to choose the interaction that she prefers. Here Cassatt wittily satirizes the woman as the object of the male gaze. The woman in black possesses her own subjective field despite the male visual hold on her.

Taken together, these portraits of women revive diverse aspects of women's personalities that had been obliterated, emaciated, or exaggerated in other cultural expressions. Thus, through these portrayals of women in the midst of their lives, Cassatt opens the door for the release of the woman, wife, mother, and daughter from her long interment within "male" culture. Cassatt is a woman who thinks her own identity; she sees, feels, and knows; she is not a creation of the male imagination.

Cassatt's portrayals suggest that she draws on personal images of great meaning. The portrait of her mother in old age as well as those of mothers tending to their babies evoke emotional reciprocity in us through the puntum of personal attachment transformed in a way that allows the power of the figure and the associated emotions to rise from the canvas significantly released from distortion and disavowal. Similarly, the painting "Lydia Crocheting in the Garden at Marley" (oil, 1880)[92] contrasts the vibrant Lydia with the pale sister ill and dying. Images of attachment and mourning experienced by women are allowed expression. The possibilities of the Eva or Beth persona are recalled here as well.

Out of the fullness of their self-respect, Cassatt's mothers structure their relationship to their daughter in mutual regard, avoiding the closed dyad of martyred identification. In many stages of the life cycle, as we have seen, Cassatt portrays mothers deeply involved in child rearing. Importantly, many of these children are female. Cassatt portrays mothers who from infancy on enjoy the female child's basic body self. In the pastel "Sleepy Nicole, A Mother Holding Her Baby" (1900) and "Rene Lefebvre Holding a Nude Baby" (oil, 1902),[93] mother holds her little daughter's well-modeled naked body close to her, enjoying and returning the child's physical and mental need of her. The daughter has the full attention and support of her mother.

Mother's attitude towards her baby daughter is nicely encoded in the oil "Baby Reaching for an Apple" (1893).[94] Mother and child, bathed in pink tones, set off by the greenery of the outdoor setting, suggest freedom to explore the outside world. Mother assists the little one to gain her goal as she reaches up to the apple. Cassatt had already explored the motif of plucking fruit as a symbol of gaining knowledge and of scientific interest. In her mural done for the women's building of the Chicago World's Columbia Exposition, Cassatt rectified the myth of Eve and fully gave permission for women to realize their mental vigor by reaching for the apple of knowledge. The baby painting expresses Cassatt's conviction that the future of the mother and child are promising.

In "Breakfast in Bed" (oil, 1897)[95] a chubby, rosy toddler enjoys a special and private audience with mother. As the two breakfast in bed, mother hugs her daughter, and the little girl sits confidently upright, backed by her mother's body and presence. Mother watches the little miss, who looks mischievously at the possibilities offered by, one supposes, jam and croissant. The soft brush strokes, the whiteness of the bedding, and the figures' clothing, surrounded by fresh apple green codes for us the happy, active interaction between mother and daughter. Similarly, in "Marie Looking Up At Her Mother" (pastel, 1897) and "Pensive Marie Kissed by Her

Mother" (pastel, 1897)[96] Cassatt presents toddlers as attractive, vital girls being offered security at a tender moment, when they return from a small journey into independence. Cassatt seems to be suggesting here something of the rapprochement crisis of faith as Margaret Mahler calls the experience when leaving mother, going off to explore, and coming back for reassurance and for the renewal of the relationship. [97]

In other works, mother fully shares her adult skills with an elder daughter, teaching her to crochet, or to play an instrument, providing the girl with a sense of competency and backing.[98] Again, the limitations imposed by bourgeois insularity are clearly evidenced. But from another perspective, it is here in these comfortable settings within self-conscious middle-class families that important transformations are being worked out. The characters immersed in knitting, sewing, or even painting enjoy their own activity. The emotional ambience is free from restraint, depression, and slavery. The entirely normal, sturdy girl and her young, relaxed mother in "The Crochet Lesson" (pastel, 1913)[99] abstracts the situation for the viewer.

Cassatt also presents an open, beneficial mother-daughter interaction that enhances the hatching of the self. In Stowe, mothers and daughters find themselves alienated from the relationship, as Eva's relationship to her mother makes painfully clear. Alcott's girls find opportunities for self-expansion but with limitation. Marmie is helpless to birth their authentic sexuality and assertiveness, while father refuses to acknowledge these qualities. Cassatt reports the daughter's self-evolution differently. She catches the girl's need to see herself and her own future destiny as a mature woman in her mother's face. In "Marie Looking Up At Her Mother" (pastel, 1897), the girl loves and admires her mother as a source of protection and benign power. This is one aspect of the background object container now clearly secularized. Hope for a safe and productive life radiates from the girl's loving look. The circle of mother's arms and the mutual response suggests the viable emergence of a daughter's individuality and independence of mind. As Cassatt's young girls find strength in their mother's adult presence, they also find themselves reflected in mother's eyes and reflected in the relationship.

Cassatt's oil "Mother and Child" (1905)[100] examines these processes between a mother and a girl of about two years of age. The little girl sits on her mother's lap, her mother holding a mirror for the child to study her reflection. The many images reflected or re-reflected structure the complex interactions and mergers between the two characters. The child's reflection is mirrored clearly. As the image of her face looks back at her and us, a moment of self-reflection is illuminated. Mother looks at the image too, sharing this moment and giving the image weight. As Winnicott, Lacan, Kohut, and others have noted, the child's self-image is at first mirrored in mother's face, then as the child moves gradually into the mental space of transitional relatedness or the shared space of reciprocal meaning, the child is able to find him or herself by carrying the mother's (father's) warm, enthusiastic responses inside his or her mind.[101] As mother and daughter peel apart, each carries aspects of the merger; the daughter bearing the weight of great attachment. Here, mother assists her daughter to find herself in the space of the intermediate. She invites her to move out of the envelope of infantile undifferentiation. At the same time, the two sitting together, holding the mirror and looking into it, are reflected in a larger mirror. The fuller reflection suggests opening up the space in which their relationship evolves in the continuing envelope of their dynamic relationship.[102]

The mother's dress is painted in bright, sunny tones of yellow and orange, connoting the warmth and vitality of her care. A huge yellow sunflower pinned to her dress seems to signify mother's capacity to feed, nurture, and foster the child's growth and development. The mother here is drawn very differently from Snow White's or Cinderella's stepmother or Eva's mother, Marie St. Clair. This woman is not competitive and has nothing of the vain, childish and self-centered character of the stepmother's stereotype. Recall the stepmother queen's attachment to her mirror and her hatred of the little princess's budding beauty in the story of Snow White. Cassatt's picture reveals a situation in which mother and daughter are not caught in the snare of their rivalry. On the contrary, mother's attention and attitude supplies the child with recognition and acceptance. She might well be saying, "I know you, and I like you as you are."

The small girl's uncovered body implies potential acceptance of her authentic self before socialization has clothed her. The contrast between the child's nudity and her mother's traditional dress hints at her potential freedom to depart from the mother's generation[103] and to enjoy her sensuality more freely and openly. The numerous mother-daughter portrayals full of multiple mergers, identifications, and separations explicate and illuminate the female odyssey of development, usually overshadowed by the one of male children. Here, adult and children females are portrayed in vital forms, enduring and suffering all the hazards and excitements of the journey of self-discovery. Cassatt is working out the new idea that modern families may offer support for full individuation to children of both sexes.

I believe there to be a close connection between the concept of genuine individuation articulated in Cassatt's mother and children portrayals and the shape and emotional tone of the symbol formation and signs constituting these works.[104] It seems to me the painting "Mother and Child" (1905) is built on openness and tolerance at every level of its meaning. On the surface level, the relationship explored is free of possessiveness or coercion. The mother has no agenda for her daughter other than that she find herself. Nor is the girl attempting to own or control her mother. Their relationship is indicated by the use of space; each character has her own space, while they meet physically, the mirror images suggest several possible perspectives.

At the level of family myth, Cassatt's girl children are given permission to evolve. Mothers and daughters are friends. One would not imagine these mothers sending Gretel or Snow White into the forest out of jealous pique. As yet there is no father/husband to stir competitive, jealous fires. One might infer him as a background presence providing for these comfortable couples, and Cassatt does deal more directly with the mother/father/child triad in "The Boating Party" (1893). But in these mother/daughter canvases she is holding that problem aside, the better perhaps to explore and emphasize visions of untruncated, lively development for girls but also at the risk of perpetuating polarized images of male and female.

Then too there is no evidence that these well-dressed, well-kept girls will cross the line to public life or become artists like their creator. Indeed, Cassatt has several paintings in soft bright colors in which a mother holds the baby, often a boy, while older sisters look at the new arrival with pleasure, curiosity, and anxiety. Many of these pictures carry on the tradition of the adoration, now secularized and made domestic.[105] In all these pictures, Cassatt shows the little elder sister in the new position of beginning to mother her younger siblings. These pictures reveal conventional family scenes with the outline of a conventional role for big sister,[106] but the liveliness and openness of the figures' relationships to each other imply a flexibility within the domestic field and thus potentially a softening of the rigid lines between the private and the public. With these issues in mind, I believe that Cassatt intended her mother/daughter works, including those of the mother, sister, and baby, as reparative and inventive symbols for a woman's potential. The openness and liveliness of the forms suggest the vitality of the underlying primitive signs.

In *Uncle Tom's Cabin* Stowe scrutinizes unhappy primitive two-person signs that close off meaning in violent and coercive ways. The shape of the triads is distorted by the interpretant's tumultuous relationship to the object, in which the subject obliterates the growth of pyschic space by merging with the significant character (mother or father) possessively and forcefully while blocking the evolution of the full meaning of the sign. One can imagine these triads as excessively long and skinny, filled in with the subject's inanimate sensual elements or a lifeless preverbal version of a drama of slavery and possession.[107] As she writes about these concrete semiotics, Stowe is creating symbols with full open shapes that allow for abstraction and the emergence of the unknown, though Stowe does not share with the reader her experience of the discovery of transitional space.

Alcott signifies the experience of thinking and feeling with a world of signs that have largely moved out of the prison of enslaved mental elements. Within the mental life of *Little Women*, flexibility and softness promote the opening out of thoughts and feelings into new ideas. However, morality and the omniscience of moral certitude restrain or abort the flow of connections that are part of living forms. The sexual and rebellious feelings found in the Gothic tales suggest violent attacks against imprisoning barriers and the entrance of darker feelings into the semiotic field.

In Cassatt's work we see a developmental line. The infant is in an early, sensual, tactile mode of experience, but it is clearly evident that there is mental life going on, signifying the presence of psychic space. As discussed earlier, Alfred Silver's exploration of the phenomenology of the formation of signs, traces the opening of psychic space through Firstness, Secondness, and Thirdness.[108] In normal development, the infant moves into the space of his/her own mental life as he/she is gradually able to relinquish the mother as part of him/herself. Slowly, the infant leaves the phantasy of twinship to further allow mother her separate life, and finally to find her as a more separate being, which allows the complex, multi-dimensional view of the object. Tolerating the caesura or gap between the object and the sign (Pierce's Thirdness) is essential for the thinking which allows the unknown to emerge. By including Thirdness Cassatt is inventing a developmental relationship that is commensal, mutually beneficial to both the partners.[109] The other extreme of the container/contained relationship depicted by Stowe is a spiral of greedy parasitism in which the interpretant (the baby) finds him or herself within a mental landscape devoid of trust or compassion. The subject experiences his/her relationship as a series of prey-predator spirals. Within the commensal relationship between container and contained, mother and baby, and interpretant and object, the baby moves out of the overlap of mentalities toward the openness or the space between him/herself and mother/father. This is the play space of meaning and signification. Cassatt paints in this space and dramatizes the evolution toward it. She is providing the infant-child thinker with a thinking partner, thus making the journey into open thinking possible.

Cassatt as a modernist voyages away from the certitude of the vision of a single perspective. Like the infant interpretant, she faces the challenge of leaving the safe shores of security for the unknown waters of multiperspective and the ambiguities of the object. She is willing to live in the intangible state of emotional life in which being and thinking are constantly transformed into new patterns of will, desire, and meaning. She is one of the artists of the late nineteenth century who recognize the need for strategies to signify a universe seen more and more as relative and indeterminate.

Cassatt's exploration of mental space in her restorative and reparative visual essays are limited by confusion in regard to men. They illustrate protected mother and child units which are free to function in important ways, but the support that allows these families to stay afloat physically and psychologically is unclear. Cassatt continues to reflect the drastic, bourgeois separation of the sexes found in several Western countries at this time. She no more pictures men functioning inside the home, within the nexus of the family relationship, than women in politics and economic activities. One can only infer husband/father backing and protecting the unit, just as one might infer that the public world is made possible by wives and mothers; although the depth and honesty of the emotional life portrayed and the richness of the signs convey that these two-person relationships are important structures for allowing messiah thoughts to emerge and to repair those aspects of Western culture that deal with family issues. Not until "The Boating Party" of 1893[110] does Cassatt take the step of working explicitly on the three-person relationships.

Within Victorian familial patterns, the father sign evolves into a Legree for the little daughter attempting to emerge into selfhood. Such an imagined figure grows in the soil of oppression but is made more spectacular by the artist of impassioned internal response. The father image is a likely candidate for the character of sinister stranger because the father is easily confused with the rude awakening into separate mental life. In addition, the more a culture inhibits father from participating in the upbringing of his infant or child, the less his offspring will be disabused of a fantastic portrayal of him. Even more important, however, the more the culture bears down on the family to buffer the force of new ideas and the resultant emotional turbulence, the more the internal figures are filled with that force and turbulence. Thus, the father inside the mind becomes victimized by what cannot be thought about, now further disguised into its opposite so that love is hidden behind hatred of love, and the recognition of dependency twists into a hatred of weakness.[111]

And once communication itself has been attacked, emotions spiral into extreme oppositional forces. Since these child/parent, father/daughter phantasies are largely disavowed, they have few constraints. If reality and reasonable logic are to temper them, they need the benefit of hermeneutic dialogue.[112] The relationship between Legree/father and slave-woman/daughter (concubines and wives) is enacted out of the Third dimension. The powerful all-or-nothing quality of extreme binary opposition suggests the First dimension.[113] The latter is the world of the line in which all ideas and feelings are expressed on one side of the line or the other, black or white, good or bad, right or wrong, and in which experience is forced into rigid configurations. The normal infant thinks in this mode, but the relationships in Stowe's novel imply an inability to go beyond the First dimension. Further, since these relationships are based on the impossibility of emotional experience or truth evolving, they also may take place at times in the negative First dimension, in which disavowal is so extreme that love and compassion have long since died. Legree's plantation is a place where existence itself has been destroyed, a place where existence used to be.[114] If these are the elements that create and constitute the terrible mythic father, the task of overcoming them requires enormous amounts of courage and insight.

Cassatt's approach to the father came at a logical point in her development as an artist. Having recovered the two-person relationship in Thirdness, she could then move on to the structure for the containment and integration of the problematical father issue. Then Cassatt was able to begin to re-think both male and female, mother and father/child relationships.

The setting of "The Boating Party" announces immediately that it will be a departure from her previous works. By expanding the vista of her usual outdoor settings (in the garden or the park) to a large body of water, she is reaching out to a world beyond privacy and domestication. In other words, the painting depicts women emerging from the confining boundaries of domestic life, a move being made in the 1890s by many women in Western countries. The woman of the painting, having left the interior world to journey along with a man, is mingling her destiny with his. She is also working tentatively to overcome her fearfulness and distrust of men, slowly coming to terms with the dark male specter who has haunted her little girl dreams with sexuality, power, and terror,[115] although the viewer can say with justice that there are no signs of Cassatt's rage and sexual desire. At the moment depicted in the painting, the woman regards the man thoughtfully, as if to see him in a new way, as part of her and her family. But the darkness of his clothes in contrast to the blue of the water, the pastels of the mother's and child's clothing, and the yellow of the boat itself suggest that this male figure remains somewhat ominous and distant. Although he is looking back at the mother and child, returning their gaze, we have only a partial glimpse of his face. The result is a sense of mystery. The fact that the male figure is in reality a strange boatman; not the child's father or the woman's husband, leads us to believe that the father is not yet part of the family. He is on a continuum with the invisible persona of the mother/child picture, protecting and providing for the couple, but from a distance. Now he visibly steers the family, keeping it afloat, and begins to study the alienated realm of his feelings as well. The tension surrounding acceptance and rejection of the three-person family group is visually signified. As Griselda Pollock points out, the high angle of vision, cutting out most of the blue Mediterranean sky, pulls the viewer into the family, as does the space created among the main figures by their mutual gaze. At the same time, the powerful back and shoulders of the boatman, caught in the action of rowing, push the viewer out of the picture's space.[116] This visual push-pull enacts the painful difficulty, and the ambivalence involved in bringing all the members of the family together. The trio nevertheless represents a family in transition, the members of which are not yet intimate and familial.

Cassatt's woman in the boat has left the world of interior settings, but she brings her child with her on her journey. She seems interested in finding new patterns within the family. Indeed, the place of the child has remained a thorny issue for the women's liberation movement. But Cassatt has her woman take a radical and different posture. The child, dressed in a pink dress, adopts something of her mother's attitude, cautiously observing the stranger, as if beginning to overcome a darker stranger inside. The painting is remarkably forward-looking and confronts issues that are often avoided by both men and women. Cassatt's family group seems to exhort us to understand that in order for the child to work out his/her future, he/she must be included within the family, including mother's journey into the outside world. Cassatt uses her Impressionist eyes to step outside history and myth as she found them to make the statement that men, women, and children share the same destiny (are in the same boat).

The painting thus provides us with a record of a modernist Oedipus myth. It also suggests the presence of an Oedipal preconception which is being realized without severe distortion. Bion calls the primary level of the Oedipal configuration an Oedipal preconception and describes it as an innate structure in the mind which is part of the mind's apparatus for contact with emotional reality. The surface myth grows out of the realization that comes from the mating of the innate preconception with experience and gives rise to a conception of parents. If the preconception is mutilated by frustration, hatred, or greed (uncontained emotions), the infant loses part of the apparatus essential for gaining a conception of him or herself as an individual and as a member of a group. And if the infant loses the apparatus essential for gaining a conception of the parental relationship and consequently for resolving Oedipal problems, he or she not only fails to solve those problems, but never even reaches them.[117] Stowe's presentation of the Oedipal semiotic implies destruction at two levels: preconception and realization. "The Boating Party" records a crucial moment in the recent history of familial emotions, a moment of separation, reconciliation, and tolerance of the unknown. Coming as it does at the close of the Victorian era, the picture works to integrate fragments of the family myth and preconceptions to restore the capacity for tolerating the powerful emotions implicit in family life.

Cassatt's "The Boating Party" integrates and heals elements of the myth in several ways. The man and woman approach each other thoughtfully. That they include their child in their journey suggests that they wish to develop a viable containing function to overcome the need for sacrifice. Further, as guiding backing figures, mother and father are helping the child to gain a useful realization-conception of parents in which feelings of uncertainty, competitiveness, and desire for potency are balanced by respect and tolerance for the parental relationship. Finally, the commensal, mutual mode of relating provides the infant/child with the ground for the growth of self-respect and the capacity for toleration of his/her own emotions and thoughts.

As handed down to us in Western culture, the Oedipus myth suggests more potential for tragedy than opportunity for emotional growth. Yet an important interpretation of the Oedipus myth is that it signifies the pain of mental life. Since Oedipus's parents are unable to think about or take responsibility for emotional significance, Oedipus is deprived of the apparatus for achieving self-knowledge. His name signifies his dilemma. Though often translated as "swollen foot," Oedipus can also be understood as "knowing foot."[118] In this way, Laius and Jocasta's act of casting out their son and ordering that his feet be pierced can be read as an attack on his ability to know.

In both *Oedipus Rex* and *Oedipus at Colonus*, Oedipus painfully searches for the truth of his emotional biography. In the second play he passes beyond the exclusive view of his personal culpability to a more complex view of his family history. At Colonus, responding to Creon's accusations of incest and murder, he says:

"The bloody death, the incest, the calamities you speak so glibly of, I suffered them, by fate against my will. It was God's pleasure or perhaps our race has angered him long ago. In me myself you could not find such evil as would make me sin against my own. How could you justly blame it upon me—on me who was yet unborn, unconcerned? If then I come into the world as I did come, in wretchedness, and met my father in flight and knocked him down, not knowing that I killed him, and when I killed again, how could you find guilt in that unmediated act? . . . If someone tried to kill you here and now, you righteous gentleman, what would you do? Inquire first if the stranger was your father, or would you not first try to defend yourself?"[119]

In this speech Oedipus overcomes the curse of ignorance and stupefaction. His release from bondage permits a journey into the mind. As with Tiresias, his blindness brings him the knowledge that comes from his inner life. Helen Bacon interprets Oedipus's sojourn into the grove of the Furies as an epiphany of integration and realization:

The welcome that he (Oedipus) finds in the grove of the Furies is confirmation of his assertion, accepted by Athens, but rejected by Thebes, that though he killed his father and committed incest with his mother, he is blameless because he acted in ignorance. This understanding of himself and his crime transforms his relation with the mother goddesses. He no longer alternates between the role of victim and victimizer in relation to women.[120]

Bacon, like Campbell, finds the experience of transcendence for the individual in the moment of integration. She suggests that Oedipus finds harmony and truth through the reconciliation of the male and female way of being.[121]

Cassatt, a woman raised in a period of extreme separation of maleness and femaleness comes, like Oedipus, to her own grove of the Furies, discovering there archaic experiences of infancy: the ancient image of mother the mysterious image of dark, stranger father. "The Boating Party" is the grove of her growth. She uses it to give a view of that experience, a view that begins to heal ruptures and provides a vision for the twentieth century

CHAPTER

6

OTHER MADONNAS

My first step from the old white man was trees,
then air, then birds, then other people. But
one day when I was sitting quiet and feeling
like a motherless child, which I was, it come
to me; that feeling of being part of everything, not separate at all. . . .
    God love everything you love—and a
mess of stuff you don't. . . .
    People think pleasing God is all God care
about. But any living thing can see it's always
trying to please us back.

—Alice Walker

Cassatt's archaeological excavations into the buried strata of familial emotions, particularly women's internal reality, allowed her to suggest the beginnings of a more balanced family mythology. By venturing into the
psychic space of toleration of the universal polar oppositions of me/not-
me, hard/soft, male/female, independent/dependent, and life/death, Cassatt invented new visual semiotic structures suitable for repairing the emotional concepts of family relations and for the revitalization of the
intersubjective field. Tillie Olsen and Alice Walker continue this creative
assault on the fortress of "male" culture from the perspective of women
who, although still confined within symbol systems of oppression, bigotry
and violent oppositions, enjoy more of the privileges of an expanding self-
awareness.

Olsen's Eva of *Tell Me a Riddle* and Walker's Shug Avery of *The Color
Purple*[1] are strong heroines, who in the tradition of Cassie, Jean Muir, and
Cassatt's self-reflecting women, protest the mutilation and underestimation
of the concepts of women and children. However, they speak and act from
a somewhat different configuration of family mythologies. As twentieth-
century women, they draw on nearly a hundred years of women's protest
activities in the arts, politics, and social movements, and while immersed

in their own synchronic experiences, they view their situation from the perspective of their history.

Eva's and Shug's present is made possible by the future concepts of the earlier women. Their present is the realization of the unborn dreams of an earlier time. Eva, a Russian immigrant born in prerevolutionary Russia, offers us the perspective of a Jewish radical and intellectually vigorous individual. Her protests are molded by the strengths of tradition, religion, and class, as well as sex. Shug and Celie share with us the history of Black women in American reaching back to slavery and looking forward to a cosmopolitan society that extends out to black people in Africa in the present. The women of *The Color Purple* speak from the vertex of race and class. However, the weight and meaning of Eva and Shug's narrative derives from their revelation of startling changes in the presentation of women's thoughts and feelings.

Olsen elaborates the changes from exile from the symbolic order to participation in its making revealed in a series of outspoken critical essays in *Silences*, a feminist collection of essays and writing.[2] In the essay entitled "Silences," Olsen brings her now powerful voice to the work of scrutinizing women's enforced muteness. She opens her argument through the use of an analogy between the processes of oppression and the silence of the artist. Olsen begins by noting that "literary history and the present are dark with silences"[3] and asks, "What is it that happens to the creator in the creative process within that time? What are creation's needs for full functioning?" Olsen explains that these are special silences, what Keats called "agonie ennuyeuse (the tedious agony), that necessary time for renewal, lying fallow, gestation and the natural cycle of creation. The silences I speak of here are unnatural; the unnatural thwarting of what struggles to come into being but cannot. In the old, the obvious parallel: when the seed strikes stone; the soil will not sustain; the spring is false; the time is drought, or blight, or infestation; the frost comes premature."[4] While on the contrary, conditions for art, as for the human infant, must be nurturant.

> To pass from conception to execution to produce, to bring the idea to birth, to raise the child laboriously from infancy, to put it nightly to sleep surfeited, to kiss it in the mornings with the hungry heart of the mother, to clean it, to clothe it fifty times over in new garments which it tears and casts away, and yet not revolt against the trials of this agitated life, this unwearying maternal love, this habit of creation, this is execution and its toils."[5]

The implication here is that the writing and the infant/female creator are deprived of the minimum conditions for growth.

In her second essay, "One Out of Twelve; Writers Who Are Women in Our Century," Olsen sorts out the conditions of what she calls the differing past of women. Today's women avoid the difficulties of compulsory child-

ɔearing while offered more educational opportunities, protection from
work, and increasing longevity. Yet, Olsen warns, these changes are recent.
Cultural change is extremely halting; scars etched so deeply are slow to
heal:

> True for most women and most of the world still.
> Unclean; taboo, the devil's gateway. The three steps behind; the girl
> babies drowned in the river; the baby strapped to the back. Buried alive
> with the Lord. Burned alive on the funeral pyre, burned as a witch at the
> stake. Stoned to death for adultery. Beaten, raped. Bothered. Bought and
> sold. Concubinage, prostitution white slavery. The hunt the sexual prey.[6]

Olsen's critical view forever moves us out of the moral vision of Stowe
and Alcott and even beyond Cassatt's gentle discovery of secular family life
to a landscape in the aftermath of an earthquake in which many buried
psychic and social elements are thrown to the surface and laid bare. Olsen's
critical essays are part of that process, and as they are, they speak without
reserve of crucial omissions and silences.

In *In Search of Our Mothers' Gardens*,[7] Walker traces the processes of re-
ease. In the essay "The Civil Rights Movement; What Good Was It?" (1966–
57), Walker opens up for us her experience of an escape from an enclosure
within the imprisoning shell of white racism. Trapped in the limited consciousness that comes with the designation of otherness, Walker comes to
ife under the gaze of the TV image of Martin Luther King.

> When we are children growing up in our parents' care, we await the spark
> from the outside world. Sometimes our parents provide it if we are lucky.
> Sometimes it comes from another source far from home. We sit paralyzed
> surrounded by our anxiety and dread hoping we will not have to grow
> up into the narrow world and ways we see about us. We are hungry for
> a life that turns us on; we yearn for knowledge of living that will save us
> from our innocuous lives that resemble death. We look for signs in every
> strange event. We search for heroes in every unknown face.
>
> It was just six years ago that I began to be alive. I had a life before but
> I did not know it. Six years ago, after half-heartedly watching my mother's
> soap operas and wondering whether there wasn't something more to be
> asked of life, the Civil Rights movement came into my life. Like a good
> omen for the future, the face of Dr. Martin Luther King, Jr. was the first
> Black face I ever saw on our new television screen and as in the fairy tale,
> my soul was stirred by the meaning for me of his mission. At the time he
> was being rather ignominiously dumped into a police van for having led
> a protest march in Alabama, and I fell in love with the soulful determined
> face of the movement.[8]

In the essay "Choice; A Tribute to Dr. Martin Luther King, Jr." (1972),
given as an address delivered at a Jackson, Mississippi, restaurant that had
been desegregated by the civil rights workers, Walker links her new ap-

preciation of her identity as a black woman with her new appreciation of her roots. She says, "My great, great, great grandmother walked as a slave from Virginia to Eatonton, Georgia, which passes for the Walker ancestral home, with two babies on her hips. She lived to be 120 years old, and my own father knew her as a boy. It is the memory of this walk that I choose to keep and to embrace my maiden name, Walker."

As Walker writes her own history as a black woman artist, she places herself within the freshly surfacing history of women and women artists. Like Olsen, Walker finds an analogy between the oppression of a class, a race, a sex, and the oppression of the artist's mind. The essay "In Search of Our Mothers' Gardens" extends the analogy into metaphor. Black women pursuing their spirit throughout their ordeal of slavery and sexual abuse "waited for the unknown thing that was in them"[9] to be made known. "For these grandmothers and mothers of ours were not saints, but artists; driven to numb and bleeding madness by the springs of creativity in them for which there was no release."[10]

As Walker probes for her history, she finds a web of connectedness between motherhood and creativity and motherhood and social oppression.

> Did you have a genius of a great, great grandmother who died under some ignorant and depraved white overseer's lash, or was she required to bake biscuits for some lazy backwater tramp when she cried out in her soul to paint watercolors of sunsets or the rain falling on the green and peaceful pasture lands. Or was her body broken, forced to bear children who were more often than not sold away from her, eight, ten, fifteen, twenty children, and her one joy was the thought of modelling heroic figures of rebellion in stone or clay?[11]

In the context of their history, Olsen and Walker both look to Virginia Woolf as the patron saint of their artist selves. Olsen draws on Woolf's analysis of the angel in the house as a symbol of the obstacles that stand between the woman artist and her realization of her gifts. She quotes Woolf: "It was she who used to come between me and my paper, who bothered me and wanted my time and so tormented me that at last I killed her, or she would have plucked out my heart as a writer."[12] Walker continues the analysis of the relationship between the artist's situation and the metaphor of women's thoughts and feelings. Drawing on Woolf, Walker suggests that a woman artist needs a room of her own in the same way that a mind must have a space for freedom of thought.

As Olsen and Walker examine the history of their women artist forebears, they realize themselves to be at a powerful crossroads. Virginia Woolf had given them a room of their own, in the same way that their grandmothers, mothers, and sister artists had broken through the barrier of silence and provided them with the thoughts and feelings of self-awareness. With the gift of speech and self-consciousness, they now articulate the angry criticism of racial, sexual, and generational bias but find themselves still caught up in those webs. From this vertex, Eva of *Tell Me a Riddle* and Shug of *The Color Purple* are forthright women who are able to speak for themselves. They no longer hide behind offstage alter egos to express their darker feelings. Their critical analysis of cultural attitudes towards black women, working-class women, and their children comes from their own experience and is articulated in their own words.

Olsen argues that motherhood, as it is structured, prohibits the full flowering of the serious artist. As mother bears the major share of responsibility for child rearing, and children's needs may not be postponed, the priorities of the artist fall more and more into the background. Olsen adds that since society itself offers little protection and aid to families, the family (largely mother) must provide most of the needs of the next generation.[13] She reveals that her own costs have been heavy.

> As for myself, who did not publish a book until I was 50, who raised children without household help or the help of the 'technological sublime,' (the atom bomb was manufactured before the first automatic washing machine); who worked outside the house on everyday jobs as well (as nearly half of all women do now, though a woman with a paid job except as a maid or a prostitute is still rarest of any in literature); who could not kill the essential angel (there was no one else to do their work) would not if I could have killed the caring part of the Woolf angel; as distant from the world of literature most of my life as literature is distant (in content to) from my world.[14]

In "Tell Me a Riddle," Olsen fashions an alter ego who shares the same dilemma. The main character Eva's intellectual life is made irreconcilable with her experience of motherhood as it is organized around the segregation of the sexual spheres. Eva, now a grandmother, bitterly accuses her husband David of robbing her of time to reflect, to think, and to read. Drawn in the style of Cassatt's self-respecting woman, she personifies women's individuality and mental strength and brings to us the history of many women. As a youngster in Russia, she gained her literacy and education through sacrifice and tragedy. A friend, an upper-class woman, defied authority and tradition to teach Eva to read. The woman was executed for her treason while Eva herself spent a year in prison. Thus, reading was a highly valued activity, a costly gift, and a means to her self-realization. Critical of traditional culture that crushes individuality, Eva vehemently rejects the lifeless shell of ritual and superstition. In response to religious practices, Eva says of her conventional daughter:

> Swindler. Does she look back on the dark centuries, candles bought instead of bread and stuck into a potato for a candlestick? Religion that stifled and said, 'In paradise, woman, you will be the footstool of your husband,' and in life poor chosen Jew ground under, despised, trembling in

cellars and cremated heritage. How have we come from our savage past. How no longer to be savages, this to teach—to look back and learn what humanizes. This to teach—to smash all ghettos that divide us. Not to go back, not to go back. This to teach—learned books in the house. Will humankind live or die? And she gives her boys superstition.[15]

Throughout the narrative and the long years of difficult child rearing, Eva maintains her freedom of mind, her conviction, and her anger. Despite the many obstacles she encounters and the pain she endures, her vitality and steadfastness are a legacy to her children. "Old scar tissues ruptured and the wounds festered anew. She thought without softness of that young life in the deep night hours while she nursed the current baby and perhaps held another in her lap or tried to stay awake for the only time to read."[16]

Olsen, exploring the parameters of motherhood and female identity at mid-century faced the monster of urban industrial indifference rather than the old Victorian moral persecution. She found women and their children, particularly those of immigrants and working class origins lost and forgotten in the urban industrial culture, which she characterized as an extension of frontier values and manifest destiny and one in which actions and influence were to be realized largely in the possession of economic and military power. In one of Olsen's other pieces in the collection *Tell Me a Riddle* called "I Stand Here Ironing," she centers on the dangerous descent of a child reared on meager nurture. The working mother, like Harriet Beecher Stowe's earlier slave mothers, is forced to abandon her infant child to the blight of marasmus-like depression.

> She was a beautiful baby. She blew shining bubbles of sound. She loved motion, loved life, loved color and music and textures. She would lie on the floor in her blue overalls patting the surface so hard in ecstasy her hands and feet would blur. She was a miracle to me, but when she was eighteen months old I left her with a woman downstairs to whom she was no miracle at all, for I worked or looked for work.[17]

As part of Olsen's rethinking family myths, she presents clearly the conflict between the mother self and the woman self or between the self and maternal obligation as well as the male/female tensions about women's mind and independence. Eva reminds her husband, the breadwinner father, of his indifference: "How cleverly you hid that you heard. Eighteen hours a day I ran and you never scraped a carrot or knew a dishtowel."

As Olsen presents the nuclear family structured on the painful and forced segretation of male and female, she connects the patterns to societal values which discount the plight of women and children who are without access to political and economic power, a culture of hard with an aversion to soft. "But for those years she had had to manage old humiliations and terrors rose up, lived again, and forced her to relive them. The children's needings, that grocer's face or the merchant's wife that she had had to beg credit from when credit was a disgrace. School coming and the desperate going over the old to see what could yet be remade; the soups from meatbones begged for the dog one winter."[18]

Olsen reminds us of the importance of the experiences of reciprocity in their blissful as well as painful aspects. Despite the pain of her isolated situation, Eva has generously shared with her children her commitment to significance, awareness, and freedom of mind. The experience is wrenching and draining. Eva has given her mind and body to shelter her children from the searing edge of cultural indifference. Now, past the child-rearing tasks, she cherishes the vision of tranquility, of solace, of a time for herself. She says, "Never again to be forced to move to the rhythm of others, being able at last to live within and not move to the rhythm of others." She is painfully reminded by her grandchildren of the old experiences of attachment. "Now they put a baby in her lap. 'Do not ask me,' she would have liked to say, 'I cannot. Cannot. Cannot. Cannot.' What an unnatural grandmother not to be able to make herself embrace a baby."

Olsen turns her powerful lens on the demands of the maternal experience. Sex, power, and material reassurances fall away before the flood of these vivid memories. "It was not that she had not loved her babies, her children. The love, the passion of tending had risen with the need like a torrent, and like a torrent drowned and immolated all else." Olsen/Eva reminds us of the inevitability of the tearing weaning and the return to separate existence after intense reciprocity.

> But when the need was done, all the power that was lost and the painful damming back and drawing up of what still surged but had nowhere to go, only the thin pulsing left that could not quiet, suffering over lives one felt but could no longer hold or help.
>
> On that torrent she had born them to their own lives and the river bed was desert long years now. Nor there would she dwell, a memoried waif; somewhere an older power that beat full of life, somewhere coherence, transport and meaning.[19]

Olsen/Eva reminds us of the need for solitude as a time for rediscovery of the inner self. But they put a baby in her lap. The old claims of overflowing intimacy threatened to engulf her.

> Needlessly to embrace and the breath of that past: warm flesh like this that had claims and nuzzled away all else and with lovely mouths devoured; hot living like an animal intensely and now; the turning maze; the long drunkenness, the drowning into needing and being needed. Severely, she looked back, and the shudder seized her again, and the sweat. Not that way. Not there. Not now could she. Not yet. In all that visit she could not touch the baby.[20]

Yet, Eva's generosity of spirit and maternal capacities radiate out into the next generation of mothers and children. Vivian, now grown, makes this connection with gratitude. "Nursing the baby my friends marvel, and I tell them, 'Oh, it's easy to be such a cow. I remember how beautiful my mother seemed nursing my brother and the milk just flows.' "[21] The reciprocity moves over the generations.

As Olsen inherited the building blocks of a personal myth from her artist ancestors, her signs became filled with the released elements of their personal myths; and standing on the foundation of the work of Stowe, Alcott, and Cassatt, she rethinks cultural and personal themes of mothers and children from a less limited vertex. Her angry protests against the treatment imposed on women and children is not confined, but expands out into chains of meaning which reach backward and forward in time, across national barriers, generations, and overcomes biased oppositions. The semiotic chain of *Riddle* is made up of several relational structures. Eva, much like the signifiers Eva St. Clair/Cassie or Beth/Jo, or Irma/Freud, is not only at the center of the narrative, holding together many juxtapositions, but goes beyond the danger of sacrifice. Eva's experience as a young person in Russia contrasted with that of her old age in America illuminates her capacity to endure change and grow and influence the lives of three generations. As a woman escaped from tyranny, her life interfaces with her children and grandchildren, born and raised in a democracy. Eva's relationship to her husband David illuminates the contrast or juxtaposition between radical feminism and the traditional Jewish patriarchy. The most crucial juxtaposition of the piece, which provides a sign of the continuity of growth and bonding, is that of Eva's radicalism and devotion to revolutionary causes, with the commitment of her granddaughter Jeannie to work as a nurse for the poor and elderly. The emotional force of these juxtapositions breaks into the linear tidiness of the narrative and releases the meaning of Eva's life from saturated cultural preconceptions and from social customs and laws and from history and time. The significance and power of her feelings and attitude extend out for sixty years, sustained by her determination to survive.

At a still deeper level, the story finds its force in the processes of transformation of overflow, ecstasy, and being, which support and fill the symbolic juxtapositions. The transformations flow out of Eva's thoughts and images.[22] A central image is of her grandchildren; their freshness, liveliness, and desire to know in contrast to her own difficult childhood and youth under tyranny and the hardship of raising her own children in a strange land without emotional and economic support. It is Eva's capacity for endurance and fidelity that has made their lives possible.

At the end of her life, Eva has only a few months to live, and she makes a last journey to visit her grandchildren, first at the house of her son, and then to her daughter's, and finally to her granddaughter's home. Her son's children are of latency age and enjoy grandmother immensely. They ask Eva to play, and to listen, and to tell them a riddle. Their excited love and appetite for companionship releases opposite images and circumstances in Eva's mind. She relives the conditions of her own education, the arrest and execution of her beloved mentor Lisa. Here, enthusiasm, love, and eager curiosity are counterposed to the conditions of tyranny in which love of knowledge is crushed. One side of this juxtaposition is the protection and nurture of children; the other, the hard container of tyranny which seeks to destroy authentic expressiveness and curiosity.

The second stop of Eva's last journey brings her to her daughter's family and a new baby. The snug, everyday family life laced with baby smells and sounds again evokes terrifying dreams and memories for Eva, not only the taxing experience of nursing and tending but of the insistent nightmare of the partial abortion of her own child self, of her creative thoughts, and of the death of the Lisa aspect of herself. How much of the authentic dreams had she been able to save for herself and for her children and their children?

The story also works throughout its course with the overflow between husband and wife. The turbulent relations between Eva and David are partly fed on the social prescriptions of what male and female must be. Eva, as the keeper of infantile life, and David, as the breadwinner father forced out of the mother-child sphere as she is kept out of the public sphere, antagonize each other from their oppositional priorities. Hard and soft, me and not-me, private and public clash and war in Eva and David's relationship. Another element of their dissension is Eva's private self. Eva as a talented intellectual and revolutionary fights for her privacy to think, read, and write. David cannot understand her interests and feels shut out. The needs of babies and husbands and the priority of intellectual and political commitment compete for Eva's attention.

Sitting loyally beside Eva as she lies dying, David reflects painfully on the gap between them. Prompted by the sound of her whimpers, death swallows, and pageant of halfdreamt memories, David realizes the jagged edge of their differences. Reflecting on her love for books, David says,

"It helps, Mrs. Philosopher, words from books, it helps." But he felt pushed out—that for seventy years she had hidden a tape recorder infinitely microscopic within her, that it had coiled infinite mile on mile, trapping every song, every melody, every word heard and spoken and that maliciously she was playing back only what said nothing of him, of the children, and of their intimate life together.[23]

Eva's nostalgic journey into her revolutionary activities and interests painfully reminds David of Eva's private self.

The cards fell from his fingers without warning the bereavement and betrayal he had sheltered—compounded through the years—hidden even from himself—revealed itself,

uncoiled

released

sprung

And with it the monstrous shapes of what had actually happened in the century.[24]

Olsen moves us from opposition to integration inside the male mind who loves his children and his wife. Continuing the death vigil with Eva, David views the enormity of her life. Empathetically responding to Eva's vivid parade of memories, David begins to journey with her:

> . . . and instantly he left the neat old woman poring over the Book of the Martyrs; went past the mother treading at the sewing machine; past the girl in her wrinkled prison dress, hiding her hair with scarred hands, lifting to him her awkward chain imploring eyes of love; and took her in his arms, dear, personal, fleshed, and all the heavy passion he had loved to rouse from her.[25]

As Eva lies dying at Jeannie's Santa Monica apartment, the generational interface is explored in its final form. Olsen studies the mother–child feelings at the close of the parent's life. "Now one by one the children come, those that were able. Hannah, Paul, Sammy. Too late to ask; and what did you learn from your loving mother and what do you need to know."[26]

The oldest child Clara, silent, reviews her bitterness. " 'Pay me back, mother. Pay me back for all you took from me. Those others you crowded into your heart. Is this she, noises the dying make, the crab-like hands crawling on the covers?' "[27] Another child deplores the irrevocable rift between them. " 'I do not know you mother. Mother I never knew you.' " Still another experiences her death compassionately and mourns not only for himself but for that which never lived. For him, too, unspoken words, " 'Goodbye mother, who taught me to mother myself.' "[28]

The surfacing and articulation of the feelings and attitudes that take place between the generations transform the nature and function of the familial myth. In this case, the myth instructs and offers reconciliation.

In the last days of Eva's life, her capacity to bond centers on the relationship to her granddaughter and to her husband David. She allows them to chaperone her to her death, and a new family group is created. Eva and Jeannie reveal themselves to each other in these painful last days. As Jeannie's anguish about her abortion is met by Eva's empathy (she too has lost children, one in Korea and one by abortion), Eva opens her life and mind to Jeannie to provide support and a sense of continuity, but also to pass on to Jean the values and history of her life. Later Jeannie tells her grandfather that Eva has the need to share her legacy and to pass on her knowledge. She particularly wants to pass on not only the legacy of attachment within the family but its implications in the social sphere. Her vision includes more than the politics of the Russian revolution; it extends to a personal politics of her own mind, a politics of freedom in which infantile mental life and its emotional forces as well as new ideas can survive without fear of the tyranny, torture, exile that stems from unintegrated hardness.

The Eva/David, Eva/Jean relationships are brought together powerfully by the imminence of Eva's death. Jean and her grandfather form a bond of solace to help Eva and him through the tearing separation. Jeannie accepts the legacy of Eva's political and social experiences and personal knowledge. In Eva's mythic odyssey within the Eva/Jean/David structure, all oppositions are brought together and integrated. Age and youth, male and female, weakness and strength, sickness and health, and of course finally life and death. Jeannie's mind takes on the responsibility that her grandmother's had held. She assumes the task of containing and integrating the powerful elements of her familial and personal myth. Similarly, Olsen takes on these tasks to create new cultural myths, meanings, and interpretations which value the female and child in all of us. Through this effort, no issue is hidden, nor disavowed. Eva as a white goddess, the mother of origin, provides us with the knowledge and the strength by which to make sense of the experience of the developmental journey of the self into individuated mental life.

Among all the thematic connections between the Victorian generation of artists and the contemporary figures, Harriet Beecher Stowe and Alice Walker have the closest ties. Each constructs a mythic tale around the problem of bias and confusion about gender and race. Walker's *The Color Purple* acknowledges the similarities as part of the continuing history of American culture and responsibly takes on the task begun by Stowe of interpreting and exorcising encapsulating pseudosymbolic structures of fear, oppression, and bigotry.

Walker's novel opens in a social and mental landscape not unlike those of *Uncle Tom's Cabin.* Although separated by a hundred years, in which slavery had long been abolished, black women and black children of both sexes remained locked within a deadly caste system. The protection offered by emancipation had achieved pathetically little in the face of racial and sexual bias. The early chapters of *The Color Purple* reveal Celie and Nettie, Walker's heroines, not only within a system of discrimination of race and class, but in a nightmare family situation in which women and children are "enslaved" by the men in their extended family.

Walker's family tales also differ in emphasis from Stowe and the others, for placed inside a black world, black people enact important roles. It is their thoughts and feelings and problems which center the novel. "White" culture remains an outside influence, abstracted into social, political, and religious forces which operate through imperialism, domination, and bigotry. White characters are bit characters and are portrayed in the style of

Stowe's Rev. Packwood as outrageous hypocrites sunk into a malicious, if not a delusional, ideology. The book reveals the thoughts and feelings of black people through the device of a series of letters between the two sisters, Celie and Nettie, and between Celie and God. The historical and personal transformations take place within the subjective experience of several black women as they slowly reclaim the occupied territory of their inner subjective world.

The opening letter is Celie's plea for help and understanding. She is in extreme distress and danger. She writes, "Dear God, I am 14 years old. I have always been a good girl. Maybe you can give me a sign letting me know what is happening to me."[29] An abused child, Celie searches for consolation and direction. Her mother failing, her pa "turns his demands on Celie 'Never had a kine word to say to me. Just say you gonna do what mammy wouldn't. First he put his thing up gainst my hip and sort of wiggle it around. Then he grab hold of my titties. Then he push his thing inside my pussy. When that hurt I cry. He start to choke me saying you better shut up and get used to it.' "[30] Like Tom, Celie plunges into a nightmare bereft of sanity's moderation. Mother, impotent, dies of overwork and excessive pregnancies. "Father," drawn as a black Legree or Haley prototype, represents the male antipathy toward the madonna and her child. " 'When I start to hurt and when my stomach start movin' and then that little baby come out of my pussy chewin' on its fist, you could have knocked me over with a feather.' "[31] Celie's two children, like Oedipus, are taken away and as far as Celie knows put into great danger, either killed or sold. She says, "He took it while I was sleeping, kill it out there in the woods. Kill this one too if he can. He took my other baby, a boy this time, but I don't think he killed it. I think he sold it to a man and his wife over in Monticello. I got breast milk running down myself."[32]

Since we are now inside black experience, the social and psychological meaning of Celie's brutal Pa poses a puzzle to be solved. Walker portrays the Kronus father as a black man. In her book of short stories, *In Love and Trouble*,[33] several more black American women are endangered and betrayed by black men who are part of their family circle. These stories and the novel *The Color Purple* reveal to us a profound historial and cultural change. The signifier Uncle Tom has disappeared from the cultural stage and has been replaced by a black Legree. The Uncle Tom/Legree exchange is a parallel structure which encodes the change from an *emphasis* on racial oppression to one based on familial sexual oppression. Walker, drawing on Stowe's mythic structures, revises them to interpret the cultural familial scenes of her own era, and discovers within the black family the presence and power of the mythology of self-hatred which is in itself a transformation of racial hatred, now transformed again and translocated onto the plane of generational and sexual differences. Black men enslave and oppress black women and children while disowning their own vulnerability and assigning it to women and children, following the contours of the mentality of the Legree ideology. Walker's revised familial myth suggests a chain of shifts and transformations within American culture. The white/black, superior/inferior oppositions signifying the polar opposition enslavement/liberty metamorphosizes into black male/black female (or black children) signifying patterns of self-hatred or a polarized relationship between the aggressor/victim polarity.

The narrative of incest, rape, and infanticide told from the vertex of the black woman functions as a radium implant and maps for us the spread of our cultural malignancy. In Walker's view, our race phobia is a phobia of vulnerability which has infected the black family while it continues in white male/female relations and in racial relations.

Walker's mythic tale begins as a tragedy, but as its mythic narrative unfolds, the character of Shug Avery appears as a significant challenge to the existing mythic and semiotic structures. Shug finds her own path out of hopelessness by the usual route for black Americans: she sings the blues, and being blessed with an abundance of charisma and sensuality, leads herself to the Promised Land, carrying along with her some of the other characters and opening up their consciousness and lives. Shug suggests the evolution of one of Stowe's strong black women. Warm, sexy, tolerant, and self-confident, she personifies at once the new women of the '80s and an ancient black goddess of female power. Shug's body openly offers comfort and sensuality. Not a vehicle for exploitation by others, it is a source of her bounty shared freely with those she loves. Celie finds both her past and her future in this body, and a world of loving sensuality. " 'First time I got the full sight of Shug Avery's long black body with its black plum nipples look like her mouth, I think I had turned into a man. I wash her body, and it feels like I'm praying. My hands tremble, and my breath is short.' "[34]

While Walker's Shug Avery seems to fulfill the criteria for a maternal goddess, we come to know her as a very human person in many ways, burdened with her own human history. When Celie and the reader are introduced to Shug, she is very ill and in trouble, unable to eat, recklessly chainsmoking, and alone. Though she dominates the narrative with her maternal power and generosity, at times her character suggests emotional anorexia. Unlike Celie, who has lost her children unwillingly, Shug is cool to maternal feelings. " 'My kid's with grandma,' she said. 'She could stand the kids. I had to go.' " Celie wonders if Shug doesn't miss her children, to which Shug replies, " 'Nah, I don't miss nothing.' "

As Celie and Shug's relationship deepens, they come to understand each other's wounds. Each mothers the other. Celie nurses Shug back to health when she has been abandoned by almost everyone else. Shug begins to eat again and regains her strength. On the other hand, Shug tends to Celie's psychological wounds of loss, of abuse, deprivation, and above all, enforced ignorance. Shug and Celie begin to form a small community of womanly love in which they reflect, choose, and become the authors of their own lives. Celie brings Shug sisterly comradeship and love, but the elder woman

offers her younger companion motherly love and support and a sophisticated view of the possibilities of Celie's life. As part of their relationship,
Shug functions as Celie's guide into self-knowledge. Like Oedipus's Tiresias, she searches for the truth of Celie's past. Celie, responding to Shug's
queries about her pregnancies and sexual experiences, responds,

> 'It hurt me, you know. I was just goin' on 14 and I never thought about
> me having nothing down there so big. It scare me just to see it and the
> way it poke itself and grow. After he through he make me finish trimming
> his hair.'[35]

Shug holds Celie and eases her through her reflective odyssey, enabling
her to realize her pain in the safety of this bond. " 'I start to cry, too, I cry
and cry and cry. Seems like it all comes back to me, laying there in Shug's
arms. How it hurt and how much I was surprised, how it stang while I
finished trimming his hair, how the blood ran down.' " And more of Celie's
painful history emerges: her mother's death and the loss of her sister (Nettie
is driven away by Celie's husband). " 'He get me to take care of him, get
me to take care of his rotten children. He never ask me nothin' about myself.
He just climb on top of me and fuck even when my head was bandaged.
Nobody ever love me.' "[36] The two women comfort each other and provide
illuminating channels to interpret their situation. Thinking and speaking
from a position of the disavowed, Shug and Celie begin to draw strength
from their relationship. Celie remarks, "Then I feel something real soft
and wet on my breast. Feels like one of my lost babies' mouths. Way after
a while, I act like a little lost baby myself.' "[37]

In the person of Sophie, Stowe and Walker find much in common. Sophie
is Walker's Cassie; angry, resourceful, reckless, and endangered. Sophie
continues to carry the burden of the woman outcast, in the tradition of
Hester, Zenobia, and Cassie. By following Sophie's odyssey, we are taken
into the inner vault of women's oppression. Inside the chambers of Sophie's
confinement, we find the location of an American internal battleground.
Sophie fights for her life, oppressed by her Legree enemies, both black and
white. Sophie explains, " 'All my life I had to fight. I had to fight my daddy,
I had to fight my brother. I had to fight my cousins and my uncles. A girl
child ain't safe in a family of men, but I never thought I'd have to fight in
my own home.' "[38] Sophie becomes another teacher to Celie, urging her to
be less passive. Sophie explains to her about her own difficult family background, reminding us clearly of the polar oppositions between male and
female seen in Stowe's novel. Speaking of her mother to Celie, she explains,
" 'She under my daddy's thumb. Now she under his foot; anything he says
go. She never say anything back. She never stand up for herself. Try to
make a little half stand sometime for her children, but that always backfire.
More she stand up for us the harder time he gives her. He hate children,

and he hate where they come from though from all the children he got, you'd never know it.' "³⁹

Sophie, like her predecessor Cassie, questions and rejects the role of victim, but is scarred deeply by taking up her battles. Refusing to bow and scrape to white royalty in the person of the mayor's wife, Sophie is beaten and jailed and separated from her children for years. But much like Cassie, Sophie maintains her anger and her cunning. It is at the interface between Cassie/Legree and Sophie/black man/white power that important cultural battle lines are drawn between the forces of slavery and disavowal and the forces that challenge these arrangements. At the level of symbols and signs we are inside the conflict between the growth and formation of meaning and its destruction.⁴⁰ In this way, the persons of Shug and Sophie represent not only social and cultural challenges, but chains of meaning which challenge chains of anti-meaning.⁴¹ As part of this process, Shug's character brings us into the processes of restoration of the female body and its functions. She enjoys her body and generously shares it with others, and teaches Celie to enjoy hers and to recover respect and control of her sexuality. Surfacing with the resurrection of the maternal body and the liberation of the female mind is the possibility for the integration of polarized splits and the recovery from malignant chains of false semiosis.

Nettie's odyssey is also part of this process as it carries us from provincialism and bias to an open-minded world view. At the beginning of the novel, Nettie is caught in the same circumstances as her sister Celie. She runs away and, through a series of gratuitous coincidences, travels thousands of miles from the rural South to her ancestor's land, Africa, with her own niece and nephew. Although Walker pushes Nettie to psychological and geographical regions far from home, the letters between the two sisters form a net of historical and personal connections. Returning to Africa, Nettie discovers on the one side the outrages of the origins of slavery, including the betrayal of blacks by other Africans, and on the other the destruction of the African social system by contemporary imperialistic forces. Nettie's letters to Celie work like Shug's worldly views to expand both the sisters' consciousness, filling in the gaps of their history. The experiences of personal history are linked to political history and American cultural patterns are linked with those of other cultures and nations. Personal suffering and oppression are revealed to be part of a pattern of world affairs.

At times Walker's black family resembles all too well George and Eliza Harrison's family history. Exposed to dangerous anti-family forces, family members torn apart, and children stolen from their parents, the two families seem doomed. However, Walker and Stowe share a tenacious optimistic view. Both authors imagine that the work of families is to endure and to come together. Cassie, after a series of tragic losses, is reunited with her child and grandchild in Canada. Nettie loses Celie, but is united with Celie's children and accompanies them and their adoptive parents on a missionary junket to Africa. Nettie and the children form an extended family, and Nettie's letters back to Celie ensure the continuance of their family ties from one end of the world to the other. As in *Uncle Tom's Cabin*, some men interfere with these ties, particularly those between mother and child. Celie's Pa steals her children, but they are not dead, as their young mother feared, but stolen away. Nettie's letters are intercepted by Celie's husband as an act of revenge on Nettie for her independence. The mythic structures of *The Color Purple* and *Uncle Tom's Cabin* share this configuration. The Legree father who defiles the mother-child bonds is indicative of primitive, turbulent sign systems. However, in Walker's tale, the psychic space of tolerance and knowledge replaces the closed structure of violence and slavery.

Like Cassatt's woman in "The Boating Party," Nettie passes beyond the familiar shores of the status quo to new continents, people, and values, leaving behind the closed triadic structures of dominance-submission, Nettie breaks through the shell of enforced ignorance. She says, " 'Oh, Celie, there are colored people in the world who want us to know, want us to grow and see the light. They're not all mean like Pa and Albert, or beaten down like Ma was. . . . Did you know there were great cities in Africa, greater than Milledgeville or even Atlanta thousands of years ago? That the Egyptians who built the pyramids and enslaved the Israelites were colored? That Egypt is in Africa? That the Ethopia we read about in the Bible meant all of Africa?' "[42] As Nettie's letters are finally read by Celie, thanks to the intervention of Shug, they are the means to her self-discovery by returning to her her lost history that had been repressed by historical, social, and psychological forces. Nettie informs Celie of the real narrative of their life. She says that "Pa" is not their pa. Their real father, a gentle, enterprising Southern black, was hanged for the sin of operating a successful dry goods store, an activity reserved for white folks. Soon after this tragedy, their mother married their stepfather, and soon after that, she died, too.[43] Celie, provided with the data of her history, begins to integrate the banished elements of her self-knowledge. At first she is disturbed. She writes, "Oh, dear God, my daddy lynched, my mamma crazy. All my little brothers and sisters no kin to me. My children not my sister and brother. Pa not pa. You must be asleep. "[44] Celie is greatly changed by these powerful new realizations. She can no longer write to her old male God. She writes, "Dear Nettie, I don't write to God no more. I write to you."[45]

As Celie rejects what she now associates with the mean men in her life, Shug pushes her to expand her vision further and provides her with the support to go beyond her anger. Shug allows that she, too, rejected the old God. " 'Ain't no way to read the Bible and not think white. And when I found out God was white and a man, I just about lost interest.' "[46] Shug reveals that she had found a new God and a new perspective. For her, God is a sense of support and of love that is inside. From this new position, Shug finds herself released into a personal sense of being, no longer circumscribed by social myths. Shug explains her God to be a god who protects the individual like a mother against the indifferences and separations of modern society. " 'My first step from the old man was trees, then air, then birds, then other people. But one day when I was sitting quiet and feeling like a motherless child, which I was, it come to me; that feeling of being part of everything, not separate at all. I knew that if I cut a tree, my arm would bleed. And I laughed, and cried, and I ran all around the house.' "[47]

Shug's new realization of God provides new realizations of mother, father, child, and container-contained in which loving respectful equality is possible within the intersubjective field. In this context, Shug maintains to Celie that sin is the obviation of personal experience. She says, " 'I think it piss God off if you walk by the color purple in a field somewhere and don't notice it.' "[48] Furthermore, Shug insists to Celie that God needs love, too. The conception of God as a royal tyrant inhibits expressive flow between two lively subjectivities. " 'People think pleasing God is all God care about. But any fool living in the world can see it always trying to please us back. Everything wants to be loved. Us sing, dance, make faces, and give flower bouquets trying to be loved.' "[49]

Walker creates an allegory of parent/child relations centered around Shug's new concept of God. Shug herself represents the resurrection of the maternal goddess, and her fresh religious philosophy signifies the functions and modes of relationships which enhance rather than oppress the processes of self-discovery and the expansion of the self. Walker's allegory also signifies the processes of healing and integration of much needed potential in American democratic culture. Men, as well as women, find opportunity for self-revision and self-discovery. The character of Adam makes clear the possibility of new attitudes between the generations and between the sexes. Walker's allegory is part of a new Oedipal myth, which overcomes disavowal, blindness, and alienation, and allows for all the children and the child in the adult to be welcomed and liberated. Celie's last letter portrays the several levels of integration. Her letter begins, "Dear God, dear stars, dear trees, dear people, dear everything, dear God. . . . " Celie's prayer of lively gratitude is inspired by the return of her lost family, but also by her new vision. She tells the reader that she is now happy and vital. In the scene that she describes, the sexes and generations have come together. While the races remain separate, women and blacks have come into their own, overcoming the many oppositions found in Uncle Tom's Cabin and *Little Women*.

As Shug, Celie, and Nettie break through the cultural patriarchal shell into a state of mind and perspective that is tolerant and open, and allows for the mingling of male and female qualities, Walker provides us with a rather happy ending which contradicts many of the brutal facts of black American life today. I think this contradiction can be understood if we read *The Color Purple* as a fresh realization of the Oedipal myth with many new potential realizations and possibilities. Celie and Shug break through the barrier of self-hatred and self-denigration, while Albert and Harpo and Samuel reach radical new realizations of themselves as well, leaving behind a self-organization based on sexual prejudice. Adam, Celie's son, is the new man of egalitarian attitudes.

It seems to me that Walker's novel goes beyond the mythic structures of the other women's works. Through its characters and realizations, the mythic structures of *The Color Purple* code the transformation from the malignant prohibition against growth and development to those which promote them. In the first phase of the myth, Celie and Nettie are victims, deprived of self-respect and self-knowledge. The black male characters are organized around racial and sexual bias. They dominate and enslave their women, mirroring the oppression of blacks and other minorities by the dominant white society. As the myth unfolds, the balance between men and women, adults and children, black and white, shifts—the victims abandon self-hatred for confidence and a sense of entitlement. In addition, the myth relies on the restoration of the maternal goddess personified by Shug to restore the balance between victim and oppressor. The new equilibrium obliterates enslavement and domination as a major mode of relating by moving psychic contents from one group to another. Shug and Celie break out of the structures that define them as insignificant persons and as prey. In so doing, they expand their psychic internal space and find within themselves their power of creativity and self-respect. The male characters reclaim their disavowed infantile aspects and their rage at white oppressors which frees them from the sadistic mode of relating within their families.

Walker, like Olsen, is tracking lost aspects of our culture. Both these women link disavowal with noxious patterning of social and personal relations. Olsen links anti-Semitism and fascism with attitudes towards mothers and children. Walker emphasizes strong relationships between racial oppression and familial forms of fascism. Thus, they are reworking signification processes, which as we have seen through the Legree sign and the associated mental processes, function in a way that prohibits the formation of meaning and the development of the self.

The Color Purple contains an allegorical journey from disturbed primitive mental life to its mature and balanced forms and from distorted unconscious structures to those of equilibrium. It seems to me that the work of Stowe and Alcott are constructed on the same allegorical structure, and it is their bridging of the unspeakable with language that promotes the gradual surfacing of undiscovered or banished elements of the Oedipus myth.[50] Cassatt's ideographs function within the same allegorical structure connecting the invisible with the visible, but with more success in bringing forward aspects of the power and necessity of the bonding experience. Olsen unearths the contradictions between the bonding experience and the needs of mothers by breaking through the autism of women buried in the tomb of the paternal birth. She takes up these contradictions in the modernist context, emphasizing an imbalance between mothering and outer society and between modern technological power and the vulnerability of the weak and the small.

With the benefits of these earlier explorations, Walker creates an allegory that is more complete and takes us further out of the morass of bias and oppression. At the beginning of the narrative, Walker finds herself and her characters in a nefarious universe haphazardly reconstructed out of the elements of disavowal.[51] In this vision, the double difference is annihilated; neither sexual nor generational differences function properly to structure benign differentiation.[52] Women and children of both sexes, as the signifiers of the double difference, seen as a threat to the world view of reductionism, are objects of horror.[53]

Gradually, Walker's characters are released from the prison of undifferentiated space. The infantile solution of abolishing the spatial and significant difference between the infant and the mother's (father's) body is relinquished. These transformations are made possible through the intelligent and empathetic container function of Walker's mind. Drawing on the gradual assemblage of meaning derived from the thinking of the earlier women, Walker's capacity to contain expands. Like the parent interpreting and detoxifying the frightened screams of their offspring, the author locates, accepts, and transforms the horror, the disavowed, and the unknown.[54] In Walker's *The Color Purple*, the structures of disavowal within the Oedipal or familial myths are reclaimed, and their contents are returned to their rightful location.

Walker's allegorical pilgrimage brings us inside the structures of disavowal. As we descend into the vault of the repudiated, Walker relocates for us the affective contents of the disavowed: fear, loneliness, rage, hatred, and self-mutilation are shared between the sexes, races, and generations, and as they are, they are transformed into love and need. The parent's respect for the double difference facilitates the infant's toleration of differences of time, space, and generation. The new generation of characters, Adam, Olivia, and Tashe, reintegrated into their extended family, papoosed snugly within a balanced mythic tale, elude the old fate of sacrifice and slavery and are offered instead the opportunities of an open, lively odyssey into self-knowledge. This transformation reiterates and mirrors the larger transformation of the myth itself from slavery and oppression to equality and the liberty of open mental space.

Notes

PREFACE

1. Nellie Furman, "The Politics of Language," in *Making a Difference: Feminist Literary Criticism*, ed. Gayle Green and Coppelia Kahn (New York: Methuen, 1985).
2. Ibid.
3. Terence Hawkes, *Structuralism and Semiotics* (Berkeley/Los Angeles: University of California Press, 1977), pp. 123–25.
4. Ibid., p. 131.
5. Roland Barthes, *Mythologies*, selected and translated by Annette Lavers (New York: Hill & Wang, 1972).
6. Roland Barthes, *Image Music Text*, selected and translated by Stephen Heath (New York: Hill & Wang, 1977), p. 40.
7. Barthes, "The Face of Garbo," *Mythologies*, pp. 56–57.
8. Hawkes, *Structuralism and Semiotics*, p. 126.
9. Alfred Silver, "A Psychosemiotic Model: An Interdisciplinary Search for a Common Structural Basis for Psychoanalysis, Symbol-Formation, and the Semiotic of Charles S. Peirce," in *Do I Dare Disturb the Universe?*, ed. James S. Grotstein (Beverly Hills: Caesura Press, 1981); Hawkes, *Structuralism and Semiotics*, p. 129.
10. Sigmund Freud, *The Interpretation of Dreams, Standard Edition*, vols. 5 & 6 (London: Hogarth Press, 1957).
11. W. R. Bion, "Notes on Schizophrenia," in *Second Thoughts* (New York: Jason Aronson, 1967).
12. W. R. Bion, *Learning from Experience*, in *Seven Servants* (New York: Jason Aronson, 1977).
13. Bice Benvenuto and Roger Kennedy, "The Instance of the Letter (1956)," in *The Works of Jacques Lacan: An Introduction* (New York: St. Martin's Press, 1986), pp. 120–21.
14. Umberto Eco, *Semiotics and the Philosophy of Language* (Bloomington: Indiana University Press, 1984), p. 24.
15. Catherine Millot, "On Hysteria, the Phallic Function, and Jouissance," *International Journal of Critical Psychology and Psychoanalysis* 2:1 (1987), pp. 25–33.
16. Daniel N. Stern, *The Interpersonal World of the Infant: A View from Psychoanalysis and Developmental Psychology* (New York: Basic Books, 1984).

1. THE MATERNAL METAPHOR

1. Michel Foucault quoted in "Mind Mother: Psychoanalysis and Feminism" by Judith Kegan Gardiner in *Making a Difference: Feminist Literary Criticism*, ed. Gayle Greene and Coppelia Kahn (New York: Methuen, 1985).
2. See W. R. Bion's "Attacks on Linking" (1959), in *Second Thoughts* (New York: Jason Aronson, 1967); Heinz Kohut, "The Bipolar Self," in *The Restoration of the Self* (New York: International University Press, 1977).
3. See, for example, Nancy Chodorow, *The Reproduction of Mothering: Psychoanalysis and the Sociology of Gender* (Berkeley/Los Angeles: University of California Press, 1978); Dorothy Dinnerstein, *The Mermaid and the Minotaur: Sexual Arrangements and Human Malaise* (New York: Harper & Row, 1976); Greene and Kahn, eds., *Making a Difference*, Julia Kristeva, *Powers of Horror: An Essay on Abjection* (New York: Columbia University Press, 1982); Julia Kristeva, *Desire in Language: A Semiotic Ap-*

proach to Literature and Art, ed. Leon S. Roudiez, tr. Thomas Gora, Alice Jardine, and Leon Roudiez (Oxford: Basil Blackwell, 1980); Hélène Cixous and Catherine Clément, *The Newly Born Woman*, tr. Betsy Wing, Foreword by Sandra M. Gilbert (Minneapolis: University of Minnesota Press, 1986 [1975]); Mary Jacobus, *Reading Women: Essays in Feminist Criticism* (New York: Columbia University Press, 1986); Jane Gallop, *The Daughter's Seduction: Feminism and Psychoanalysis* (Ithaca: Cornell University Press, 1982); Hester Eisenstein and Alice Jardine, eds., *The Future of Difference* (New Brunswick, N.J.: Rutgers University Press, 1985); Claire Duchen, *Feminism in France: From May '68 to Mitterand* (London: Routledge & Kegan Paul, 1986); Elizabeth Able and Emily Kay Able, eds., *The Signs Reader: Women, Gender, and Scholarship* (Chicago: University of Chicago Press, 1983); Elaine Marks and Isabel de Courtivron, eds. and Introduction, *New French Feminisms: An Anthology* (New York: Schocken Books, 1981); Josephine Donovan, *Feminist Theory: The Intellectual Tradition of American Feminism* (New York: Ungar, 1985); Luce Irigaray, *Speculum of the Other Woman*, tr. Gillian C. Gill (Ithaca: Cornell University Press, 1985 [1974]); Nancy Kay Miller, ed., *The Poetics of Gender* (New York: Columbia University Press, 1986); Hester Eisenstein, *Contemporary Feminist Thought* (Boston: G. K. Hall, 1983); Juliet Mitchell and Jacqueline Rose, eds., *Feminine Sexuality: Jacques Lacan and the École Freudienne*, tr. Jacqueline Rose (New York: W. W. Norton, 1968).

4. Simone de Beauvoir, *The Second Sex*, tr. H. M. Parshley (New York: Knopf, 1953); Adrienne Rich, *Of Woman Born: Motherhood as Experience and Institution* (New York: Bantam Books, 1976).

5. Roland Barthes, *Mythologies* (New York: Hill & Wang, 1972).

6. Sigmund Freud, *Interpretation of Dreams*, Chapters 6 and 7, *Standard Edition*, vol. 5 (London: Hogarth Press, 1957).

7. Chodorow, *The Reproduction of Mothering*, p. 28.

8. Freud, *Totem and Taboo* (1913), S.E., vol. 13.

9. Chodorow, pp. 108–10.

10. Ibid., p. 110.

11. Melanie Klein, "Schizoid Mechanisms" and "On Identification," *Envy and Gratitude* (New York: Delta Press, 1967); James S. Grotstein, *Splitting and Projective Identification* (New York: Jason Aronson, 1981).

12. Klein, "Notes on the Emotional Development of the Infant," *Envy and Gratitude*; Daniel N. Stern, *The Interpersonal World of the Infant: A View from Psychoanalysis and Developmental Psychology* (New York: Basic Books, 1984); Dinnerstein, *The Mermaid and the Minotaur*.

13. Along with Dinnerstein, I am emphasizing that here the split in the infant's mind is not one of normal divisions of good experiences and bad experiences into categories which are manageable, but rather something which is unresolved in the previous generation's unconscious which is passed on to the infant along with the milk.

14. Dinnerstein, *Mermaid*, pp. 202, 205.

15. Ibid., ("The Dirty Goddess"), p. 149.

16. Melanie Klein's theory of manic defenses is germane here. Klein theorized that these defenses are implemented to blot out or cover the feelings of the soft, vulnerable self associated with the experience of evolving separation and lack of security.

17. Thomas H. Ogden, *The Matrix of the Mind: Object Relations and the Psychoanalytic Dialogue* (Northdale, N.J.: Jason Aronson, 1986).

18. Cixous and Clément, *The Newly Born Woman*; Irigaray, *Speculum of the Other Woman*; and Kristeva, "Place Names" and "Motherhood According to Bellini," both in *Desire in Language*.

19. Duchen, *Feminism in France*, pp. 74–75.

20. Jonathan Culler, "Saussure on Deconstruction," *On Deconstruction: Theory*

and Criticism After Structuralism (Ithaca: Cornell University Press, 1983); Duchen, *Feminism in France*. pp. 78–79.

21. Claude Lévi-Strauss, *Overture to the Raw and the Cooked: Structural Anthropology*, tr. Claire Jacobson and Brooke Grundfest Schoepf (London: Allen Lane, 1968).

22. Duchen, *Feminism in France*, p. 78; Jane Gallop and Carolyn Burke, "Psychoanalysis and Feminism in France" see especially Carolyn Burke, "Rethinking the Maternal," in *Making a Difference*, p. 110.

23. Ibid.; Duchen, *Feminism in France*, p. 178.

24. Ibid., pp. 78–79.

25. Ibid., p. 79.

26. D. W. Winnicott, "Transitional Objects and Transitional Phenomena," in *Playing and Reality* (New York: Basic Books, 1971).

27. Donovan, *Feminist Theory*, p. 112; and Burke, "Rethinking the Maternal," p. 111.

28. Jacques Lacan, "The Signification of the Phallus," in *Écrits: A Selection* (London: Tavistock Publications, 1980 [1966]).

29. See Jonathan Culler's "Institutions and Inversions," *On Deconstruction*, pp. 172–73. Culler discusses the critique of logocentrism from within the system itself.

30. Jane Gallop, "Of Phallic Proportions: Lacanian Conceit," in *The Daughter's Seduction*, p. 19.

31. Ibid. (Gallop, quoting from Lacan's *Écrits*).

32. Ibid., p. 22.

33. Ibid., p. 24.

34. See Freud's *Totem and Taboo* and *Civilization and Its Discontents* as examples of this bifurcation.

35. Gallop, "Of Phallic Proportions," p. 27.

36. Gallop quotes from Freud's *Civilization and Its Discontents* to make her argument.

37. Ibid., pp. 27–28.

38. Michelle Montrelay quoted in ibid., pp. 27–28.

39. Ibid., p. 28.

40. Ibid.

41. Ibid., pp. 30–31; Culler, *On Deconstruction*, pp. 58–59.

42. Bice Benvenuto and Roger Kennedy, "The Instance of the Letter," *The Works of Jacques Lacan: An Introduction* (New York: St. Martin's Press, 1986), p. 113.

43. Jacqueline Rose, Introduction II, *Feminine Sexuality*, p. 31.

44. Ibid., p. 40.

45. Culler, *On Deconstruction*.

46. Donovan, "Feminism and Freudianism," *Feminist Theory*, pp. 112–14; and Culler, *On Deconstruction*, p. 172. Culler quotes Derrida's *Avoir L'Oreille de la Philosophies*.

47. Duchen, *Feminism in France*, p. 75.

48. Ann Rosalind Jones, "Inscribing Femininity: French Theories of the Feminine," in *Making a Difference*; Donovan, *Feminist Theory*, pp. 114–16.

49. Jones, "Inscribing Femininity," p. 81; Nellie Furman, "The Politics of Language," p. 75, both in *Making a Difference*.

50. Domna Stanton, "Difference on Trial," in *The Poetics of Gender*, ed. Miller, p. 160; Jones, "Inscribing Femininity," pp. 85–89; Cixous, "Sortie," in *The Newly Born Woman*: Luce Irigaray, "The Mechanics of Fluid," in *The Sex Which Is Not One*, tr. Catherine Porter (Ithaca: Cornell University Press, 1985).

51. Stanton, "Difference on Trial."

52. Ibid.

53. Cited in ibid.

54. Quoted in ibid. Also "Le Corp à corp de la mère," 1981.

55. Stanton, "Language and Revolution," in *The Future of Difference*, ed. Eisenstein and Jardine, p. 74; Duchen, "The Concept of the Feminine," *Feminism in France*, p. 88.

56. Ibid., p. 88.

57. From *The Sex Which Is Not One*; also quoted in Jones, "Inscribing Femininity," p. 84.

58. "And the One Doesn't Stir Without the Other," tr. Helene Vivienne Wenzel, *Signs* 7:1 (1981).

59. Ibid., p. 64.

60. Ibid., p. 67.

61. Jones, "Inscribing Femininity," p. 88.

62. Irigaray, "When Our Lips Speak Together," in *The Sex Which Is Not One*, p. 205.

63. Ibid., p. 209.

64. Ibid., p. 210.

65. Furman, "The Politics of Language," p. 61.

66. Jones, "Inscribing Femininity," p. 88; Cixous quoted in Jones, from Hélène Cixous, 1977, "La Venue à L'Ecriture," with Annie Le Clerc and Madeline Gagnon, Paris.

67. Stanton, "Difference on Trial," p. 65.

68. See Freud's "Feminine Sexuality" (1931), S.E., vol. 21.

69. Stanton, "Difference on Trial," p. 165.

70. Cixous, "Illa," 1980, quoted in ibid.

71. Ibid. and Duchen, *Feminism in France*, pp. 88–89.

72. Cixous, "Sortie," p. 93; and Stanton, "Difference on Trial," p. 167.

73. "Sortie," p. 93.

74. Stanton, "Difference on Trial," p. 168.

75. K. K. Ruthven makes the distinction between Kristeva's *le sémiotique* (baby talk) and *la sémiotique* (semiotics) in *Feminist Literary Studies* (London: Cambridge University Press, 1984), p. 98.

76. Stanton, "Difference on Trial," p. 166; Burke, "Rethinking the Maternal," p. 111; Mary Jacobus, "Dora and the Pregnant Madonna," *Reading Women*, p. 148.

77. Alfred Silver, *The Oedipal Structure of Signs*, unpublished paper. Silver explores C. S. Peirce's theory of signs as moving from the concrete to the abstract through three main phases.

78. Julia Kristeva, *Revolution in Poetic Language*, intro. by Leon S. Roudiez, tr. Margaret Waller (New York: Columbia University Press, 1984), pp. 25, 78–79; Kristeva, "Place Names," pp. 276–77; Gallop, "The Phallic Mother: Fraudian Analysis," *The Daughter's Seduction*, p. 125.

79. Kristeva, "Place Names," p. 276.

80. Kristeva, *Powers of Horror*.

81. Ibid., pp. 12–13.

82. Kristeva, "Motherhood According to Bellini," *Desire in Language*, p. 238.

83. See Mary Jacobus's splendid essay, "Dora and the Pregnant Madonna," especially p. 168. She quotes from Kristeva's "Héréthique de la Mor" (*Tel Quel*, Winter 1977).

84. Mary Daily, *Inventing Motherhood: The Consequences of an Ideal* (London: Burnett Books Ltd., 1982), pp. 25–26; Philippe Ariés, *Centuries of Childhood* (New York: Vintage Books, 1963); and Lloyd DeMause, "The Evolution of Childhood," in *The Foundations of Psychohistory* (New York: Creative Roots, Inc., 1982).

85. Daily, "Death and Motherhood," *Inventing Motherhood*, p. 26.

86. Ibid., p. 27.

87. DeMause, "Evolution," pp. 16, 26–27, 25–28; Daily, *Inventing Motherhood*, p. 5.

88. DeMause, "Evolution," pp. 35–38.

89. Ariés, Centuries of Childhood.

90. Stern, The Interpersonal World of the Infant; Frances Tustin, Autistic Barriers in Neurotic Patients (London: Karnac, 1986); and Robert M. Emde, "The Affective Self and Transformations in Infancy" in Frontiers in Infant Psychiatry, ed. Justin E. Call, Eleanor Galenson, and Robert L. Tyson (New York: Basic Books, 1983); Emde, "Levels of Meaning for Infant Emotion: A Biosocial View," in Development of Cognition, Affect, and Social Relations, ed. W. A. Collins (Hillsdale, N.J.: Analytic Press, 1980); Virginia Demos, "Empathy and Affect: Reflections on Infant Experience," in Empathy, ed. J. Lichtenberg, M. Bernstein, and J. Silver (Hillsdale, N.J.: Analytic Press, 1985).

91. Robert D. Stolorow, Bernard Brandchaft, and George Atwood, Psychoanalytic Treatment: An Intersubjective Approach (Hillsdale, N.J.: Analytic Press, 1987), see especially "Bonds that Shackle, Ties That Free"; Bion, "Theory of Thinking," in Second Thoughts, and Elements of Psychoanalysis, in Seven Servants (New York: Jason Aronson, 1977); and D. W. Winnicott, Babies and Mothers, Introduction by Benjamin Spock, ed. Clare Winnicott, Ray Shepherd, and Madeline Davis (Reading, Mass.: Addison-Wesley Publishing Company, 1987).

92. Melanie Klein, "The Development of the Child" [1921], "Symposium on Child Analysis" [1927], "Early Stages of the Oedipus Conflict" [1928], "Personification in the Play of Children" [1929], "The Importance of Symbol Formation in the Development of the Ego" [1930], "The Early Development of Conscience in the Child" [1933], "Love, Guilt and Reparation" [1937], and "The Oedipus Complex in the Light of Early Anxieties [1945], all in Love, Guilt, and Reparation and Other Works 1921–1945 (New York: Delta Books, 1975). Also see "Notes on Some Schizoid Mechanisms" [1946], "Some Theoretical Conclusions Regarding the Emotional Life of the Infant" [1952], "On Observing the Behavior of Young Infants" [1952], "Envy and Gratitude" [1957], "Our Adult World and Its Roots in Infancy [1959], all in Envy and Gratitude and Other Works 1946–1963.

93. Phyllis Groskruth, The Life of Melanie Klein (New York: Knopf, 1986).

94. Sigmund Freud, Three Essays on the Theory of Sexuality (1905), S.E., vol. 7, The Introductory Lectures 1916–1917, S.E., vol. 16, pp. 370–71, and Totem and Taboo (1913), S.E., vol. 14.

95. See, for example, Klein, "Some Theoretical Notes Regarding the Emotional Development of the Infant" and "Schizoid Mechanisms."

96. Ibid.

97. See Ogden, The Matrix of the Mind.

98. Bion, "Theory of Thinking" and Learning from Experience (Seven Servants).

99. Didier Anzieu, Freud's Self-Analysis, tr. Peter Graham (Madison, Conn.: International University Press, 1986).

100. Ogden, The Matrix of the Mind, p. 33.

101. Kristeva, "Motherhood According to Bellini" and Powers of Horror.

102. Bion, Learning from Experience; James Grotstein, "The Borderline as a Disorder of Self-Regulation," with an additional contribution by Pamela Scavio, The Borderline Patient, Vol. 1, ed. James S. Grotstein, Marion F. Solomon, and Joan A. Lang (Hillsdale, N.J.: Analytic Press, 1987).

103. See, for example, Stern, The Interpersonal World of the Infant, pp. 47–48, in which he cites the cross-modal studies of Melzoff and Boston, 1979.

104. Stern, Interpersonal World, cites Stern (1978), Casper (1980), and Burn (1984.)

105. Stern, Interpersonal World, p. 21. Stern cites Allen et al. (1977), and De May et al. (1977).

106. Stern, Interpersonal World, p. 27.

107. James S. Grotstein, "The Psychology of Powerlessness: Disorders of Self-

Regulation and Interactional Regulation as a Newer Paradigm for Psychopathology," *Psychoanalytic Inquiry* 6:1, pp. 104–105.

2. THE MYTHOLOGY AND SEMIOTICS OF FAMILIAL BONDS

1. W. R. Bion, "Theory of Thinking," in *Second Thoughts* (New York: Jason Aronson, 1967), and *Elements of Psychoanalysis*, in *Seven Servants* (New York: Jason Aronson, 1977). Bion proposed that thoughts evolved from unmentalized mental elements to abstract symbolic sign systems. Also see his grid.

2. Sigmund Freud, *Interpretation of Dreams* (1901), chapters 2, 5, 6, a 7, *S.E.*, vols. 4 and 5.

3. *The Works of Jacques Lacan: An Introduction* by Bice Benvenuto and Roger Kennedy, pp. 110–14.

4. See, for example, Joseph Campbell, *The Flight of the Wild Gander* (New York: Gateway Edition, 1951), pp. 106–137. Campbell cites breastlike objects out of which the jaw of a huge boar protrudes, or an object shaped as two griffin vultures sealed within a pair of breasts with the beaks protruding from the open, red-painted nipples. These objects suggest a myth of the mother who eats back her young. These objects are from 6200 B.C. at Çatal Hüyük.

Lloyd DeMause, in his article "The Fetal Origins of History," in *The Foundations of Psychohistory* (New York: Creative Roots, Inc., 1982), suggests the presence of mother-child relationships in the cave paintings at Lasceaux. The presence of these objects is the effort to signify the drama of the family from the earliest origins of culture.

5. Bion, *Elements of Psychoanalysis*. Bion substitutes emotional linkages for libidinal cathexis as Fairbairn had before him. Bion understands the links as made up of varying emotional colors and functions—the link K signifies the search for knowledge; L, loving ties and needs; and H, hate or defense against an unpleasing or dangerous object relationship.

6. See Joseph Campbell, *The Masks of God: Primitive Mythology* (New York: Penguin Books, 1959), p. 63.

7. Nellie Furman, "The Politics of Language: Beyond the Gender Principle?," in *Making a Difference: Feminist Literary Criticism*, ed. Gayle Green and Coppelia Kahn (New York: Methuen, 1985), pp. 60–61.

8. Didier Anzieu, *Freud's Self-Analysis* tr. Peter Graham (Madison, Conn.: International University Press, 1986). See especially "The Discovery of the Oedipus Complex" and "The Discovery of the Primal Scene."

9. Helen Bacon, "Woman's Two Faces: Sophocles' View of the Tragedy of Oedipus and His Family," *Science and Psychoanalysis, Vol. X: Sexuality of Women* (New York: Grune & Stratton, 1966).

10. Campbell, *Primitive Mythology*, p. 66.

11. Christine Downing, *The Goddess: Mythological Images of the Feminine* (New York: Crossroad, 1), p. 12.

12. Ibid., p. 21.

13. Charlene Spretnack, *The Lost Goddesses of Early Greece: A Collection of Pre-Hellenic Myths* (Boston: Beacon Press, 1978).

14. Jane Ellen Harrison, *Themis* (Cleveland: World Publishing Co., 1962 [1912]), pp. 522–23, 480.

15. Ibid., pp. 494–96.

16. Ibid., p. 500.

17. Ibid., p. 501.

18. Campbell, *The Flight of the Wild Gander*, pp. 51–52.

19. D. W. Winnicott, *Playing and Reality* (New York: Basic Books, 1971). Winnicott suggests that transitional objects and phenomena take place in the interface between the mother and the child and between me and not-me, and also function as an illusion of an overlap between their two bodies which protects the infant from jarring awareness of post-natal experience.

20. Campbell, *The Flight of the Wild Gander*, pp. 53 and 59, and Bion, "Theory of Thinking."

21. Bion, "Theory of Thinking" and *Learning from Experience* (*Seven Servants*).

22. Campbell, *Primitive Mythology*, p. 48.

23. Campbell, *The Flight of the Wild Gander*, p. 108.

24. Ibid., p. 70.

25. I am using sublimation not in the traditional way that Freud has used it, as a reasonable channel for instinctual desire, but in the sense of Julia Kristeva's notion that sublimation is a way of transforming powerful preverbal experience which cannot ever be fully put into words, but is somehow transformed into some structure which partly integrates it into the conscious part of the personality.

26. James S. Grotstein, *The Sins of the Fathers: Human Sacrifice from the Social Perspective of the Oedipal Complex*, pp. 36–37. Manuscript submitted for publication.

27. Ibid.

28. Geza Roheim, *The Riddle of the Sphinx*, tr. Money-Kyrle (New York: Harper Torchbooks, 1974).

29. Ibid., p. 1; Grotstein, *The Sins of the Fathers*, section on the Sphinx.

30. Roheim, *Riddle*, p. 1.

31. Freud, "The Schreber Case" (1911), *S.E.*, vol. 12; Bion, "Differentiation Between Psychotic and Non-Psychotic Personalities," in *Second Thoughts*; Frances Tustin, *Autistic Barriers in Neurotic Patients* (London: Karnac, 1986); James S. Grotstein, "The Borderline as a Disorder of Self-Regulation," in *The Borderline Patient: Emerging Concepts in Diagnosis, Psychodynamics, and Treatment*, ed. James S. Grotstein, Marion F. Solomon, and Joan A. Lang (Hillsdale, N.J.: Analytic Press, 1987).

32. Melanie Klein, *The Psychoanalysis of Children* (New York: Delta Books, 1975); and Klein, "On Observing the Behavior of Young Infants" (1952) in *Envy and Gratitude* (New York: Delta, 1967).

33. Grotstein, *The Sins of the Fathers*; and Roheim, *The Riddle of the Sphinx*.

34. Bion, "Theory of Thinking." Bion proposes in this paper that, in the absence of the maternal container, the infant's particles of experience are dashed against an impervious maternal mind, and are felt to be hurled back at the infant at increasing speeds, rather than contained and signified. He explains that this is an important element in the etiology of psychosis.

35. Janine Chasseguet-Smirgel, "Perversion and the Universal Law," in *Creativity and Perversion*, foreword by Otto Kernberg (London: Free Association Books, 1985); Peter L. Rudnytsky, *Freud and Oedipus* (New York: Columbia University Press, 1987). Rudnytsky explains that many important figures in nineteenth-century Europe, such as Schiller, Hegel, and Nietzsche were compelled by Sophocles' Oedipus trilogy. He proposes that the dual nature of Oedipus's internal and external experiences intrigued these major thinkers as they increasingly perceived the complex layers of the mind, especially the double nature of consciousness.

36. Anzieu, *Freud's Self-Analysis*, p. 247.

37. By signification processes, I have in mind signification in the sense of the capacity of the mind to give meaning to experience through the relationships of signifiers in their metaphoric and metonymic relationship. I'm using symbols as an entity which gathers together many meanings (many signifiers) and condenses them into one structure.

38. Freud, *Interpretation of Dreams*, p. 255.

39. Ibid., pp. 260–61.

40. Ibid., p. 261.
41. Ibid., p. 263.
42. Ibid., p. 256.
43. Freud, *Psychopathology of Everyday Life* (1901), *S.E.*, vol. 6. p. 218.
44. *Moses and Monotheism* (1939), *S.E.*, vol. 23, p. 114.
45. Freud, *Interpretation of Dreams*, pp. 263–64.
46. Freud, *Moses and Monotheism*, p. 89.
47. Paul Ricoeur, *Freud and Philosophy* (New Haven: Yale University Press, 1970), p. 6.
48. Ibid., p. 22.
49. Freud, "Some Psychical Consequences of the Anatomical Distinction Between the Sexes" (1925), *S.E.*, vol. 19; "The Dissolution of the Oedipus Complex" (1924), *S.E.*, vol. 19; and "Feminine Sexuality" (1931), *S.E.*, Vol. 21.
50. Carl Schorske, *Fin-de-Siècle Vienna: Politics and Culture* (New York: Vintage Books, 1981 [1961]); Peter Gay, *A Life for Our Time* (New York: Norton Books, 1988).
51. Schorske, *Fin-de-Siècle Vienna*; Meltzer's article on Bion, "The Reversal of Alpha Function" in *The Kleinian Development* (Perthshire: Clunie Press, 1978); Bion, "Differentiation Between the Psychotic and Non-Psychotic Personalities," in *Second Thoughts*; and Grotstein, "A Proposed Revision of the Psychoanalytic Concept of Primitive Mental States, Part I," *Contmporary Psychoanalysis* 16, (Nov. 1980), *Journal of the Willian Alanson White Society*.
52. Schorske, *Fin-de-Siècle Vienna*, pp. 227–28.
53. Ibid., pp. 221–28.
54. Freud, *Interpretation of Dreams*.
55. Ibid., p. 169.
56. Ibid., pp. 170–71.
57. Ibid., pp. 171–72.
58. Anzieu, *Freud's Self-Analysis*, p. 287.
59. Freud, *Interpretation of Dreams*, p. 172.
60. Anzieu, *Freud's Self-Analysis*, pp. 286–88.
61. Freud, *Interpretaion of Dreams*, p. 173.
62. Anzieu, *Freud's Self-Analysis*, p. 288.
63. Heinz Kohut, *The Analysis of the Self* (New York: International University Press, 1971). Kohut's notion of the idealizing and mirroring transferences are germane here toward understanding Freud's need for recognition.
64. Freud, Chapter 5: "The Material and Sources of Dreams," *Interpretation of Dreams*.
65. Freud, Chapter 2: "An Analysis of a Specimen Dream," *Interpretation of Dreams*.
66. Anzieu, *Freud's Self-Analysis*, p. 173.
67. See for example, Thomas Mann, *The Magic Mountain*, and Friedrich Nietzsche, *Beyond Good and Evil* and *The Birth of Tragedy*. Mann and Nietzsche also probed the experiences of living in a culture which was losing its belief system.
68. Freud, Chapter 2: "An Analysis of a Specimen Dream," *Interpretation of Dreams*.
69. See June Rachuy Brindel, *Ariadne* (New York: St. Martin's Press, 1980); Harrison, *Themis*; Downing, *The Goddess*; and Robert Graves, *The White Goddess* (New York: Farrar, Straus & Giroux, 1948).
70. See Michael Waltzer, *Revolution of the Saints* (Cambridge: Harvard University Press, 1965); Schorske, *Fin-de-Siècle Vienna*; and Peter Gay, *The Bourgeois Experience* (New York: Oxford University Press, 1984).
71. See Klimt's paintings "Pallas Athena" and "Judith and the Water Snakes."
72. Sigmund Freud, *The Theme of the Three Caskets* [1913], *S.E.*, vol. 13.

73. Ibid., p. 291.
74. Ibid., p. 301.
75. Sophocles, *Oedipus Rex*.
76. Oedipus would surely have died had it not been for the compassion of the shepherd.
77. James S. Grotstein, "A Proposed Revision for the Psychoanalytic Concept of the Death Instinct," *The Year Book of Psychoanalytic Psychotherapy*, ed. Robert J. Langs (Hilldale, N.J.: Analytic Press, 1986).
78. Ibid. Grotstein draws on Lorenz and Tinbergen to emphasize that in humans, adaptive patterns are species-typical, and as such are subject to modification. This modification suggests the possibility of various realizations in Bion's sense of the term.
79. Grotstein suggests, drawing on the theories of John Bowlby, that without a sense of bonding, the infant's warning system is overstimulated. Tustin also explains that children without comforting mental attachment feel themselves to be prey to an infinite number of possibilities of horrendous danger.
80. Grotstein, "Death Instinct."
81. See Melanie Klein, "Notes on the Emotional Development of the Infant," *Envy and Gratitude* (1956) and her "Stages of the Early Oedipus Complex" (1928), *Love, Guilt, and Reparation*.
82. Freud, *Moses and Monotheism*, pp. 10–11.
83. Ibid., p. 11.
84. Ibid., p. 12.
85. Julia Kristeva, "Place Names," *Desire in Language* (Oxford: Basil Blackwell, 1980); Susanne K. Langer, *Feeling and Form: A Theory of Art Developed From Philosophy in a New Key, Part II: The Making of a Symbol* (New York: Charles Scribner's Sons, 1953); Jacques Lacan, "The Signification of the Phallus," *Écrits: A Selection*; Frances Tustin, "The Threat of Dissolution," Proceedings of Conference "Transformation in Psychoanalysis: The Uses of Interpretation in the Clinical Setting and in the Arts, Humanities, and Social Services," presented by the Psychoanalytic Center of California in association with the Department of Psychoanalysis, California Graduate Institute, March 1984.
86. The mythic figure Hainuwele is taken up by Campbell in *Primitive Mythology*, pp. 182–90. It is a myth from a cannibal culture of West Cerum near New Guinea.
87. Ibid., p. 177.
88. Ibid., pp. 176–77.
89. Ibid., p. 188.
90. Ibid., "The Imprints of Experiences," pp. 81–118. DeMause, "The Fetal Origins of History," p. 283.
91. DeMause, "Fetal Origins of History," p. 283, and Campbell, *Primitive Mythology*, pp. 370 and 372.
92. DeMause, "Fetal Origins of History," p. 283. Campbell, *Primitive Mythology*, pp. 370–72. Michelle Zimbalist Rosaldo, "Women, Culture, and Society: A Theoretical Overview"; Nancy Chodorow, "Family Structure and Feminine Personality,"; Sherry B. Ortner, "Is Female to Male as Nature is to Culture?"; and Joan Bamberger, "The Myth of Matriarchy: Why Men Rule in Primitive Society"; all in *Women, Culture, and Society*, ed. Michelle Zimbalist Rosaldo and Louise Lamphere, Stanford University Press, 1974). Patricia Meyer Spacks, *The Adolescent Idea* (New York: Basic Books, 1981).
93. Mariette Nowak, *Eve's Web: A Revolutionary New View of the Female* (New York: St. Martin's Press, 1980), Chapter 5: "A New Perspective," pp. 121–24.
94. See ibid. and Peggy R. Sanday, "Female Status in the Public Domain," in *Women, Culture, and Society*.

95. Joseph Campbell, *The Masks of God: Occidental Mythology* (New York: Penguin Books, 1964), p. 22.

96. Ibid., p. 22.

97. Klein, "Early Stages of the Oedipus Complex" (1928) in *Love, Guilt, and Reparation*.

98. Freud, "Instincts and Their Vicissitudes" and "On Narcissism"; Klein, "Envy and Gratitude" and "Notes on the Emotional Development of the Infant."

99. Klein theorized that a series of primitive defenses and anxieties were organized in what she called the paranoid-schizoid position in which splitting and manic denial were paramount. This was followed by the onset of a different kind of cluster of phantasies and thoughts called the depressive position in which splitting and omnipotence were not as paramount and were replaced by a sense of reality and a sense of compassion toward whole separate objects.

100. Bion was a distinguished psychoanalyst, practitioner, and theoretician writing up through the 70s. He died in 1980.

101. Bion, "Theory of Thinking," *Learning From Experience* [1962], *Transformations* [1965], *Attention and Interpretation* [1970], in *Seven Servants*; and *Memoir of the Future* (Rio de Janeiro: Imago Editoria Ltd., 1975), ed. Jayme Salomao.

102. Bion, "Theory of Thinking" and *Learning from Experience*. Alpha function is somewhat equivalent to primary process, though Bion emphasizes its capacity to organize meaning rather than its capacity to find discharge.

103. See, for example, John Bowlby, *Attachment and Loss*, vol. 1 (New York: Basic Books, 1969), especially "The Child's Tie to the Mother."

104. Bion, *Learning From Experience*, *Elements of Psychoanalysis*, and *Transformations*.

105. Bion, *Elements of Psychoanalysis*, p. 92.

106. Alfred Silver, "The Oedipal Structures of Thought" (unpublished paper); and Claude Lévi-Strauss, "The Structure of Myths," *Structural Anthropology* (New York: Basic Books, 1963).

107. Ibid. Lévi-Strauss explains that myths function like the rest of language, through the relations of constituent units.

108. Lévi-Strauss, "Overture" to *The Raw and the Cooked*.

109. Ibid., p. 18.

110. Lévi-Strauss, "Structural Study of Myth," pp. 213–15.

111. Ibid., p. 215.

112. Many of these ideas are inspired by Michael Paul, "A Mental Atlas of the Process of Psychological Birth," in *Do I Dare Disturb the Universe?* ed. James S. Grotstein (Beverly Hills: Caesura Press, 1981). Paul posits the existence of an encapsulated fetal aspect of the mind which has not yet experienced birth and which does not participate in ordinary existence. This aspect is unable to understand feeling or thinking, much like the "savage," who is unable to understand the function of a street sign, let alone read its letters. Paul discusses the myth of Palinurus as an exemplum of the unborn self's desire to sleep.

113. Lévi-Strauss, "Structural Study of Myth," p. 216.

114. Julia Kristeva, *Powers of Horror* (New York: Columbia University Press, 1982). Kristeva defines the abject as that which cannot be tolerated as being inferior or sordid, or so unclean that it is unbearable. Jacques Derrida and many of the French feminists have argued with Lacan's notion of the transcendental signifier as the logic that perpetuates a kind of disavowal of unbearable states of mind.

115. Frances Tustin, "Psychological Birth and Psychological Catastrophe," *Autistic States in Children* (London: Routledge & Kegan Paul, 1982).

116. Melanie Klein, "The Importance of Symbol-Formation in the Development of the Ego (1930), in *Love, Guilt and Reparation*; and Hanna Segal, "Notes on Symbol Formation" (1957), *International Journal of Psycho-Analysis* 38, pp. 391–97.

117. Alfred Silver, "A Psychosemiotic Model: An Interdisciplinary Search for a Common Structural Basis for Psychoanalysis, Symbol Formation, and the Semiotic of Charles S. Peirce," in *Do I Dare Disturb the Universe?*

118. These ideas are from Alfred Silver's important article "The Psychoanalytic Semiotic and the Oedipal Structure of Thought" (unpublished) and "A Psychosemiotic Model."

119. Grotstein, "A Proposed Revision of the Psychoanalytic Concept of Primitive Mental States, Part I."

120. Silver, "A Psychosemiotic Model," pp. 290–92. Silver argues that this fore-knowing is necessary so the sign can know what to point to in order to represent an object to an interpreter.

121. See Pierre Guirad, "Significant Form and Substance of the Sign," *Semiology* (1975):26. Guirad says that while personal motivation does not exclude convention, it tends to free the sign from content, as in a poetic system.

122. Silver, "A Psychosemiotic Model," p. 283.

123. Melanie Klein, "Notes on the Emotional Development of the Infant" and "On Identification" in *Envy and Gratitude*.

124. Bion, *Attention and Interpretation.*

125. Melanie Klein, "Some Reflections on the Orestia," in *Envy and Gratitude*, and Langer, *Feeling and Form.*

126. Grotstein, "A Proposed Revision of the Psychoanalytic Concept of Primitive Mental States, Part I"; Tustin, "Psychological Birth and Psychological Catastrophe," *Autistic States in Children*; Tustin, *Autism and Child Psychosis* (London: Science House, 1972); Donald Meltzer, *Explorations in Autism* (Perthshire: Clunie Press, 1975); and Esther Bick, "The Experience of Skin in Early Object Relations," *International Journal of Psychoanalysis (London)* 49, pp. 484–86. These authors have termed this stage the stage of adhesive identification, in which the infant's sense of mental skin boundary (a sense of inside and outside, hence the formation of the early self) is nurtured by skin-to-skin contact.

127. See Tustin's "Autistic Objects" and "Confusional Objects" in *Autistic States in Children* for a phenomenological approach to these early experiences.

128. Winnicott's notion of the environmental mother in "Transitional Objects and Transitional Phenomena," *Playing and Reality* and Bion's notion of the container-contained explore the mental processes of early bonding. Also see Robert M. Emde, "Development Terminable and Interminable, Part I: Innate and Motivational Factors from Infancy," *International Journal of Psychoanalysis* 69 (1986), pp. 23–42; and Jacqueline Rabain-Jamin, "Survey of the Infant's 'Sound Envelope' and Organization of Parent-Child Communication," in *Frontiers of Infant Psychiatry*, ed. Justin D. McCall, Eleanor Galenson, and Robert L. Tyson (New York: Basic Books, 1984).

129. John Bowlby, "The Nature of the Child's Tie to the Mother," *International Journal of Psychoanalysis* (1958), pp. 35–36; Justin D. McCall, "From Early Patterns of Communication to the Grammar of Experience and Syntax and Infancy," *Frontiers of Infant Psychiatry.*

130. Kohut, *Analysis of the Self; Advances in Self Psychology*, ed. Arnold Goldberg, (New York: International University Press, 1980); Pauline F. Kernberg, "Reflections in the Mirror," "Mother-Child Interactions," "Self-Awareness and Self-Recognition," in *Frontiers in Infant Psychiatry.*

131. Grotstein, "A Proposed Revision of the Psychoanalytic Concept of Primitive Mental States, Part I," and "Who is the Dreamer Who Dreams the Dream?" in *Do I Dare Disturb the Universe?* Grotstein has termed this monumental selfobject the subject or object of primary identification, or the background presence. He suggests that at-one-ment experiences grow from the infant's experience with the powerful holding mother (father).

132. Grotstein, "A Proposed Revision of the Psychoanalytic Concept of Primitive Mental States, Part II," *Contemporary Psychoanalysis* 19:4 (October 1983).
133. Alfred Silver, "The Psychoanalytic Structure of Thought"; and Bion, *Learning from Experience* and *Transformations*.
134. Winnicott, Lacan, and Kohut.
135. In this sense, the Oedipus complex begins in the earliest weeks of life and involves difficulty in bonding. See Melanie Klein, "Early Stages of the Oedipus Complex," [1928] in *Love, Guilt, and Reparation*. This is further elaborated by W. R. Bion, Hanna Segal, Donald Meltzer, and James Grotstein.
136. Tustin, *Autistic States in Children*, pp. 6–8.
137. Silver, "Oedipal Structures of Thought."
138. Secondness denotes a beginning to tolerate the space between the self and the other; although the concept of two is still incipient. Thirdness is a concept which designates the ability to tolerate signification; in other words, the sign of the interpretant-object relationship.

3. *UNCLE TOM'S CABIN:* A MYTH OF
FAMILIAL RELATIONS

1. Constance Rourke, *Trumpets of Jubilee* (New York: Harcourt, Brace & Co., 1963 [1927]), and Charles Edward Stowe, *Life of Harriet Beecher Stowe: Compiled From Her Letters and Diaries* (Boston: Houghton Mifflin & Co., 1889).
2. For a superb discussion of language and writing as a continuation of the male domain, see Nellie Furman, "Textual Feminism," in *Women and Language in Literature and Society*, ed. Sally McConnell-Ginet, Ruth Borke, and Nellie Furman, (New York: Praeger, 1980); Nellie Furman, "The Politics of Language: Beyond the Gender Principle?" in *Making a Difference: Feminist Literary Criticism*, ed. Gayle Green and Coppelia Kahn (New York: Methuen, 1985).
3. See Edmund Morgan, *The Puritan Family* (New York: Harper & Row, 1966 [1944]); John Demos, *A Little Commonwealth: Family Life in Plymouth Colony* (London: Oxford University Press, 1970); and Joseph Kett, *The Rights of Passage: Adolescence in America 1970 to the Present* (New York: Basic Books, 1977).
4. See, e.g., Henry James, *Daisy Miller* and *Portrait of a Lady*; Edith Wharton, *House of Mirth* or *The Mother*; Kate Chopin, *The Awakening*; Nathaniel Hawthorne, *The Scarlet Letter*; Willa Cather, *My Antonia*; Herman Melville, *Pierre*; Mark Twain, *Tom Sawyer*; F. Scott Fitzgerald, *The Beautiful and the Damned* and *The Great Gatsby*; Eugene O'Neill, *Desire Under the Elms* and *Mourning Becomes Electra*; and Arthur Miller, *Death of a Salesman*.
5. Elaine Showalter, "Introduction: The Feminist Critical Revolution" in *Feminist Criticism: Essays on Women, Literature, Theory* (New York: Pantheon Books, 1985), and *A Literature of Their Own: British Women Novelists from Bronte to Lessing* (Princeton: Princeton University Press, 1977); Ellen Moers, *Literary Women: The Great Writers* (Garden City, N.Y.: Doubleday, 1976); Adrienne Rich, "When We Dead Awaken: Writing as Revision," *College English* 34 (October 1972); Annette Kolodny, "Dancing Through the Minefield: Some Observations on the Theory, Practice and Politics of a Feminist Literary Criticism" in *Feminist Criticism*; Nellie Furman, "The Politics of Language"; Peggy Kamuf, "Writing Like a Woman," in *Woman and Language in Literature and Society*; Sandra M. Gilbert and Susan Gubar, *The Madwoman in the Attic: The Woman Writer and the Nineteenth Century Literary Imagination* (New Haven: Yale University Press, 1979); Mary Jacobus, "Is There a Woman in the Text?" in *Reading Women: Essays in Feminist Criticism* (New York: Columbia University Press, 1981); and Tillie Olsen, *Silences* (New York: Delta/Seymour Lawrence, 1965).
6. E.g., Henry Nash Smith, *The Myth of the Garden* (David Noble); Leo Marx,

The Machine in the Garden: Technology and the Pastoral Ideal in America (New York: Oxford University Press, 1964); and Alexis de Tocqueville, *Democracy in America* (New York: Vintage Books, 1945).

7. D. W. Winnicott, "Ego Distortion in Terms of a True and False Self" (1960), *The Maturational Processes and the Facilitating Environment* (London: Hogarth Press, 1965).

8. Louisa May Alcott, *Behind a Mask: The Unknown Thrillers of Louisa May Alcott*, intro. by Madeline Stern (New York: William Morrow & Co., Inc., 1975) and *Plots and Counterplots: More Unknown Thrillers of Louisa May Alcott*, intro. by Madeline Stern (New York: William Morrow & Co., Inc., 1976). See also Gilbert and Gubar, *The Madwoman in the Attic*.

9. See Carl Schorske, *Fin-de-Siècle Vienna: Politics and Culture* (New York: Vintage Books, 1981 [1961]) for a splendid analysis of the loss of authority and stability in turn-of-the-century Europe.

10. W. R. Bion, "Theory of Thinking," in *Second Thoughts* (New York: Jason Aronson, 1967); James S. Grotstein, "Who is the Dreamer Who Dreams the Dream," in *Do I Dare Disturb the Universe?* (Beverly Hills: Caesura Press, 1981). Bion and Grotstein emphasize the birth of meaning or the processes of signification that function through the mating of a preconception with a realization. The realization births new meaning or aborts it according to the subject's ability to withstand the turbulence of change and the psychic pain of growth.

11. The serial was called *Uncle Tom's Cabin, or The Man That Was a Thing*.

12. Jane P. Thompkins, "Sentimental Power: Uncle Tom's Cabin and the Politics of Literary History" in *Feminist Criticism*.

13. Ellen Moers, *Harriet Beecher Stowe and American Literature* (Hartford, Conn.: Stowe-Day Foundation, 1978), p. 3.

14. Moody E. Pryor, "Mrs. Stowe's Uncle Tom," *Critical Inquiry* 5 (Summer 1975), p. 635.

15. Edmund Wilson, "Harriet Beecher Stowe," in *Patriotic Gore* (New York: Oxford University Press, 1954), p. 117.

16. Harriet Beecher Stowe, *Uncle Tom's Cabin* (New York: New American Library, 1966 [1855]), pp. 24–28.

17. Ibid., p. 29.

18. Ibid., p. 26.

19. Ibid., p. 125.

20. Ibid., p. 19.

21. Bion, "Theory of Thinking," *Second Thoughts*, and *Learning From Experience*, in *Seven Servants* (New York: Jason Aronson, 1977). Bion defines concept in the special sense of a cognitive structure which properly or improperly signifies emotional experience. Concept in this sense names and carries emotional meaning. Kristeva uses the thetic in this way.

22. See an analysis of the universal tendency towards separating public and private by Sherry Ortner in "Is Female to Male as Nature is to Culture," in *Woman, Culture, and Society*, ed. Michelle Zimbalist Rosaldo and Louise Lamphere (Stanford: Stanford University Press, 1974).

23. Stowe, *Uncle Tom's Cabin*, p. 75.

24. The second level of the myth combines aspects of the cultural customs and the workings of the unconscious.

25. Stowe, *Uncle Tom's Cabin*, p. 66.

26. Joseph Campbell, *The Masks of God: Occidental Mythology*, (New York: Penguin Books, 1964), pp. 27–28.

27. Ibid., p. 158.

28. Melanie Klein proposed that the ego's capacity to integrate the polar opposites of experience is the mark of maturity and sanity.

29. Studies of ancient culture inform us of the repeated effort to disavow vulnerability and mortality by disavowing the infant-mother (father) experience. See Robert Graves, *Greek Myths I and II* (New York: Penguin Books, 1955) and Joseph Campbell, *The Masks of God: Occidental Mythology* and *The Masks of God: Primitive Mythology* (New York: Penguin Books, 1959).

30. George Atwood, and Robert D. Stolorow, *Structures of Subjectivity: Explorations in Psychoanalytic Phenomenology* (Hillsdale, N.J.: Analytic Press, 1984). Atwood and Stolorow posit that the self develops out of the phenomenology of infant-mother interactions. They state: "From the perspective of psychoanalytic phenomenology personality structure is the structure of a person's experiencing." Thus the basic units of personality are *structures of experiences*, the distinctive configurations of self and object that shape and organize a person's subjective world (p. 33).

31. Stowe, *Uncle Tom's Cabin*, p. 30. Elaine Showalter, "Piecing and Writing," *The Poetics of Gender*, ed. Nancy Kay Miller (New York: Columbia University Press, 1986). Showalter interprets *Uncle Tom's Cabin* as an allusion within the referential system of women's culture to the log cabin quilt—itself a creative sign of women's internal and external world (pp. 234–35).

32. Stowe, *Uncle Tom's Cabin*, p. 31.

33. Ibid., p. 149.

34. Michael Waltzer, *Revolution of the Saints* (Cambridge: Harvard University Press, 1965).

35. Bion, "Theory of Thinking," and *Learning from Experience*. See footnote #21 above.

36. All of these cultural processes define men as well, but their situation requires an entirely different analysis.

37. Stowe, *Uncle Tom's Cabin*, p. 156.

38. Ibid., p. 151.

39. I have put "male" in quotes because I am discussing cultural sign systems. Furthermore, the complex interaction between mothers and children suggests that "male" is a product of male and female minds.

40. In "Reading Reading: Echoes Abduction of Language" in *Women and Language in Literature and Society*, Caren Greenberg makes the argument that the Oedipal myth is useful only for discussion of male sexuality and development. She suggests that the elements of the myth which provide a map for reading the male odyssey denies the importance of women. Mother is structured into the myth as the text or as the mark of incest and parricide. Jocasta is a female figure onto whom men write meaning. For example, Laius is author of the text Jocasta. He provides her meaning as "she whom one must marry in order to become King" and "she who could render love making incestuous" (pp. 302–303). Or women acquire meaning only as the symbol of the father's power. In this way, Greenberg argues woman is the text in the Oedipus myth. Within this situation women like language have no intrinsic value and gain importance only as they signify something other than themselves.

While I agree that the women of the manifest Oedipus myth are intermediary figures acted upon by men, the decoding of the figures of the Sphinx and Jocasta reveals a mutation and a distortion of female or maternal potency and a radical splitting off of the first birth, out of mother's body and its significance as a signifier of the relationship between the infant and the body mother. In this context the manifest Oedipus myth is an artifact of splitting.

41. See Jane Ellen Harrison, *Themis* (Cleveland: World Publishing Co., 1962 [1912]), pp. 16–20.

42. Helen Bacon, "Woman's Two Faces," *Science and Psychoanalysis, Vol. X; Sexuality of Women* (New York: Grune & Stratton, 1966).

43. Ariés's discussion of the discovery of childhood and DeMause's theory of

the evolution of childhood also suggest the surfacing of new concepts and feelings involving parent child affective relations.

44. For women's response, see Harriet Beecher Stowe, *The Minister's Wooing* and *Dread*. See also Edith Wharton, *The House of Mirth*, *The Custom of the Country*, *The Mother's Recompense*, and *The Age of Innocence*; and Willa Cather, *My Antonia* and *Oh Pioneers!* For a discussion of the English dilemma, see the chapter on Jane Eyre in Gilbert and Gubar's *The Madwoman in the Attic*.

45. Stowe, *Uncle Tom's Cabin*, p. 291.

46. Ibid., p. 189.

47. Kathryn Kish Sklar, *Catharine Beecher: A Study in American Domesticity* (New Haven: Yale University Press, 1973) and Edmund Wilson, *Patriotic Gore*, pp. 436–438.

48. Stowe, *Uncle Tom's Cabin*, p. 175.

49. Ibid., p. 258.

50. Ibid., p. 262.

51. Ibid., p. 263.

52. Ibid., p. 267–68.

53. Ibid., p. 268.

54. C. E. Stowe, *Life of Harriet Beecher Stowe*, p. 60.

55. Marie Balmary, *Psychoanalyzing Psychoanalysis* (Baltimore: Johns Hopkins University Press, 1984); and Grotstein, "The Sins of the Fathers."

56. See, for example, Bronson Alcott, Elizabeth Peabody, and Catharine Beecher's writings.

57. See, for example, Theda S. Stowe, "The Only Lie," *Parents Magazine* (January 1841). Also recall the domestic conduct books of William Alcott and Catharine Beecher.

58. Frances Tustin, *Autistic States in Children* (London: Routledge & Kegan Paul, 1982). Her hypothesis is that the raw, fragile self insufficiently protected by maternal shelter, seeks protection in hard objects, which are meant to seal the self off from experience. She is thus discussing primitive forms of materialism and militarism.

59. C. E. Stowe, *Life of Harriet Beecher Stowe*, pp. 2–5.

60. Stowe, *Uncle Tom's Cabin*, pp. 243–44.

61. Ibid., pp. 246–47.

62. In addition to morbid moodiness, Stowe struggled with hysterical blindness, paralysis, and generalized body aches and pains. See Sklar, *Catharine Beecher*, and C. E. Stowe, *Life of Harriet Beecher Stowe*.

63. See Gilbert and Gubar, *The Madwoman in the Attic*. They discuss the characters of Sleeping Beauty and Snow White as embodying the serious limitation of female growth and self-knowledge. Also see Bion, "Differentiation of the Psychotic from the Non-Psychotic Personalities," in *Second Thoughts*. The sleep signifies a stupor of the part of the mind that no longer thinks normally. The capacities to be aware and think have been impaired through a somatic and/or psychological tragedy.

64. Eva is more identified with her grandmother; both are saintly figures of sacrifice.

65. Melanie Klein, "On Identification," *Envy and Gratitude*; and D. W. Winnicott, "The Observation of Infants in a Set Situation" (1936), in *Through Pediatrics to Psycho-Analysis* (London: Tavistock, 1975 [New York: Basic Books, 1958]).

66. I am using Silver's model of the psychosemiotic structure discussed in chapter 2.

67. Tustin, *Autistic States in Children*, and D. W. Winnicott, *Playing and Reality* (New York: Basic Books, 1971).

68. Frances Tustin, "Autistic Shapes," *International Review of Psychoanalysis* 11 (1984), p. 279.

69. Grotstein, "The Dual-Track Theorem, Part I" (in press).

70. Bion's notation of the container or interpreter may be applied to groups, which like the individual choose response to content discriminately.

71. See Tustin, "Psychological Birth and Psychological Catastrophe," *Autistic States in Children.* Tustin believes that the expressive mode of autosensuality is overflow or flowing-over at-one-ment. A precursor to projection, overflow communicates through skin-to-skin, body-to-body sensations.

72. Stowe, *Uncle Tom's Cabin*, p. 169.

73. Ibid., p. 342.

74. Ibid., p. 162.

75. Sklar, *Catharine Beecher*; Edmund Wilson, *Patriotic Gore*; Barbara Cross, ed., *The Autobiography of Lyman Beecher* (Cambridge: Belknap Press of Harvard University Press, 1951); and Rourke, *Trumpets of Jubilee.*

76. Johanna Johnston, *Run Away to Heaven: The Story of Harriet Beecher Stowe* (New York: Doubleday & Co., 1963), p. 51.

77. Rourke, *Trumpets of Jubilee*, p. 87.

78. Harriet Beecher Stowe, *Dread: A Tale of the Dismal Swamps* (London, 1856), p. 377.

79. C. E. Stowe, *Life of Harriet Beecher Stowe*, p. 149.

80. Stowe, *Uncle Tom's Cabin*, p. 283.

81. Grotstein, "A Proposed Revision for the Psychoanalytic Concept of the Death Instinct," *The Year Book of Psychoanalytic Psychotherapy*, ed. Robert J. Langs (Hillsdale, N.J.: Analytic Press, 1986).

82. Children of both sexes are sacrificed, although Stowe seems to be concentrating on the female version.

83. See the passage in *Little Women* in which Jo's Marmy counsels her to curb her aggressiveness, as she had all her life. Also see Edith Wharton, *House of Mirth*, and Alfred Silver, *The Oedipal Structure of Thought.* Silver calls attention to triadic signs which do not allow vital expressiveness to flow into the manifest structure.

84. Catharine Beecher, *Principles of Domestic Science as Applied to the Duties and the Pleasures of the Home* (New York: Harper Brothers, 1870), p. 13; *The Duty of American Women* (New York: Harper Brothers, 1845); and *The Evils Suffered by American Women and Children* (New York: Harper Brothers, 1847). Also see Jane Thompkins's discussion of Beecher's tracts, "Sentimental Power," pp. 98–99. Thompkins argues that the belief system behind these writings was the reformation of the human race through the family and superior mothering.

85. See Bion, "Theory of Thinking" and *Attention and Interpretation*, in *Seven Servants* (New York: Jason Aronson, 1977). In these works Bion argues that when the container function is damaged, the child must get rid of emotional significance by destroying the ability to make meaning. Also see R. E. Money-Kyrle, "Instinct in the Child," *Man's Picture of His World* (New York: International University Press, 1961) and Michael Paul, "An Atlas of Mental Birth," in *Do I Dare Disturb the Universe?*

86. Bion, "Theory of Thinking" and *Transformations.*

87. Bion, *Experience in Groups* (London: Tavistock Publications, 1961) and *Attention and Interpretation.*

88. Gandhi or Luther may be understood as figures who embody the leadership and the sacrificial aspects of the messiah.

89. Stowe, *Uncle Tom's Cabin*, p. 297.

90. Ibid., p. 75.

91. Ibid., p. 358.

92. Ibid., p. 77.

93. Ibid., p. 77.

94. Ibid., p. 78.
95. Ibid., p. 367.
96. Ibid., p. 369.
97. Note, for example, Cassie's tragic dilemma: rather than see her child grow up a slave, she murders him.
98. See James S. Grotstein, "A Proposed Revision of the Psychoanalytic Concept of Primitive Mental States, Part I," *Contemporary Psychoanalysis* 16 (Nov. 1980).
99. Bion, *Learning from Experience*, in *Seven Servants*, and "Differentiation of the Psychotic from the Non-Psychotic Personalities," in *Second Thoughts*; and Grotstein, "Primitive Mental States."
100. Bion, "Attacks on Linking," *Second Thoughts*, and *Transformations*, in *Seven Servants*.
101. Silver, "The Psychoanalytic Semiotic and the Oedipal Structure of Thought."
102. W. R. Bion, *Transformations*. If the individual's mental processes are severely disturbed, the transformation taking place would be what Bion calls a projective transformation, which is characteristic of -K, in contrast to a rigid motion, which operates similarly to normal transference. The former is delusional and its system put together out of the fragments of a psychotic break.
103. Harold Searles, "The Patient as Therapist to His Analyst," in *Classics in Psychoanalytic Technique*, ed. Robert Langs (New York: Jason Aronson, 1981) and Lloyd DeMause, "The Evolution of Childhood" in *Foundations of Psychohistory* (New York: Creative Roots, Inc., 1982); Joseph Lichtenberg, "Some Analogies Between Findings in Infant Research and Clinical Observations of Adults, Particularly Patients with Borderline and Narcissistic Disorders," and James S. Grotstein, "The Borderline as a Disorder of Self-Regluation" (with additional contribution by Pamela Scavlo), both in *The Borderline Patient* (Hillsdale, N.J.: Analytic Press, 1987).
104. Stowe, *Uncle Tom's Cabin*, p. 375.
105. Eva and Tom can be seen as alter egos or twins, like the mother/child twins of early symbiosis. Tom and Eva exchange roles, each playing mother to the other.
106. Stowe, *Uncle Tom's Cabin*, pp. 376–77.
107. Ibid., p. 384.
108. Ibid., p. 402.
109. Ibid., p. 398.
110. Ibid., pp. 398–99.
111. Ibid.
112. Bion, *Learning From Experience*; James S. Grotstein, "A Proposed Revision for the Psychoanalytic Concept of the Death Instinct," *The Year Book of Psychoanalytic Psychotherapy*, ed. Robert J. Langs (Hillsdale, N.J.: Analytic Press, 1986).

4. *LITTLE WOMEN:* A STUDY IN ADOLESCENCE AND ALTER EGOS

1. Also see, for example, Ann Douglas (Wood), "The Scribbling Women and Fanny Fern: Why Women Wrote," *American Quarterly* 23 (Spring 1971); William R. Taylor and Christopher Lasch, "Two Kindred Spirits: Sorority and Family in New England, 1839–1843," *New England Quarterly* 36:2 (March 1963); and Madeline Bedell, Introduction to *Little Women* by Louisa May Alcott (New York: Modern Library, 1983).
2. Carroll Smith-Rosenberg, "The Female World of Love and Ritual: Relations Between Women in Nineteenth Century America," and "Beauty and the Beast and the Militant Woman: A Case Study in Sex Roles and Social Stress in 19th Century America," in *Disorderly Conduct: Visions of Gender in Victorian America* (New York:

Alfred A. Knopf, 1985); Nancy F. Cott, *The Bonds of Womanhood: Women's Sphere in New England, 1780–1835* (New Haven: Yale University Press, 1977); Ann Douglas, *The Feminization of American Culture* (New York: Alfred A. Knopf, 1977).

3. Also see Nina Auerbach, "Waiting Together Two Families: *Pride and Prejudice* and *Little Women*," *Communities of Women: An Idea in Fiction* (Cambridge: Harvard University Press, 1978); Auerbach emphasizes *Little Women* as centered around a community of women, and as a female society so powerful that it draws art and politics and men themselves into its orbit. Furthermore, the female characters are admired by men, reversing the usual pattern seen in the conventional view portrayed in the relationships between men and women in *Pride and Prejudice*.

4. Frances Tustin, *Autistic States in Children* (London: Routledge & Kegan Paul, 1982). In her chapter entitled "Psychological Birth and Psychological Catastrophe," Tustin posits that the birth of the self or its hatching involves a phenomenology far deeper and more primary than the early signs of autonomy such as entertaining oneself with toys, sitting up, toddling, and so on. She suggests, following on Bion's notions of the container/contained, that the readiness for psychological birth grows out of the protection of the "second womb" of mother's mind. The subtle but powerful emotional interactions that are carried on in this phase of at-one-ment, overflow, and ecstasy allow primary integrations of comfortable and uncomfortable, soft and hard sensations to be made. In turn, a firm viable self comes together out of these processes which can handle awareness and significance. I am suggesting that the integration and hatching processes are emotional maps on which all psychological change depends.

5. Alcott, *Little Women*, p. 18.

6. Ibid., p. 18.

7. Joseph Hartounian, *From Piety to Moralism* (New York: Harper & Row, 1970).

8. George E. Haefner, "A Critical Estimation of the Educational Theories and Practice of Bronson Alcott" (Ph.D. diss., Columbia University, 1937); Elizabeth Peabody, *Record of Mr. Alcott's School Exemplifying the Principles and Methods of Moral Culture*, 3rd ed. (Boston, 1824), p. 214.

9. Alexis de Tocqueville, *Democracy in America, Vol. II* (New York, 1969); Ben Benfield, "The Spermatic Economy," in Michael Gordon, ed., *The American Family in Social Historical Perspective* (New York: St. Martin's Press, 1973).

10. Quentin Anderson, *The Imperial Self* (New York: 1971).

11. On narcissism and omnipotence, see Heinz Kohut, *The Analysis of the Self* (New York: International University Press, 1971); Melanie Klein, *Psychoanalysis of Children* (New York: Delta Books, 1975); Donald Meltzer, Sexual States of Mind (Perthshire: Clunie Press, 1973).

12. Charles Strickland, "A Transcendental Father: The Child Rearing Practices of Bronson Alcott," *History of Childhood Quarterly, The Journal of Psychohistory 1* (Summer 1973), p. 15.

13. Also see Judith Plotz, "The Perpetual Messiah; Romanticism, Childhood and the Paradoxes of Human Development" in *Regulated Children, Liberated Children; Education and Psychohistoric Perspective*, ed. Barbara Finklestein (New York: Psychohistory Press, 1979). Plotz argues that similar notions were part of the Romantic movement in Europe, and she cites Coleridge, Shelley, Byron, Rousseau, and others who defined childhood as ideally sublime and important for its potential to reach perfection. This notion is a somewhat secular concept which replaces religious explanations of the divine. Alcott read many of these figures as well as Kant, from whom he drew his ideas about a higher reality.

14. Strickland, "Transcendental Father," p. 8.

15. Haefner, "Critical Estimation," p. 36.

16. Ibid., pp. 63–64.

17. Honore Morrow, *Father of Little Women* (Boston: Little, Brown & Co., 1927), pp. 113–14.

18. W. R. Bion, "Theory of Thinking," in *Second Thoughts* (New York: Jason Aronson, 1967). Alcott is suggesting a process similar to Bion's notion of the container/contained although not as sophisticated in terms of emotional complexity.

19. Strickland, "Transcendental Father."

20. Tustin, "Psychological Birth and Psychological Catastrophe" in *Autistic States in Children*. Tustin is connecting sensual modes of experience to primitive states of mind which may reveal something of the etiology of the Victorian fear of sensuality.

21. Morrow, *Father of Little Women*, p. 103.

22. Tustin, "Psychological Birth and Psychological Catastrophe" and "The Asymbolic Nature of Autistic States," both in *Autistic States in Children*.

23. Morrow, *Father of Little Women*, p. 114.

24. Tustin, "Normal Primary Autism and Pathological Autism," in *Autistic States in Children*.

25. Donald Meltzer et al., *Explorations in Autism*.

26. Grotstein, "A Proposed Revision of the Psychoanalytic Concept of Primitive Mental States, Part II."

27. G. Stanley Hall, *Adolescence and Its Relation to Physiology, Anthropology, Sociology, Sex, Crime, Religion and Education I and II* (New York: D. Appleton & Co., 1901).

28. Twain's *Tom Sawyer* and *Huckleberry Finn* mark the emergence of the concept of individuality in the stage of early adolescence.

29. See Kenneth Keniston, "Youth Change and Challenge," *Challenge of Youth*, ed. Erik Erikson (New York: Anchor Books, 1965); and Joseph F. Kett, *Rites of Passage*.

30. Philippe Ariés, *Centuries of Childhood: A Social History of Family Life* (New York: Vintage Books, 1963); David Bakan, "Adolescence in America: From Idea to Social Fact," *Daedalus* (1969); and Patricia Meyer Spacks, *The Adolescent Idea: Myths of Youth and the Adult Imagination* (New York: Basic Books, 1981).

31. Joseph Campbell, *The Masks of God: Primitive Mythology* (New York: Penguin Books, 1959); Jane Ellen Harrison, *Themis* (Cleveland: World Publishing Co., 1962 [1912]); and Louise Kaplan, *Adolescence: The Farewell to Childhood* (New York: Simon and Schuster, 1984).

32. I am suggesting here that adolescence recapitulates earlier phases and stages of development that lead from symbiosis to individuation. See Margaret S. Mahler, Fred Pine, and Annie Bergman, *The Psychological Birth of the Human Infant: Symbiosis and Individuation* (New York: Basic Books, 1975). Also see Jay R. Greenberg and Stephen H. Mitchell, *Object Relations in Psychoanalytic Theory* (Cambridge: Harvard University Press, 1983); and *Rapproachment: The Critical Subphases of Separate Individuation*, ed. Ruth F. Flax, Sheldon Bach, and J. Alexis Burland (New York: Jason Aronson, 1980)—see especially "Adolescent Psychopathology and the Rapproachment Process," Aaron Esman. Also see Melanie Klein, "Notes on the Emotional Development of the Infant," in *Envy and Gratitude*.

33. Campbell and Harrison; also Christopher Lasch, *The Minimal Self: Psychic Survival in Troubled Times* (New York: W. W. Norton, 1984); see especially "The Inner History of Selfhood."

34. Paul John Eakin, *The New England Girl* (Athens: University of Georgia Press, 1976).

35. Alcott, *Little Women*, pp. 9–10.

36. Ibid., p. 177.

37. Ibid.

38. Ibid., p. 178.

39. Ibid., p. 175.

40. The relationship between growth↔stasis that I am suggesting is based on

Wilfrid Bion's notion of PS↔D in which there is a reciprocal relationship between an uncertain or ungathered state of mind and the realization of meaning (splitting and integration); PS being the former, D being the latter. I'm suggesting that there's an analogous reciprocal relationship here between growth and stasis. See Bion, *Elements of Psychoanalysis* (1963), p. 35.

41. Louisa May Alcott, *An Old Fashioned Girl*, (New York: Grosset & Dunlap, 1973 [1894]). The adolescent in this novel, Polly, is modeled on the type of the good New England country girl, who resists the temptations of city life.

42. Alcott, *Little Women*, p. 226.

43. Ibid., pp. 460–61.

44. See Mary Poovey's *The Proper Lady and the Woman Writer: Ideology as Style in the Works of Mary Wollstonecraft, Mary Shelley, and Jane Austin* (Chicago: University of Chicago Press, 1984), pp. 40–42, for a discussion of the act of writing as a method for gathering the self and exploring its inner dimensions.

45. W. R. Bion, *Learning from Experience* (1962), *Elements of Psychoanalysis* (1963), *Transformations* (1965), and *Attention and Interpretation* (1970), all in *Seven Servants* (New York: Jason Aronson, 1977).

46. Alcott, *Little Women*, p. 51.

47. Ibid., p. 265.

48. Hartounian, *From Piety to Moralism.*

49. For another view of the emphasis on home and family, see Joy Marsella, *The Promise of Destiny* (Westport, Conn.: Greenwood Press, 1983). Marsella argues that Alcott wrote from the strength of her identity drawn from women's sphere. She uses Daniel Scott's term "domestic feminism" to bolster her argument. On the other hand, Gilbert and Gubar suggest in *Madwoman in the Attic* that Alcott's writing was adversely affected by her devotion to the domestic madonna.

50. Grotstein, "A Proposed Revision of the Psychoanalytic Concept of Primitive Mental States, Part I," *Contemporary Psychoanalysis* 16 (Nov. 1980).

51. Kohut, *Analysis of the Self.* Kohut's notion of transmuting internalization is useful here; however, as I am using the concept, it suggests that there are inner processes which must be negotiated in order for these internalizations to take place. See also D. W. Winnicott, "Contemporary Concepts of Adolescent Development" in *Playing and Reality* (New York: Basic Books, 1971); Donald Meltzer, "The Emergence From Adolescence" and "Identification and Socialisation in Adolescence," both in *Sexual States of Mind.* Also see John Demos and Virginia Demos, "Adolescence in Historical Perspective," *Journal of Marriage and the Family* 31:4 (1963) for a discussion of the development of adolescence in America.

52. Alfred Silver, "A Psychosemiotic Model," in *Do I Dare Disturb the Universe?* (Beverly Hills: Caesura Press, 1981); and "The Psychoanalytic Semiotic and the Oedipal Structure of Thought" (unpublished paper).

53. Grotstein, "Newer Perspectives in Object Relations Theory," *Contemporary Psychoanalysis* 18:1, January 1982.

54. Grotstein, "Inner Dimensions of Space," *International Journal of Psychoanalysis* 59 (1978); and Meltzer, *Explorations in Autism.*

55. Sydney Blatt, "Developmental Modes of Representation," in *The Developmental Modes of Representation: Continuity and Change in Art* (New York: Lawrence Erlbaum Associates, 1984).

56. Personal Communication, John Lundgren. Lundgren's hypothesis is that the feelings of insecurity that are aroused in family members when one member pulls out of the value system evokes in the other family members the image of the teenager as a potential messiah or devil. A wish to crucify that individual develops out of these experiences. These intense unconscious interactions within a family system which is being challenged provokes a state of panic and upheaval which can in some cases literally drive the youngster insane or to suicide. Also John Lundgren,

"The Management of Dependency; Sexual Acting Out as a Stimulus for Intergroup Work Between Hospitalized Adolescents, Their Families, and Staff," unpublished manuscript.

57. Alcott, *Behind a Mask*, ed. Madeline Stern, and Alcott, *Plots and Counterplots*, ed. Madeline Stern.

58. Leslie Fiedler, *Love and Death in the American Novel*, revised edition (New York: Dell Publishing, 1966).

59. Ibid., p. 129.

60. Ibid., p. 132.

61. Louisa May Alcott, quoted by Madeline Stern in her Introduction to *Behind a Mask*.

62. Alcott, *Little Women*.

63. See Fiedler, *Love and Death*, especially pp. 296–308. Jean of *Behind a Mask*, Pauline of *Pauline's Passion*, Virginie of *Plots and Counterplots*, and Edith Snowden in *The Abbot's Ghost* represent the Eve-like character, while Gladys in *A Modern Mephistopheles*, Octavia Treherne in *The Abbot's Ghost*, and Lilian Trevlyn in *The Mysterious Key* typify a Mary-like person. All of these characters, with the exception of Gladys, are to be found in Madeline Stern's recent editions of Louisa May Alcott's short stories, entitled *Behind a Mask* and *Plots and Counterplots*.

64. Louisa May Alcott, *A Modern Mephistopheles* (New York: Praeger, 1987), p. 196.

65. Alcott, *Behind a Mask*, p. 51.

66. Ibid., pp. 50–51.

67. Ibid., p. 54.

68. Ibid., p. 98.

69. Ann Douglas, "Mysteries of Louisa May Alcott," in *Critical Essays on Louisa May Alcott*, ed. Madeleine B. Stern (Boston: G. K. Hall, 1984). Douglas suggests Alcott's heroine Jean Muir uses deception to infiltrate a closed world (p. 236) while Alcott used deception too by writing under a pseudonym.

70. Alcott, *Plots and Counterplots*, p. 43.

71. Ibid., p. 43.

72. Ibid., p. 122.

73. Sigmund Freud, *Moses and Monotheism* (1939) S.E., vol. 22, and *On Narcissism* (1914), S.E., vol. 14.

74. Melanie Klein, "Notes on the Emotional Development of the Infant," and "On Identification," both in *Envy and Gratitude*; W. R. Bion, "Notes on the Theory of Schizophrenia and Development of Schizophrenic Thought" and "Differentiation of the Psychotic from the Non-Psychotic Personality," in *Second Thoughts* (New York: Jason Aronson, 1967); and James S. Grotstein, "The Psychoanalytic Concept of Schizophrenia; I. The Dilemma, and II. The Reconciliation," *International Journal of Psychoanalysis* 53 (1977).

75. James S. Grotstein, "The Experience of Splitting," *Splitting and Projective Identification* (New York: Jason Aronson, 1980), p. 65.

76. Sandra Gilbert and Susan Gubar, *The Madwoman in the Attic* (New Haven: Yale University Press, 1979). They cite other examples: Heathcliff and Cathy in the chapters "Horror's Twin," and "Mary Shelley's Monstrous Eve."

77. Ibid., pp. 361–62.

78. Alcott, *Behind a Mask* and *Plots and Counterplots*; Tustin, *Autistic States in Children*; and Heinz Kohut, *How Does Analysis Cure?* (Chicago: 1984). Tustin and Kohut focus on the concept of empathetic interpretation in regard to the clinical problem of the individual's tactic of surrounding him/herself with extreme hardness and cruelty. This suggests that the more the being and sense of self is placed in jeopardy, the more requirement for hardness, callousness, and cruelty.

79. Tustin, *Autistic States in Children*, p. 166.

80. Alcott, *Little Women*, p. 438.

81. Ibid., p. 512.

82. Donald Meyer, *Positive Thinkers* (Garden City, N.Y.: Doubleday & Co., 1965). Meyer uses Christian Science as a superb example of the gospel of love and the declension of Protestant piety into a one-dimensional split aspect, the all-good separated from any sense of evil; God is love and only goodness and kindness are real while evil is nonexistent.

83. Alcott, *Little Women*, p. 513.

84. Ibid., p. 532.

85. Ibid., p. 596.

86. Louisa May Alcott, *Little Men* (New York: Grosset & Dunlap Publishers, 1871), p. 278.

87. Louisa May Alcott, *Jo's Boys* (Boston: Little, Brown & Co., 1896), pp. 77–78.

88. Ibid., p. 329.

5. MARY CASSATT

1. Linda Nochlin, *Realism* (Englewood Cliffs, N.J.: Prentice-Hall, 1966), p. 15.

2. Nancy Hale, *Mary Cassatt* (New York: 1978), pp. 91–92.

3. Arnold Hauser, *The Social History of Art*, vol. 4, (London: Routledge & Kegan Paul, 1862), p. 195.

4. Nochlin, *Realism*, p. 3. Also see Degas's "The Dance."

5. Carl Schorske, *Fin-de-Siècle Vienna* (New York: Vintage Books, 1981 [1961]), Plate III, p. 225.

6. Ibid., Plates I, p. 223, and II, p. 224, respectively.

7. Tim Clark, personal communication.

8. Nochlin, *Realism*, p. 53.

9. I am not suggesting that icons of the mother function cannot help to clarify issues of the family; I merely wish to point out that the American use of the madonna figure and mother character was sterile because it was designed to interpret experience in limited and very selective ways.

10. Joseph Campbell, *The Masks of God: Primitive Mythology* (New York: Penguin Books, 1959).

11. Merlin Stone, *When God Was a Woman* (New York: Harcourt Brace Jovanovich, 1976), p. 17.

12. Robert Graves, *The Greek Myths* (Baltimore: Penguin Books, 1955); Stone, *When God Was a Woman*, pp. 22–23; Campbell, *Primitive Mythology*; Jane Ellen Harrison, *Themis* (Cleveland: World Publishing Co., 1962 [1912]).

13. Elaine Pagels, *The Gnostic Gospels* (New York: Vintage Books, 1981).

14. Julia Kristeva, "Motherhood According to Bellini," *Desire in Language* (Oxford: Basil Blackwell, 1980); also Anna Brownwell Jameson, *Legends of the Madonna as Represented in the Fine Arts* (New York: Houghton, Mifflin, 1895), p. 50.

15. Jameson, *Legends of the Madonna*, pp. 115 and 126; Leo Steinberg, "The Sexuality of Christ in Renaissance Art and in Modern Oblivion," *October* (Summer 1983), pp. 82–83.

16. John O'Malley, "Praise and Blame in Renaissance Rome," p. 9. Quoted in Steinberg, "The Sexuality of Christ."

17. Steinberg, "The Sexuality of Christ," p. 10.

18. Ibid., pp. 128, 129. See for example, Figure 140, Chima Da Conegliano, "Madonna and Child," circa 1510; and Figure 142, Joos van Cleve Shop, "Holy Family," 1520.

19. Also see Philippe Ariés, *Centuries of Childhood* (New York: Vintage Books,

1963). Ariés' argument that cultural artifacts of babies do not appear to resemble a real infant until it is safe to invest them with earthly value applies here. He suggests that the recognition of infancy takes many centuries but real infants appear in the Renaissance.

20. Sigmund Freud, *Leonardo da Vinci and the Memory of His Childhood*, S.E., vol. 11, p. 82. Freud mistakenly identified the shape in the painting and the cartoon as a vulture. In fact, it was a Kite, but the infant's relation to the bird as interpreted by Freud remains tenable.

21. Ibid.

22. Kristeva understands Freud's interpretation of Leonardo's "St. Anne and Two Others" as a fetishistic (possessive and controlling) relation to the mother's body. She compares his work to Bellini's painting which signifies the pulsing, rhythmic elements of the infant's relation to mother's body through luminous chromatic differences beyond and despite corporeal representation. See also Mary Jacobus, "Dora and the Pregnant Madonna," in *Reading Women* (New York: Columbia University Press, 1986), pp. 150–51.

23. Susanne K. Langer, *Feeling and Form* (New York: Charles Scribner's Sons, 1953).

24. Ibid., pp. 24, 25.

25. Ibid., pp. 32 and 51.

26. Harrison, *Themis*, pp. 31–32.

27. Julia Kristeva, "Poetry That is Not Murder," *Revolution in Poetic Language* (New York: Columbia University Press, 1984).

28. Harrison, *Themis*, p. 36.

29. Ibid., pp. 34–35.

30. Ibid., p. 35.

31. Ibid., p. 36.

32. Marina Warner, *Alone of All Her Sex: The Myth and the Cult of the Virgin Mary* (London: Picador, 1985 [1976]), p. 286.

33. Pagels, *The Gnostic Gospels*, pp. 29–50.

34. Ibid., p. 50.

35. Julia Kristeva, "About Chinese Women," *The Kristeva Reader*, ed. Toril Moi (New York: Columbia University Press, 1986), pp. 146–47. Also see Donald Meltzer, *Sexual States of Mind* Clunie Press, 1973), and Janine Chasseguet-Smirgel, "Perversion and the Universal Law," *Creativity and Perversion* (London: Free Association Books, 1985).

36. Susanne K. Langer, *Philosophy in a New Key*, p. 89. Langer takes the position that all mental life begins with sensory awareness. "A tendency to organize the sensory field into groups and patterns of sense data; to perceive forms rather than a flux of light impressions, seems to be inherent in our reception apparatus just as much as in the higher nervous system with which we do arithmetic and logic. But this unconscious appreciation of forms is the primitive root of all abstraction which in turn is the keynote of rationality; so it appears that the conditions for rationality lie deep in our pure animal experience and our power of perceiving." Also see Daniel N. Stern, *The Interpersonal World of the Infant* (New York: Basic Books, 1984).

37. Rudolph Arnheim, *Visual Thinking* (Berkeley/Los Angeles: University of California Press, 1969). Arnheim posits that perception and thinking need each other: "Perception consists in the grasping of relevent generic features of the object. Inversely, thinking in order to have something to think about must be based on images of the world in which we live. The thought elements in perception and perception elements in thought are complementary." p. 53. Arnheim's notions complement Bion's theories of preconceptions. Bion states that this external stimulus known to us as perception courts the preconception which yearns for its external companion in order to be born, and it is the mating of the preconception with the

perceptual object which gives birth to significance and awareness. See W. R. Bion, *Learning From Experience* and *Transformations*.

38. Bion, *Learning from Experience*.
39. Kristeva, "Stabat Mater," *The Kristeva Reader*. Kristeva calls to our attention the appearance of the signs of milk and tears as the Byzantine icons gradually softened and the embodied mother and child emerged (p. 173).
40. T. Berry Brazelton, "Joint Regulation of Neonate-Parent Behavior," *Social Interaction in Infancy: Affect, Cognition, and Communication*, ed. Edward T. Tronic (Baltimore: Johns Hopkins University Press, 1982); and T. Berry Brazelton and H. Als, "Four Early Stages in the Development of Mother-Infant Integration," *The Psychoanalytic Study of the Child* (New Haven: Yale University Press, 1979).
41. D. W. Winnicott, "Primary Maternal Preoccupation" (1956), *Through Pediatrics to Psychoanalysis* (New York: Basic, 1975).
42. James S. Grotstein, "Primitive Mental States;" Phyllis Greenacre, "Early Determinants in the Development of a Sense of Identity," *International Journal of Psychoanalysis* 56, pp. 1–22; and Esther Bick, "The Experience of Skin in Early Object Relations," *International Journal of Psychoanalysis* 49 (1968), pp. 484–86.
43. See Margaret Breuning, *Mary Cassatt* (New York: Hyperion Press, 1944), "Mother and Baby" (drypoint, 1891), p. 45, and "Nursing" (drypoint, 1891), p. 44.
44. Melanie Klein, "Notes on the Emotional Development of the Infant," in *Envy and Gratitude*; W. R. Bion, "Theory of Thinking," in *Second Thoughts* (New York: Jason Aronson, 1967); and John Bowlby, "The Nature of the Child's Tie to the Mother," in *Attachment*; and Daniel Stern, *The Interpersonal World of the Infant*. Also, Frances Tustin, "Spilling and Dissolving," in *Autistic Barriers in Neurotic Patients* (London: Karnac, 1986).
45. Griselda Pollock, pp. 13–14. Also, John Bullard, *Mary Cassatt: Oils and Pastels* (New York: Watson-Guptill Publications, 1972), Plate 8, p. 36.
46. Pollock, p. 14.
47. Brazelton, "Joint Regulation."
48. Stern, *The Interpersonal World of the Infant*; Diane Coton Fletcher, *Development in Four-to-Five-Month Infants Who Were Irritable as Newborns; A Biopsychosocial Interaction*, dissertation (California, 1985); and Brazelton, "Joint Regulation."
49. Fletcher, *Development*; Brazelton, "Joint Regulation," and "Why Early Intervention," in *Frontiers of Infant Psychiatry II*; and Frances Tustin, "The Rhythm of Safety," in *Autistic Barriers in Neurotic Patients* (London: Karnac, 1986).
50. Fletcher, *Development*, p. 5. With the parents, the newborn sets up and is part of a finely tuned biologically structured feedback system which insures the release, expansion, and differentiation of the hierarchically organized interacting subsystems of behavior.
51. T. Berry Brazelton, "Joint Regulation" and "Why Early Intervention;" and Fletcher, *Development*, pp. 267–69.
52. Brazelton, "Why Early Intervention," p. 272.
53. Fletcher, *Development*.
54. Ibid., p. 6.
55. Ibid., p. 7.
56. Daniel Stern, *Affective Attunement*; and Jacqueline Rabain-Jamin, "Survey of the Infant's Sound Envelope" and "Organization of Parent-Infant Communication," both in *Frontiers of Infant Psychiatry II*.
57. Brazelton, "Why Early Intervention," and Rabain-Jamin, "Survey" and "Organization."
58. Rabain-Jamin, "Survey" and "Organization."
59. Ibid.
60. Stern, *Affective Attunement*.
61. André Green, "The Double Limit Between Inside and Outside and Be-

tween Conscious and Unconscious," unpublished paper presented at Conference on Roots of Psychopathology: Theory and Practice (Paris, 1985).

62. D. W. Winnicott, "Mirror Role of Mother and Family in Child Development," in *Playing and Reality* (New York: Basic Books, 1971).

63. Pauline Kernberg, "Self-Awareness and Self-Recognition," in *Frontiers of Infant Psychiatry II.* Also Lacan's famous 1949 article, "The Mirror Stage as Formative of the Function of the I," suggests similar phenomenology. Lacan's theory of the mirror stage is somewhat different. He describes the mirror stage as part of the infant's awareness of lack. The not yet integrated infant sees his/her self as integrated and whole in the mirror. Paradoxically, also in the mirror phase the infant is aware of his/her incompleteness. That he/she is found elsewhere in the mothering one or in the mirror reminds him/her of his/her deficiency. Lacan states, "The mirror stage is a drama with internal thrust, which is precipitated by insufficiency to anticipation, and which manufactures for the subject caught up in the lure of spatial identification, a succession of fantasies that extends from a fragmented body ego to a form of its totality" ("The Mirror Stage as Formative of the Function of the I" [1949], *Ecrits*, p. 4).

64. Victor Burgin, "Re-reading Camera Lucida," *Creative Camera* 25 (November 1982), p. 734.

65. Jacques Lacan, "The Signification of the Phallus," in *Ecrits*, and Julia Kristeva, "Place Names," in *Desire in Language*.

66. Burgin, "Re-reading Camera Lucida," p. 74.

67. Pissarro and Cassatt were excluded from the exhibition of the Société de Peintres-Graveurs Française because of the strict construction of the word Français. An artist had to be born in France to qualify as a member. Pissarro and Cassatt arranged for an exhibition of their own, which gave Cassatt an opportunity to show her excellent interpretation of Japanese printmaking. Frank Getlein, *Mary Cassatt's Paintings and Prints*(New York: Abbeville Press, 1980), p. 76.

68. Ibid., pp. 76, 88, and 90, respectively. Also see *The Omnibus*, p. 82.

69. Bion, "Differentiation of the Psychotic from the Non-Psychotic Personalities," *Second Thoughts*.

70. James S. Grotstein, "The Inner Dimensions of Space"; Alfred Silver, "A Psychosemiotic Model;" and Donald Meltzer et al., *Explorations in Autism: A Psychoanalytic Study* (Strathtay, Scotland: Clunie Press, 1975), Chapter: "Disturbed Geography of Life Space in Autism."

71. See Renoir's and Morisot's renderings of mothers and children. See for example, Renoir's "Maternity" (1885), in which the mother faces out, away from the baby, and has very little emotional connection with him. Also, Berthe Morisot's "The Balcony" (1872) and Claude Monet's "In the Cubicle" (1867).

72. Getlein, *Cassatt's Paintings and Prints*, p. 148.

73. Bullard, *Mary Cassatt*, Plate 25, p. 70; and Pollock, Plate 48, p. 115.

74. Jay Roudebush, (New York: Crown, 1979), pps. 73 and 85, respectively.

75. See Munch's "The Scream," Kafka's *The Trial* and *Metamorphosis*, and Klimt's "Jurisprudence, Medicine, and the Law," in which all sense of order and linear continuity is felt to be lost, and authority is symbolized as crumbling and bizarre.

76. Bion, *Attention and Interpretation*, and Bion, *A Memoir of the Future, Book Three: The Dawn of Oblivion* (Strathtay, Scotland: Clunie Press, 1979); also *A Memoir of the Future; The Dream* (Rio de Janeiro: Imago Editoria, 1975); and Langer, *Philosophy in a New Key*, p. 85. Langer explains these changes as the loss of belief in certain metapsychological propositions. She states that the problems of first cause, unity, and substance are insoluble, because they derive from a misconception; we attribute to the world what really belongs to logical projections in which we conceive it. Many issues that seem to concern the sources of knowledge, for instance, now appear to turn partly or wholly on the forms of knowledge or even the forms of expressionist

symbolism. The recognition of the intimate relation between symbolism and experience is a key idea for the understanding of knowledge and interpretation.

77. W. R. Bion, *Experience in Groups.*

78. Bion, *Attention and Interpretation*; also see Grotstein, "Who Is the Dreamer Who Dreams the Dream and Who Is the Dreamer Who Understands It?"

79. Grotstein, "Who Is the Dreamer . . . ?" and *Primitive Mental States: Part I.*

80. Many American writers wrote from the identity of the archetypal female and the sense of the good woman, either representing it or trying to overcome it. See for example, Margaret Fuller, Harriet Beecher Stowe, Emily Dickinson, and Louisa May Alcott. For male views on this issue, see Ben Benfield's *Horrors of the Half-Known Life.*

81. See Margaret Drabble, "Gone But Not Forgotten," *New York Times Book Review*, 6 July 1982. Drabble suggests that it was not until the eighteenth and nineteenth centuries that the idea of woman as immoral and weak formed and hardened. Moreover, women could not become writers without facing their identity as ladies, a situation which seriously informed their work.

82. Bion, *Learning From Experience.* Bion theorizes that structures of significance evolve as the immediate experience of the subject evolves, freeing both from saturated or stereotypic thinking.

83. See for example, "Mother and Child in a Boat" (1908) in Getlein, p. 147; and "By the Pond" in Adelynn Dohine Breeskin, *Mary Cassatt: A Catalogue Résumé of the Graphic Works* (Washington, D.C.: Smithsonian Institution Press, 1979).

84. Sophocles' version of the Oedipus myth is often bound together by–K and H, which deny the awareness of emotional truth and responsibility. The emotional links holding Cassatt's myth together and defining the characters and relationships are normal L, K, and H. Bion designates L as loving feelings and ties, H as hate in the sense of asserting oneself protectively or beneficially, and K as the search for Knowledge. K in these infants is not used in an omnipotent way, but rather to discover what is needed to survive and grow.

85. For this approach to generational conflicts, see Alice Miller, *Thou Shalt Not Be Aware: Society's Betrayal of the Child*, tr. Hildegard and Hunter Hannum (New York: Farrar, Straus & Giroux, 1984); Marie Balmary, *Psychoanalyzing Psychoanalysis: Freud and the Hidden Cult of the Father*, tr. Ned Lukacher (Baltimore: Johns Hopkins Univ. Press, 1982); and Grotstein, "A Revision of the Metapsychological Theory of the Death Instinct."

86. Bullard, Plate 10, p. 47; Pollock, Plate 23, p. 93.

87. Bullard, Plate 41, p. 48.

88. Ibid., Plate 3, p. 26.

89. Ibid., Plate 4, p. 28.

90. Pollock, p. 10.

91. Bullard, Plate 6, p. 32.

92. Pollock, Plate 9.

93. "Sleepy Nicole," Pollock, Plate 48, p. 115; and "Lefebvre," Bullard, Plate 25, p. 70.

94. Bullard, Plate 17, p. 54.

95. Bullard, Plate 21, p. 62.

96. Pollock, Plate 43, p. 111, and Plate 44, p. 113, respectively.

97. Margaret S. Mahler, Fred Pine, and Enid Bergman, *The Psychological Birth of the Human Infant: Symbiosis and Individuation* (New York: Basic Books, 1975); and *The Selected Papers of Margaret S. Mahler, Vol. 2, Separation and Individuation* (New York: Jason Aronson, 1979). See especially Chapter 9, "Rapproachment: Subphase of the Separation Individuation Process" (1972).

98. Kohut's theory of the idealized imago is useful here. He has theorized a stage of development in which the child draws strength from the parents, whom he/

she sees as an ideal and capable person, an imago capable of protecting him/her powerfully and benevolently. See Kohut, *Restoration of the Self*. Also see "Marie Looking Up at Her Mother" (1897) in Pollock, p. 111. Cassatt is suggesting here that daughters look up to mothers, whom they consider to be the source of their competence and self-esteem.

99. Bullard, Plate 31, p. 82.

100. Pollock, Plate 32, p. 64.

101. Kohut understands this discovery of the self through the mirroring function of the parents differently from Lacan. The baby looks to be discovered in his/her parent's eye. Kohut explains that the infant needs to show him or herself to the parent in all his/her grandiosity. The parent's task is to recognize and accept the emerging self. Failure to do so results in a severe narcissistic injury. See Kohut's *Restoration of the Self* and *Analysis of the Self*. Also see Winnicott's *Transitional Objects and Transitional Phenomena* and Harold S. Searles, "The Role of the Therapist's Facial Expressions in Psychoanalysis and Psychoanalytic Therapy," presented at the Second Annual Harry Stack Sullivan Lectures at the Shephard and Enoch Pratt Hospital, Towson, Maryland, 5 June 1982. Searles explains, "I believe that in order for any effective transference analysis to occur in any patient whether a neurotic, borderline, or psychotic, the analyst must have come to accept at least a transitional object degree if not more deeply symbiotic degree of relatedness for the particular transference image or percept which is presently holding sway in analysis." He goes on to say, "It is of the patient's symptoms and transference images of the therapist as described, so it is with the therapist and the patient's facial expressions. That is, in the therapeutically symbiotic core phase of the work with any patient, each of the two participant's facial expressions belong in a sense as much to the other as to the self. In this way the patient finds an aspect of him or herself on the analyst's face" (pp. 25–27).

102. Bullard, Plate 28, p. 76. Also see Brazelton, "Joint Regulation."

103. See Pollock's fine discussion of this painting in *Mary Cassatt*, pp. 17–18. Also see Hélène Cixous, *The New Woman*, and Lucy Irigaray, "The One Doesn't Stir Without the Other."

104. I am using symbols and signs as Alfred Silver uses them, moving from icons, indexes to symbols. He defines the first two categories as signs by positing that the infant is in a sensory mode of relating, much like Piaget's sensory motor stage or Tustin's sensory state before the overt transitional phenomena phase. The infant has not yet developed the capacity to balance sensory immediate experiences with experiences transcending the body and skin, i.e., the emotional essence and significance of a relationship. Babies stress the former. Bion develops this notion in *The Brazilian Lectures* and in *Learning from Experience*. Symbols, then, are not based only on a sensual duplication of the object. They are abstract and allow for many transformations.

105. See, for example, "The Family" (oil, 1886), Plate 19 in Pollock, or "Mother, Daughter and Son" (pastel, 1913), Plate 32 in Bullard. Also see "Mother With Two Children" (oil), p. 42 and "Children Playing With a Cat" (oil, 1908), p. 40, both in Margaret Breuning. See also "The Caress" (oil, 1902), p. 126 in Getlein.

106. See for example "The Family" (oil, 1886) in Bullard, Plate 11, p. 42 and "The Bath" (pastel, 1901) in Bullard, Plate 24, p. 68.

107. Silver, "The Oedipal Structure of Thought," p. 15, and Tustin, *Autistic States in Children*.

108. Silver, "A Psychosemiotic Model," p. 293.

109. Ibid., p. 296. Silver discussed Bion's notion of the container/contained relationship as influencing the nature of the triad's shape and development.

110. See Getlein, p. 104.

111. See James S. Grotstein's "Demoniacal Possession, Splitting, and the Tor-

ment of Joy," *Contemporary Psychoanalysis* 153 (1979), pp. 407–453, and Bion's *Transformations*. Both Catharine and Harriet Beecher seem to have had a father in mind with whom they waged a fierce battle for recognition and respect, and Louisa May Alcott seems to have been in rebellion against a mythic Bronson from her earliest years.

112. By this I mean the development of two points of view—one aspect of the self speaking to another—or the inside self listening to an externally oriented self. In addition, one side speaks and the other interprets. See R. Steele, "Psychoanalysis and Hermeneutics," *International Review of Psychoanalysis* 6, pp. 389–411.

113. Grotstein, "The Dimensions of Inner Space," *International Journal of Psychoanalysis* 59 (1978):55.

114. Bion, *Transformations* and *Elements of Psychoanalysis*. The phenomenon that Bion discusses is an attack on the space where the mother was, an attack so extreme that it becomes an attack on existence itself.

115. See Gilbert and Gubar's interesting discussions of Emily Dickinson's similar image. They discuss Dickinson's internal father as if God and Satan had united in the shape of her nobodaddy, p. 600.

116. Pollock, p. 71.

117. Bion, *Elements of Psychoanalysis*, pp. 92–93.

118. Helen Bacon, "Woman's Two Faces: Sophocles' View of the Tragedy of Oedipus and the Family," p. 20.

119. Sophocles, *Oedipus at Colonus*, pp. 133–34.

120. Bacon, "Woman's Two Faces," p. 18.

121. Ibid., pp. 22–23.

6. OTHER MADONNAS

1. Tillie Olsen, *Tell Me a Riddle* (New York: Laurel Edition, 1956) and Alice Walker, *The Color Purple* (New York: Washington Square Press, 1982).

2. Tillie Olsen, *Silences* (New York: Delacorte Press/Seymour Lawrence, 1978).

3. Ibid., p. 6.

4. Ibid.

5. Ibid., p. 12.

6. Ibid. ("One Out of Twelve"), p. 26.

7. Alice Walker, *In Search of Our Mothers' Gardens: A Collection of Feminist Prose* (New York: Harcourt Brace Jovanovich, 1983).

8. Ibid. ("Choice; A Tribute to Martin Luther King, Jr."), p. 142.

9. Ibid. ("In Search of Our Mothers' Gardens"), p. 233.

10. Ibid.

11. Ibid.

12. Olsen, *Silences*, p. 34.

13. Ibid., p. 33.

14. Ibid., p. 38.

15. Olsen, *Tell Me a Riddle*, p. 90.

16. Ibid., p. 75–76.

17. Ibid. ("I Stand Here Ironing"), p. 10.

18. Ibid., p. 76.

19. Ibid., pp. 92–93.

20. Ibid., p. 93.

21. Ibid., p. 96.

22. Frances Tustin, *Autistic States in Children.*

23. Olsen, "Tell Me a Riddle," p. 118.

24. Ibid., p. 120.
25. Ibid., p. 124.
26. Ibid., p. 116.
27. Ibid.
28. Ibid., p. 117.
29. Walker, *The Color Purple*, p. 11.
30. Ibid.
31. Ibid., p. 12.
32. Ibid., p. 13.
33. Alice Walker, *In Love and Trouble: Stories of Black Women* (New York: Harcourt Brace Jovanovich, 1973).
34. Walker, *The Color Purple*, p. 53.
35. Ibid., p. 108.
36. Ibid., p. 109.
37. Ibid.
38. Ibid., p. 46.
39. Ibid.
40. W. R. Bion, "Differentiation of the Psychotic from the Non-Psychotic Personalities," in *Second Thoughts* (New York: Jason Aronson, 1967). A useful metaphor here is the difficult interface between the psychotic part of the mind and the normal functioning part.
41. See the discussion of Legree in Chapter 2.
42. Walker, *The Color Purple*, pp. 123–24.
43. Ibid., pp. 161–62.
44. Ibid., p. 163.
45. Ibid., p. 175.
46. Ibid., p. 177.
47. Ibid., p. 178.
48. Ibid.
49. Ibid.
50. Julia Kristeva, *Desire in Language* (Oxford: Basil Blackwell, 1980) and Jacques Lacan, "Speech And Language in Psychoanalysis," *Ecrits*.
51. This process is discussed by Bion in his work on psychotic mental processes, e.g., *Second Thoughts*, especially "Notes on the Theory of Schizophrenia" and "Development of Schizophrenic Thought." Also recall Freud's discussion of the Schreber case. Bion conceptualizes this process as a mock reconstitution of psychic experience after its elements have been split, fragmented and and agglomerated/agglomerated. Bion applies these theories to the functioning of groups as well. He theorizes that the group splits and disavows unconscious forces locating them in individuals and subgroups which are transformed into enemies, messiahs, and pariahs. See Bion, *Experiences in Groups*.
52. Janine Chasseguet-Smirgel, *Creativity and Perversion* (London: Free Association Books, 1985). Chasseguet-Smirgel explains perversion as related to a series of unconscious phantasies or structures of self and object relations which seek to subvert the universe of differences; children's capacities are seen as more valuable or at the least equal to those of the parents; the anal universe is substituted for a genital procreative one; and at the extreme, differentiation between the sexes and generations is blurred into one confused mass separated off from external forces (reality)—the subject replaces God as the originator of the universe—and the parents as the procreative couple.
53. Julia Kristeva, *Powers of Horror: An Essay on Abjection* (New York: Columbia University Press, 1982).
54. W. R. Bion, "Theory of Thinking," *Elements of Psychoanalysis*, and *Transformations*.

Index

Abandonment, 30, 109
Abject, the, 19, 56, 185 n.114
Abolitionism, 74, 78
Abraham, Karl, 48
Abstraction, level of, 110
Adaptive patterns as species-specific, 184 n.78
Adolescence, 103–4, 109–10, 118–19, 194 nn. 28, 32; analogy between rites of and Gothic genre, 111, 118; portrayal in *Little Women*, 97, 102, 104–7, 108–9, 121, 123
Aggressivity, 66, 112, 116, 119
Alcott, Bronson, 96, 99–101, 104, 108, 116, 193 n.13
Alcott, Louisa May, 1–2, 24, 62–63, 65–66, 96–99, 101–2, 119–20, 195 n.49; allegorical structure of works, 174; compared with Cassatt, 124–25; Gothic/pseudo-Gothic tales, 102, 110–16, 118, 119–21, 142, 144, 196 n.63; *Jo's Boys*, 104, 108, 122; *Little Men*, 97, 104, 108, 122; *Moods*, 102, 108; *An Old-Fashioned Girl*, 97, 106, 195 n.41; quoted, 96; rebellion against father, 202–3 n.111; treatment of mother-daughter relationships, 149. See also *Little Women*
Allegory: created by Walker, 173, 174–75
Alone of All Her Sex (Warner), 132
Alpha functions, 51, 185 n.102
Alter egos, 5, 68, 104, 106, 116–18; in Alcott's Gothic tales, 112–16, 117, 144; Cassatt's in her paintings, 147; in "Tell Me a Riddle," 161; in *Uncle Tom's Cabin*, 93, 192 n.105
"Amante Marin" (Irigaray), 14
Anderson, Quentin, 99
Angel in the house, 72, 160; alter egos to, 144
Annihilation anxiety, 21, 48
Anorexia, emotional, 169
Antigone (Sophocles), 29, 32, 52
Anti-meaning, chains of, 171
Antinomianism, 108
Anxiety, infant's, 21, 47–50, 131–32
Anzieu, Didier, 39–40
Apatoria, myth of, 27
Aphrodite, 27
Archetypal female, 145, 201 n.80
Ariés, Philippe, 20, 189–90 n.43, 197–98 n.19
Arnheim, Rudolph, 198–99 n.37
Artists, 65, 66, 109–10, 158; women, 1–2, 65–66, 160
Asceticism, 65, 144
Athena, 26, 27
At-one-ment of the infant, 59, 60, 186 n.131

Attachment, xv, 100, 139; Cassatt's focus on, 134, 148; effects of not experiencing, 82–83; in "Tell Me a Riddle," 163–64, 166–67
Atwood, George, 189 n.30
Auerbach, Nina, 193 n.3
Autism, 48, 56–57, 82–83; as stage of development, 60, 92, 110
Autochthony, 54–55, 70–71, 79
Autosensuality, 56–57, 60, 82–83, 191 n.71
Avant-garde artists, 127, 130

Baby. *See* Infant
"Baby Reaching for an Apple" (Cassatt), 148
"Baby's First Caress" (Cassatt), 133–34, 138, 140, 143
Bacon, Helen, 26, 156
"Balcony, The" (Morisot), 200 n.71
Baptism, 103, 131
Barthes, Roland, x, 3–4, 140–41, 142
"Bath, The" (Cassatt), 140
Becker, Paula Modisohn, 143
Beecher, Catherine, 72, 78, 85–86, 88, 202–3 n.111
Beecher, Lyman, 64, 78, 79, 85–86
Behind a Mask (Alcott), 113–14, 116, 118, 119, 121, 196 n.63
Bellini, Giovanni, 198 n.22
Bernard, A. M., 118. *See also* Alcott, Louisa May
Binary (polar) oppositions, 25–26, 71–72, 117; in Alcott's works, 101–2, 112–16, 118, 120, 123; in *The Color Purple*, 169, 170–71; integration of, 167, 188 n.28
Bion, Wilfred R., xii-xiii, 57, 110, 185 n.100, 190 n.63, 194–95 n.40, 201 n.82; on container-contained, 191 nn.70, 85, 193 n.4, 194 n.18; definition of concept, 188 n.21; on disturbed mental processes, 192 n.102, 204 nn.40, 51; on emotional linkages, 181 n.5, 201 n.84; on infant-mother relationship, 21, 133, 182 n.34; on mental life, 50–52, 57, 185 n.102; on myths, 54; theory of ideographs, 142; theory of preconceptions, 155, 188 n.10, 198–99 n.37; on thoughts, 144, 181 n.1
Birth, 1, 9, 28, 30, 55, 131; of self, 109, 193 n.4; as signaling death of parent, 45–46. *See also* Second birth
Blacks: Stowe on treatment of, 67; Walker's perspective on, 158, 159–60, 167–75. See also *Uncle Tom's Cabin*
"Boating Party" (Cassatt), 63, 126–27, 151, 153–55, 156, 172, il. 135

"Boating Party in Argenteuil" (Monet), 126
Body, 7, 109, 143; female, 169–70, 171
Body, mother's, 73, 132, 133, 198 n.22; infant's relationship to, 14, 17–18, 21, 48–50, 60, 182 n.19; as metaphor, 9, 16–18; in Oedipal theory, 10, 11, 26; separation from, 12, 13, 131
Bonding, 142, 166–67
—between mother and child, xv, 6, 22–23, 100, 117, 184 n.79; contradictions in for Olsen, 174–75; explored in Cassatt's works, 133–34, 138, 141–42, 143; opposition to, 77; role in maturation of nervous system, 138–39; as ruptured in Oedipus myth, 30–31
Botanical Monograph, Dream of, 38–40, 41
Bowlby, John, 22, 184 n.79
Boys. See Children, male
Brazelton, T. Berry, 138–39
"Breakfast in Bed" (Cassatt), 148
Brontë, Charlotte, 117–18
Burgin, Victor, 140–41

Calvinism, 78, 85–86, 98–99, 100; child-rearing ideology, 78, 79, 80, 101
Campbell, Joseph, 52, 54, 59, 71–72, 156, 181 n.4; on earth as mother, 26; on life and death in myths, 45–47; quoted, 25; on second birth, 28–29
"Can the Immortality of the Soul be Proved by the Light of Nature?" (Stowe), 86
Caretaker, primary, 2–3, 46–47, 50–51
Cassatt, Mary, 62–63, 65–66, 124–26, 130, 144–46, 151–55, 156, 157, 200 n.67; female rebellion in works of, 121; move to Europe, 66, 124; paintings and prints, 1–2, 24, 133–38, 140–44, 145–51, 152–55, 156, 200 n.67, ils. 135–37. See also specific works by title
Castration, 10, 12, 34
Chasseguet-Smirgil, Janine, 204 n.52
Child abuse, 77, 80, 101, 168, 170
Childhood, 20, 189–90 n.43; denial of in Uncle Tom's Cabin, 70–71; idealization of, 99, 193 n.13
Child mortality in 19th century, 87
Child rearing, 1, 19–20, 28, 51; Bronson Alcott's beliefs on, 99–101; Cassatt's portrayals of, 133–34, 138, 140–42, 143, 148; as mother-dominated, 3, 4, 5–9, 161, 162–65; 19th century theories on, 72, 79–81, 88, 103. See also Mothering
Children, x, 1–2, 4, 19–20, 89,103; Bronson Alcott's beliefs on, 99–101, 108; cultural concepts of as portrayed in Uncle Tom's Cabin, 68–69, 72–74, 82, 85, 87–88, 89, 191 n.82; Olsen on treatment of, 157, 162, 164; position and concepts of in 19th-century America, 64–65, 66, 79–81; psychoanalytic theories on, xii-xv, 32–34; Walker on treatment of, 157, 167–69, 170–72. See also Infant; Mother-child/infant relationship
Children, female, 5–6, 17, 97, 104; as evolving in Cassatt's portrayals, 150–51; Oedipal theory on, 11, 34, 36, 42, 44, 76; puberty rites for, 46; Stowe's idealization of in Uncle Tom's Cabin, 76, 82, 84–85, 95
Children, male, 5–6, 10, 17; Oedipal theory on, 4, 34, 36, 44, 76; puberty rites for, 46; ritual of the second birth, 27
Child sacrifice, 80
Child-selves, 46, 141
Child's First Year, The (Bronson Alcott), 100
Chodorow, Nancy, 3, 4–6, 7–8
"Choice; A Tribute to Dr. Martin Luther King, Jr." (Walker), 159–60
Christ, 88–89, 128, 132
Christian Science, 197 n.82
"Civil Rights Movement, The; What Good Was It?" (Walker), 159
Cixous, Hélène, 3, 9, 11–12, 13–14, 16–18
Clark, Tim, 126
Class, social, 67, 158, 162
"Cleon" (Stowe), 86
Codes, ix, 2, 11, 21, 23, 54, 58
Color Purple, The (Walker), 104, 157–58, 167–75
Communication, ix–x, 91; between caretaker and child, 50–51, 57, 59, 73, 88, 139–40; infant's gazing as form of, 23
Community of womanly love: formed in The Color Purple, 169–70
Concepts, 57, 188 n.21
Condensation, xiii–xiv, 4, 32, 35, 71–72
Conscience, 78, 101, 106, 108, 117
Contact, place of: between mother and child in Cassatt's paintings, 140–41, 143
Container-contained relationship, 52–53, 83, 88, 173, 191 nn.70, 85, 194 n.18; and container function, 59, 175; denial of in Oedipus myth, 51, 56; extreme of depicted by Stowe, 152; and formation of alter egos, 117; myth as aspect of, 56; signs of in Cassatt's paintings, 144, 145; Tustin's use of notion of, 56–57, 193 n.4
Core self, development of, xv, 23
"Corps à corps avec la mère, Le" (Irigaray), 14
Creativity, 35, 127, 158, 160; compared with adolescence, 109–10; portrayal in The Scarlet Letter, 107–8; as treated in Little Women, 106–7, 120–21
Creativity myths, 45
"Crochet Lesson, The" (Cassatt), 149
Culture, 3, 28, 42, 97, 103, 131; criticism of

Culture—*continued*
traditional, 161–62; customs of as part of
second level of myth, 188 n.24; as defining
women, 75, 189 n.36; development of infant's links to, 139–40; French school on,
9, 16; of Freud's time, 37–38; as manmade,
xiv, 10, 12, 34, 35, 36; mother goddess at
center of, 127; parent-child relationship
fashioned by, ix, 1; women and children
caught in structures of, 83–84
Curse, family: in Oedipus myth, 29–30, 32

Dark ladies, portrayal of, 112, 114–16
Da Vinci, Leonardo, 128–30, 133, 142, 198
n.22. See also *Leonardo da Vinci . . .* (Freud)
Daughters, 145. *See also* Mother-daughter re-
lationship
"Dead Christ with Angels" (Manet), 127
Death, 20, 45–47; infant's anxiety about, 47–
50; portrayal in *Little Women*, 102, 110,
120–21; portrayal in "Tell Me a Riddle,"
165–67; portrayal in *Uncle Tom's Cabin*, 84,
88, 94
Death instinct, 21, 43, 48–49
De Beauvoir, Simone, 3, 4
Deception, Alcott's use of, 196 n.69
Declaration of Independence: Fugitive Slave
Law as corruption of principles, 67–68
Deconstruction, 2, 6, 9, 11–13, 14, 15
Defense organization, 43, 46
Degas, Edgar, 125–26, 127
"Déjeuner sur l'Herbe, Le" (Manet), 127
Demause, Lloyd, 20, 181 n.4, 189–90 n.43
Depressive position, 22, 185 n.99
Derrida, Jacques, 13–14, 185 n.114
Dialogue: hermeneutic, 153, 203 n.112; in-
ternal, 116–17
Dickinson, Emily, 66
Différance: Derrida's notion of, 14
Difference, toleration of, 52–53, 56
Dinnerstein, Dorothy, 3, 4, 6–8
Disavowal, structures of, 175
Disintegration anxiety, 131
Displacement, xiii–xiv, 4, 57, 71–72, 141;
role in Freud's theories, 32, 35, 38–39
Dithyramb, 131
Divine motherhood: as treated in patriarchal
mythologies, 71–72
Doctor Faustus (Marlowe), 116
Domestic angel, 105
Domestic feminism, 195 n.49
Domestic madonna, 23, 65, 72, 121, 126, 133;
for Alcott, 102, 116, 195 n.49; dual aspects
of in *Uncle Tom's Cabin*, 72–73, 94–95
Domestic sphere, 1–2, 5, 9, 72, 103, 126, 152,
154; Catherine Beecher on, 88; father
forced out of, 165; for Freud, 12, 38–39,
40; importance in *Little Women*, 97, 106,

108, 122–23; mythologization of opposi-
tion to public sphere, 46–47; as portrayed
in *Uncle Tom's Cabin*, 67, 69–70, 72–75
Dominance, 77, 86, 174
Dominance-submission: portrayal in *Uncle
Tom's Cabin*, 67, 68–69, 79–80
Dostoevski, Fyodor, 116
Double, The (Dostoevski), 116
Double identities/doubles, 116–18; in Al-
cott's Gothic tales, 113–16
Double (multiple) voices: for women, 16
Douglas, Ann, 196 n.69
Drabble, Margaret, 201 n.81
Dread (Stowe), 86
Dream images, Bion on, 142
Dreams, source of persona of, 117
Dream theory, Freudian, xi, xiii, 4, 25, 52,
130; and the Oedipal myth, 32–35, 37–42
Dyad: image of God as a, 132

Eakins, Thomas, 65, 125
Earth goddess, 28. *See also* Mother goddess(es)
Écriture féminine, 9, 14, 15–18
Egalitarianism, 74–75, 77, 99
Ego, 22, 116–17, 188 n.28
Ego ideal, 116–17
Emerson, Ralph Waldo, 66, 99
"Emmy and Her Child" (Cassatt), 133–34,
138, 140
Emotional linkages, 26, 92, 181 n.5, 201 n.84
Emotions, 66, 70, 109, 141, 142, 146; Bron-
son Alcott on children's, 100–101; distor-
tion of in *Uncle Tom's Cabin*, 95; expression
of in *Little Women*, 105, 106–7, 112; infan-
tile, 2, 7; child-rearing and 19th-century at-
titudes on, 81; relatedness of, 91. *See also*
Reciprocity
Enslavement, 92–93, 174
Epigenesis, x, 28–29, 138
Eurydice, 27
Eve/Mary polarity, 112–16, 196 n.63
"Evolution of Childhood, The" (Demause),
20
Exile, female: metaphor of, 119
Experience, 109, 130, 131, 173, 200–201
n.76, 202 n.104
Expressiveness, disruptive, 144–45
Eye contact: as punctum of "Baby's First Ca-
ress," 140

Fairy tales, 42–43, 190 n.63
Family life/relations, 1–2, 8, 24, 25–63, 67;
and adolescent change, 110, 195–96 n.56;
of the Beechers, 78; Cassatt's rethinking
and portrayals of, 125–27, 133–34, 145,
150–51, 152, 153–55; as center of mythology of American culture, 64–65, 66; in
Freud's Oedipal theory, 32–37; for Olsen,

Family life/relations—continued
157, 161–67; portrayal in Little Women, 96,
97–98, 102, 104–6, 110–11, 119–23; portrayal in Uncle Tom's Cabin, 67, 69–71, 73–
78, 82–85, 90–95; role in Alcott's Gothic
tales, 113–16; significance in Oedipus
myth, 29–32, 54–55, 75–76; Walker's portrayal, 157, 167–75
Father, law of the, 9, 10–11, 18, 131
Father/father figure, 5, 44, 51, 90, 153; Cassatt's approach to, 151, 152, 153–55;
daughters' rebellion against, 202–3 n.111;
as eclipsing divine motherhood, 71–72;
missing from Little Women, 97, 122; portrayal in The Color Purple, 168–69, 170–71,
172; portrayal in Uncle Tom's Cabin, 84, 89–
92
Father-child relationship, 5, 34, 60–61, 139–
40, 145, 153–55
Father god, 27, 131
Fatherhood, 3, 127
Fear, 7, 8, 19–20
Feeling and Form (Langer), 130–31
Female: archetypal, 145, 201 n.80; treatment
in mythology, 71–72. See also Woman;
Women
Female godhead, Christianity's refusal of a,
132. See also Mother goddess(es)
Feminists, psychoanalytic, 2–24. See also
French school of psychoanalytic feminists
Fertility, 26–27, 46, 127–28
Fielder, Leslie, 111
Firstness, 58, 152, 153
Flaubert, Gustave, 126
Fletcher, Diane Coton, 138–39
Flowers: role in Freud's Monograph dream,
39–40
Forgetting: Freud's theory on, 38–39, 40
Form, living, 130–31, 133
Freedom (Liberty), 67, 68–69, 142, 144, 145;
for mothers, 8–9; as 19th-century ideal, 66,
81; wanted by adolescents in Little Women,
102, 107
French school of psychoanalytic feminists, 3,
9, 11–24, 185 n.114. See also Kristeva, Julia
Freud, Anna, xii
Freud, Sigmund, xi–xii, xiii, 5, 12, 17, 116–
17; interpretations of Oedipus myth, 26,
29, 32–44, 52; Klein's departure from and
agreements with, 20–21, 48, 49–50; Lacan's use of theories, xiii, xiv, 9–11; Leonardo da Vinci, 129–30, 198 nn.20, 22;
psychoanalytic feminists' approach to theories of, 2–3, 4–5, 6, 9, 12–13; theory of
dream work, 25, 32–35, 37–42, 53, 130;
Totem and Taboo, 4, 5, 34, 35–36, 43–44.
See also Oedipus complex

Freudian slip, 34
Fugitive Slave Law, 67–68
Fuller, Margaret, 66

Gallop, Jane, 3, 12–13
Gandhi as messiah figure, 191 n.88
Gazing ability of infants, 23
Gender, 4, 6, 67. See also Sexual difference
Generational relations, 103, 168, 173, 175; in
Little Women, 104–5, 106; Oedipus myth
centered on, 26, 29–32, 75–76; in "Tell
Me a Riddle," 161, 163–67; in Uncle Tom's
Cabin, 67, 75–78
Gilbert, Sandra, 117–18, 190 n.63, 195 n.49
Girls. See Children, female
Gnostic Gospels, The (Pagels), 132
God, new concept of in The Color Purple, 172–
73
Good enough mothering, 22
Good woman, 97, 98, 102, 201 n.80
Gothic genre, 111; Alcott's stories within,
111–16, 118, 119–21, 144, 151
Grammar, call for innovation in, 14, 16
Graves, Robert, 127
Great goddess. See Mother goddess(es)
Greek religion, 27–28
Greenberg, Caren, 189 n.40
Grotstein, James, 59–60, 117, 186 n.131, 188
n.10; on death instinct, 43, 184 nn.78, 79
Growth: female, 80, 190 n.63; relationship to
stasis, 105–7, 194–95 n.40
Gubar, Susan, 117–18, 190 n.63, 195 n.49

Hainuwele, 45, 184 n.86
Hall, G. Stanley, 103
Hardness, 56–57, 118–19, 132, 196 n.78; as
way of supporting and protecting self, 83,
84, 190 n.58
Harrison, Jane Ellen, 27–28, 29, 131
Hawthorne, Nathaniel, 66, 98, 107–8, 112,
114
Hera, 27
Heresy, disruptive expressiveness as, 144–45
Hero, 44, 45, 72, 76
Heroine, 45, 74–75
History, 3, 35; Olsen speaking from perspec-
tive of, 158–59, 160–62; Walker speaking
from perspective of, 158, 159–60
Homeostasis: infant's ability to achieve, 139
House of Mirth (Wharton), 124
Huckleberry Finn (Twain), 104, 194 n.28
Human rights, 67, 79, 80–81
Husband-wife relationship in "Tell Me a Rid-
dle," 161, 164–67
Hutchinson, Anne, 108

Icons: Cassatt's development of modern, 134,

Icons—*continued*
142; level of, 110; of Mary and Christ, 127–30; mother-child relationship as, 127, 197 n.9
Id, 37, 116
Idealization, 1–2, 97, 99
Identification, 5, 6, 59, 145, 186 n.126; between characters in *Uncle Tom's Cabin*, 85, 86, 190 n.64
Identity, 2, 148, 162, 195 n.49
Ideographs, 42, 145, 174
Ignorance: myths as dramatizing dilemma of, 91
Imaginary, the, 14–16, 52
Imago, xii, 201–2 n.98
Imperialist Self, The (Anderson), 99
Impressionists (Independents), 125–27, 130, 134, 138, 143, 153
Imprinting, 29
Incarnation, 128
Incest in Oedipus myth, 31–32; as interpreted by Freud, 32, 34, 37, 43, 44
Independents. *See* Impressionists
Individuation, 57, 131, 143, 150; during adolescence, 103, 106, 110, 123, 194 nn.28, 32; *Uncle Tom's Cabin* as fictional account of, 64, 82. *See also* Separation/individuation
Inequality, 67, 68–69, 77
Infancy, 82–84, 99, 110, 131; concepts of, ix, xi, 20, 100–101; re-enactment of dramas of in adolescence, 103, 109 194 n.32
Infant, 6–8, 23, 28–29, 91, 197–98 n.19, 202 n.104; Cassatt's portrayals of, 133–38, 141, 151–52; development of, 20, 152–53; experience in Oedipus myth, 30–31; Klein on, 20–24, 47–50; mental life, 50–52, 57–59, 182 n.34; as messiah of joy, 89; needs, 8–9, 103, 133, 138–40; organizing capacity, 23, 53; in prey-predator relationship, 45–46; psychoanalytic theories on, xii–xv, 43; split in mind, 7, 177 n.13; warning system, 43, 184 n.79. *See also* Children; Mother-child/infant relationship
Infant-child self of mother, 88
Infanticide: committed by slave mothers, 71, 80, 91, 192 n.97
Infant mortality, 20
Infant (infantile) semiotics, 9, 21, 22–23, 24, 59, 92
Initiation, 109, 131; rites, 28, 103, 109, 131
In Love and Trouble (Walker), 168
In Search of Our Mothers' Gardens (Walker), 159–60
Instincts, 20–22
Intellectual life: conflict with motherhood, 161–62
Interpretation of Dreams (Freud), 32–34, 38–41

"In the Bath" (Cassatt), 141
"In the Cubicle" (Monet), 200 n.71
Irigaray, Luce, 3, 9, 11–12, 13–16, 17
Irma's Injection, Dream of, 38, 40–42
"I Stand Here Ironing" (Olsen), 162

Jacobus, Mary, 3
Jakobson, Roman, ix–x
James, Henry, 104
Jane Eyre (Brontë), 117–18
Japanese color prints by Cassatt, 140, 141, 200 n.67
Jo's Boys (Alcott), 104, 108, 122
Jouissance, xiv, 13
Judaism, traditional role in "Tell Me a Riddle," 158, 161–62, 164
"Judith and Holfernes" (Klimt), 38, 126
"Jurisprudence" (Klimt), 37

Kafka, Franz, 144, 200 n.75
Keats, John, 158
Kernberg, Pauline, 140
King, Martin Luther Jr., 259
Klein, Melanie, xii, 3, 6, 177 nn.16, 28, 185 n.99; influence on Bion, xiii, 50; interpretation of Oedipus myth, 29, 52; theory of mental life, 20–24, 53; version of Oedipus complex, 44, 47–50
Klimt, Gustav, 37–38, 42, 126, 144, 200 n.75
Kohut, Heinz, 195 n.51, 196 n.78, 201–2 n.98, 202 n.101
Kouros, 131
Kristeva, Julia, 3, 185 n.114, 188 n.21, 198 n.22, 199 n.39; approach to concept of motherhod, 9, 11–12, 13–14, 18–19, 22–24; quoted, 1

Lacan, Jacques, xii, xiii–xiv, 9–11, 25–26, 185 n.114, 200 n.63; French school's use and criticism of, 3, 9, 11–14
Lack, 35, 42, 200 n.63
Lactation, 4. *See also* Nursing
Langer, Susanne K., 130–31, 198 n.36, 200–201 n.76
Language, ix–x, 14–16, 18–19, 34; for Lacan, xiii–xiv, 10–11; between mother and child, 9, 11, 18–19; sexual difference in, 12, 13, 15
Law of the father, 9, 10–11, 18, 131
Leaves of Grass (Whitman), 66
Leonardo da Vinci, 128–30, 133, 142, 198 n.22
Leonardo da Vinci and the Memory of His Childhood (Freud), 129–30, 198 nn.20, 22
Lévi-Strauss, Claude, 10, 25–26, 53–56, 69–71, 185 n.107
Liberation as theme in *Dread*, 86

Liberty. See Freedom
Libido, xi, xiii, 35, 48, 129–30
Life cycle, 29–32, 103, 131, 146–47
Life instinct, 21, 43, 48–49
"Little Anne Sucking Her Fingers Embraced by Her Mother" (Cassatt), 143
Little Men (Alcott), 97, 104, 108, 122
Little Women (Alcott), 96–98, 101–3, 104–7, 108–9, 110–11, 112, 119–23; advice on aggressiveness, 112, 191 n.83; Auerbach on, 193 n.3; importance of morality in, 98, 104, 107, 110–11, 151
Log cabin quilt, 189 n.31
Love, gospel of, 86, 120, 197 n.28
Lundgren, John, 195–96 n.56
Luther, Martin: as messiah figure, 191 n.88
"Lydia, Leaning on Her Arm, Seated in a Loge" (Cassatt), 147
"Lydia Crocheting in the Garden at Marley" (Cassatt), 148
"Lydia in a Loge Wearing a Pearl Necklace" (Cassatt), 147

Madonna. See Domestic madonna; Madonna and child; Maternal figure; Mother
Madonna and child, 1–2, 23, 108, 168; evolution of iconography of, 127–30, 199 n.39; Renaissance portrayals of, 128
"Madonna and Child with Saint Anne" (da Vinci), 128–30
Madwoman in the Attic (Gilbert and Gubar), 190 n.63, 195 n.49
Mahler, Margaret, xii, 149
Males/men, 78, 85, 97, 99, 122–23; concepts of, 7, 26, 47, 189 nn.36, 39; cultural concepts of portrayed in Uncle Tom's Cabin, 69, 70–71, 76, 90, 95; place in Cassatt's family mythology, 126, 148, 152; safety and survival mythified as, 46–47; sublimations, 3, 9, 12–13; treatment in mythology, 26, 34, 71–72, 189 n.40
Manet, Edouard, 127
Manic defenses, 177 n.16
"Marie Looking Up At Her Mother" (Cassatt), 148–49, 201–2 n.98
Marlowe, Christopher, 116
Marsella, Joy, 195 n.49
Martyrdom, 81, 89, 92, 93, 97; role in Uncle Tom's Cabin, 84–85, 86–88, 94
Mary, 128, 132–33
Mary and Christ: evolution of representations of, 127–30. See also Madonna and child
"Maternal Caress, The" (Cassatt), 141
Maternal figure, xiv, 14, 86
Maternal goddess. See Mother goddess(es)
Maternal metaphor, 9, 14–18, 19, 52–53
Maternity. See Motherhood

"Maternity" (Renoir), 200 n.71
Matrilinear society, primitive, 27
Meaning, ix–x, 91, 107, 109–10, 188 n.10, 191 n.85; as drained from contemporary sign systems, 3–4; for French school, 9, 18–19; Oedipus myth as template for creation of, 34–35; second mythic level of in Uncle Tom's Cabin, 69–71; le sémiotique as structure of, 18–19; of subject's inner reality, 130
Meaning, chain of (Semiotic chain), 140–41, 164, 171
Melville, Herman, 65, 66, 98, 112, 114, 116
Memories, 109
Men. See Males/men
Mental life, 57, 82–84, 103, 116, 155, 198 n.36; Bion on, 50–52, 192 n.102, 204 nn.40, 51; of infant, 92–93, 152–53; Klein's exploration of levels of, 20–24; Lévi-Strauss on, 54, 56; myths as growing out of, 25; Silver on, 57–59
Mermaid and the Minotaur, The (Dinnerstein), 6–7
Messiah, 30, 95, 99, 110, 191 n.88; Eva functioning as, in Uncle Tom's Cabin, 78, 86–87, 88–89
Messiah thoughts, 144, 145, 152–53
Metaphor, ix, xiii, 37–38, 57; maternal, 9, 14–18, 19, 52–53; paternal, 19, 52–53; slavery as, 64, 66
Metaphorical displacement, 141
Metonymical displacement, 141
Metonymy, ix, xiii, 12, 13, 57
Meyer, Donald, 197 n.82
Millot, Catherine, xiv
Mimetic process in ritual enactment, 131
Mind, 35, 57, 185 n.112, 204 n.40; changes in adolescence, 109, 110; independence of, 103, 146
Mind, infant's, xiii–xiv, 28–29, 31, 145; splitting, 7, 117, 177 n.13
Minister's Wooing, The (Stowe), 104
Mirror images, 114, 117
Mirroring, 60, 140, 149–50, 202 n.101; stage, xiii, 18, 200 n.63
"Mirror Stage as Formative of the Function of the I" (Lacan), 200 n.63
Moby-Dick (Melville), 66
Modernism, 42, 65, 76, 128, 130, 143; of Cassatt's work, 127, 130, 141, 152, 155; context of Olsen's work as, 174–75
Modern Mephistopheles, A (Alcott), 102, 113, 196 n.63
Monet, Claude, 125, 126, 127, 200 n.71
Monster mother, 31, 32
Moods (Alcott), 102, 108
Moralism, 97, 107, 108
Morality, 35, 65, 66, 125; importance for the

Morality—*continued*
Alcotts, 101, 120; importance in *Little Women*, 98, 104, 107, 110–11, 151
Moral scrutiny in 19th-century child rearing, 80–81
Moral woman, 65, 66, 108–9
Morisot, Berthe, 200 n.71
Moses and Monotheism (Freud), 34, 35–36, 44
Mother, 7, 26–27, 46, 65, 103; concepts of, ix, x, 1–2, 3–4, 9; as eating her young, 181 n.4; effects of freedom for, 8–9; in Freud's interpretation of fairy tales, 42–43; as represented in *Uncle Tom's Cabin*, 91–94; as structured into Oedipal myth, 189 n.40; woman as, for psychoanalytic feminists, 2–8. *See also* Body, mother's; Mother-child/infant relationship
"Mother About to Wash a Sleepy Child" (Cassatt), 133–34, 138, il. 137
"Mother and Child" (Cassatt), 149–50, il. 136
Mother-child/infant relationship, 13, 20, 28, 152, 182 n.19, 193 n.4; appreciation of significance of in *Uncle Tom's Cabin*, 72–74, 75, 87; Barthes on, 3–4; Bion on, 50–51, 133; Cassatt's portrayals of, 126, 127, 133–38, 140–44, 145–46, 148–51, 152; as coded by Christian icons, 127–28; defiled in *The Color Purple*, 172; disavowal of experience of, 73, 189 n.29; for Freud, 34, 35, 36, 40; importance of sensation in, 56–57; Klein on, 20–24, 44, 47–50; for Kristeva, 18–19; in Lasceaux cave paintings, 181 n.4; myths of mother goddess culture as reflecting, 62; in pre-Oedipal, 17; as presented in *Uncle Tom's Cabin*, 77, 83–85, 88; Renoir's and Morisot's representations of, 200 n.71; self as developing out of, 91, 189 n.30; sharing of organizing capacities, 24; Silver on, 57–58; as symbiosis, 9, 192 n.105; temptation to cloister or trivialize, 37. *See also* Mother-daughter relationship; Mother-son relationship; Parent-child relationship
Mother-daughter relationship, 15, 34, 145, 149; Cassatt's treatment of, 145–46, 148–51, 201–2 n.98; portrayal in *Uncle Tom's Cabin*, 77–78, 82, 149
Mother Earth, mother as, 26–27
Mother/father/child triad, 64, 89, 151
Mother (Earth/Great/Maternal) goddess(es), 9, 26, 46–47, 62, 94, 127–28; defilement and destruction of in Oedipus myth, 29–30; devaluation or elimination of in patriarchal mythologies, 71–72; Freud on, 42, 43; personification of in *The Color Purple*, 169, 173, 174
Motherhood (Maternity), ix, 2–9, 27–28, 76, 160, 161; as a calling of significance in Cas-

satt's works, 124; as experienced in *Tell Me a Riddle*, 161–67; French psychoanalytic feminists' approach to, 9, 11–20; importance of Virgin Mary's, 132; mythification in *Uncle Tom's Cabin*, 81–82; portrayal in *The Color Purple*, 169–70
Mothering, ix, 1, 4, 8, 72, 90; of each other by women, 169–70; as function of survival, 20; good enough, 22; by maternal figure, 78–79, 84–85, 94, 192 n.105; misuse of, 15
Motherliness: phobia of in *Uncle Tom's Cabin*, 70–71; portrayal in *Uncle Tom's Cabin*, 73–74, 75, 79
"Mother Nursing Her Baby" (Cassatt), 143
Mother of all things, 26
"Mother's Kiss, The" (Cassatt), 141
Mother-son relationship: in Oeidipus myth, 26, 29–32
Mothers to their work: Victorian women artists as, 1–2
"Mrs. Robert Simpson Cassatt" (Cassatt), 146–47
Multiple (double) voices for women, 16
Munch, Edvard, 126, 144, 200 n.75
Mythemes, 53
Mythologies (Barthes), x, 304
Mythology/myths, ix–x, 3–4, 25–63, 108, 112, 117; Bion's interpretations of, 51–52; Cassatt's paintings functioning as, 142, 145, 146; *The Color Purple* functioning as, 167, 168–69, 172–75; cultural, 25, 27, 28–29; family, 64–65, 157–58, 162–75; functions of, 52–53; infantile, 49, 59; Lévi-Strauss on, 53–56, 185 n.107; *Little Women* functioning as, 96, 97–98; personal, 25, 34, 51, 164; second level of, 69–71, 188 n.24; *Uncle Tom's Cabin* functioning as, 67, 68, 69–71, 75–76, 80–81, 82–83, 89, 91; use in Freud's theories, xi, 32–44. *See also* Oedipus myth

Narcissism, 19, 50, 99
Neurosis: Freud's theories on, 32, 33, 36
New England propriety, 78–79, 104, 111–12
"Notes on the Emotional Development of the Infant" (Klein), 48
"Not-me" phenomena, 11, 56–57, 61, 82–83, 84, 119
Nursing, 4, 9, 103, 143

Object, 57, 60, 91–92, 125
Object-relations theory, 3, 4–5
Odysseys, 29–32, 42–43, 76, 97
Oedipus at Colonus (Sophocles), 26, 29, 52, 53, 155–56
Oedipus complex, 17, 26, 60–61; Freud's theory, 9–11, 32–37, 40, 42, 43–44, 47; Klein's theory, 21, 44, 47–50, 187 n.135;

Oedipus complex—*continued*
for Lacan, xiv, 9–11; psychoanalytic feminists on, 2–3, 4–5
Oedipus myth, 26–27, 28, 29–32, 52–53, 59, 61–62, 65, 189 n.40; as applicable for male and female development, 75–76, 189 n.40; Bion's interpretation of, 51–52; Cassatt's version of, 146, 155, 201 n.84; credit for Oedipus's survival, 184 n.76; female version in *Uncle Tom's Cabin*, 75–76, 80; Freud's interpretation of, 29, 32–44; Klein's interpretation of, 29; Lévi-Strauss's analysis of, 54–56, 69–71; as mapping triadic structure, 61, 91; Sophocles' interpretations of, 26, 29, 32, 34, 43, 182 n.35, 201 n.84; Walker's allegory as new version of, 173–75
Oedipus Rex (*Oedipus Tyrannus*) (Sophocles), 29, 39, 52, 53, 155–56
"Of Phallic Proportions: A Lacanian Conceit" (Gallop), 12–13
Old-Fashioned Girl, An (Alcott), 97, 106, 195 n.41
Olsen, Tillie, 157–59, 174–75; *Silences*, 158–59, 161; *Tell Me a Riddle*, 157–58, 161–67
"One Doesn't Stir Without the Other, The" (Irigaray), 15
"One Out of Twelve" (Olsen), 158–59
Oppositions. *See* Binary oppositions
Original sin, doctrine of, 99; effects on concepts of child rearing, 78, 79, 81; effects on Lyman Beecher's daughters, 78
Other, 3, 9, 82–83

Pagels, Elaine, 132
"Pallas Athena" (Klimt), 38, 126
Paranoid-schizoid position, 21, 24, 185 n.99
Parent-child relationship, ix, 19–20, 58–59, 138–40, 189–90 n.43, 199 n.50; Bion on importance of, 51; Bronson Alcott on, 100; communication in, 57; cultural changes in, 97; life and death theme in myths of, 45–46; mirroring, 202 n.101; as revealed in Oedipal structure, 35, 36; sensuousness of, 61; *Uncle Tom's Cabin* as myth about, 77; Walker's allegory of, 173. *See also* Father-child relationship; Mother-child/infant relationship
Parenting. *See* Child rearing; Mothering
Parents, 103, 109, 201–2 n.98; containing function of, 52–53, 145
Parler femme, 16
Parricide, 30, 31, 32, 34, 36, 37, 43
Paternal metaphor, 19, 52–53
Patriarchal culture, 11, 69, 127–28, 131; mythologies, 47, 71–72
Patrilinear society, 27–28
Paul, Michael, 185 n.112
Pauline's Passion (Alcott), 113, 116, 196 n.63

Peirce, Charles Sanders, x–xi, 57
"Pensive Marie Kissed by Her Mother" (Cassatt), 148–49
Perception: for the Impressionists, 125, 127, 130; relationship to thinking, 198–99 n.37
Persecutory anxiety, 49
Persephone, 45
Personality, 2, 189 n.30; women's, 96, 147–48
Perversion, Chasseguet-Smirgil on, 204 n.52
Phallic mother, Sphinx as, 26
Phallocentrism, 3, 9, 12, 13–14, 19
Phallus of Christ as signifier in Renaissance portrayals, 128
Phantasies, 28, 130; role in Freud's Oedipal theory, 33, 34–35, 36, 41; role in Oedipus myth, 30–31, 53
Phantasies, infantile, xii–xiii, 6–7, 19, 22, 24, 52; importance for Klein, 20–22, 23, 24, 47–50, 185 n.99
"Photograph of an American Family" (Van der Zee), 140–41
Pierre (Melville), 116
Pilgrims: Alcott's characters as, 98, 105, 106–7
Pissarro, Camille, 200 n.67
Plots and Counterplots (Alcott), 113, 114–16, 118, 119, 120–21, 196 n.63
Plotz, Judith, 193 n.13
Polar oppositions. *See* Binary oppositions
Pollock, Griselda, 154
Portrait of a Lady (James), 104
Potency/power, 8, 103, 109; male, 26, 69, 71, 93–94
—female/maternal, 73, 127–28; in Alcott's gothic tales, 112–16, 118, 119; in Mary as the madonna, 132–33; in Oedipus myth, 26, 30; portrayed in *The Color Purple*, 169–70; portrayed in *Uncle Tom's Cabin*, 72, 74–75, 76, 93–94
Powerlessness of women, children, and slaves, 69, 83
Preconceptions, 54, 57–58, 59, 188 n.10; Bion's theory of, 51–52, 155, 198–99 n.37
Pregnancy, 1, 4, 9, 17, 18, 103; in *The Color Purple*, 168, 170
Prelinguistic. *See* Preverbal/prelinguistic/presymbolic
Pre-Oedipal, 3, 5–6, 8; French school's emphasis on, 9, 17–19; Klein's exploration of, 20–24
Presence, 9–10, 12, 13
—maternal, 30, 44, 110; in Cassatt's paintings, 134, 148, 149; in Mary as the madonna, 132
Preverbal/prelinguistic/presymbolic, 30, 36, 38, 59, 117; French school on, 9, 14, 16, 17–18, 19
Prey anxiety, 131

Prey-predator relationship, 32–33, 46, 47, 55, 152
Primary process, 51, 185 n.102
Private sphere. *See* Domestic sphere
Procreation, 45, 128, 132
Protestantism, 133, 197 n.82
Psychoanalysis (Psychoanalytic theory), xi–xv 20, 57–59, 116–17, 189 n.30, 202 n.101. *See also* French school of psychoanalytic feminists; Freud, Sigmund; Klein, Melanie
Psychoanalytic feminists, 2–24
Psychopathology of Everyday Life (Freud), 34
Psychosis, 48, 182 n.34
Puberty rites, 46
Public sphere, 46–47, 67, 69, 74, 106; entry into for males, 5, 10, 47; separation of women and family life from, 2, 7, 65, 103, 152, 165
Puntum: in Cassatt's mother and child paintings, 140–41, 148; etiology of, 140–41, 142
Puritanism, 108

Quest for self, 103
Quiet alert state of consciousness, 139

Rabain-Jamin, Jacqueline, 139–40
Race, perspective of in *The Color Purple*, 167–75
Racial hatred, 159; self-hatred among blacks as transformation of, 168–69
Rank, Otto, 44
Rapprochement, 60, 149
Raw and the Cooked, The (Lévi-Strauss): overture to, 54
Reading, importance to heroine in "Tell Me a Riddle," 161–62
"Reading LeFigaro" (Cassatt), 146
Realism, 125, 127
Rebellion, 86, 93–94, 103, 104–5, 121
Rebirth. *See* Second birth
Reciprocity, 88, 100, 138–40, 149–50, 163–64; explored in Cassatt's paintings, 133–34, 146, 148
Reciprocity dance, 138–40, 142
"Reine Lefebvre Holding a Nude Baby" (Cassatt), 143
Religion, 35, 65, 79–80, 108; Greek, 27–28; protests against traditions of, 158, 161–62
Renoir, Auguste, 125, 127, 200 n.71
Representative Men, The (Emerson), 66
Repression, 10, 12, 19, 38–39, 40, 112
Reverie, 7, 51, 91, 117
Rich, Adrienne, 3, 4
Ricoeur, Paul, 35–36
Riddle of the Sphinx, 31
Rites/rituals, 27, 28–29, 46, 103, 131; inner, 103, 109–10, 112, 118
Ritual murder, 45–46
Rudnytsky, Peter L., 182 n.35

Sacrifice, 32, 44, 45, 80, 105; of individual needs, 5; Oedipus in role of, 30, 43; in *Uncle Tom's Cabin*, 86, 87–88, 93, 191 n.82
"Saint Anne and Two Others" (da Vinci), 133, 142, 198 n.22
Saussure, Ferdinand de, ix–x, 10, 25
Scarlet Letter, The (Hawthorne), 66, 107–8
"Schizoid Mechanisms" (Klein), 48
Screen memories, 39–40, 129
Searles, Harold S., 202 n.101
Second birth (Rebirth), 30, 42, 44, 76, 97, 110; Campbell on, 28–29; rites of, 27, 29, 131, 142
Secondness, 58, 61, 152, 187 n.138
Self, 91–92, 101, 116–17, 131, 203 n.112; assertiveness, 66; awareness, 157, 160; birth, 109–10, 193 n.4; development in childhood and adolescence, 103, 109–10, 118–19; development in infancy, 23, 47–48, 59, 109–10, 138–40, 189 n.30; doubled in Alcott's Gothic tales, 113–16, 118; female, 98, 102–3, 104, 120; realization, 161, 162; as seeking protection in hardness, 83, 190 n.58; sense of, 1–2, 5, 99
Self-aggrandizement, male quest for, 7, 98
Self-alienation, 82
Self-analysis, Freud's, 32–33
"Self-Awareness and Self-recognition" (Kernberg), 140
Self-control, 66, 88, 101, 106, 112
Self-creation, 70–71, 109, 125
Self-determination, 68–69, 142
Self-discovery, 81, 82, 125, 163, 202 n.101; for Oedipus, 30, 52; portrayal in *The Color Purple*, 172, 173; *Uncle Tom's Cabin* as account of processes of, 64, 75
Self-exploration, 107–8, 109, 120–21
Self-expression, 102, 107, 109
Self-government, 70, 100–101
Self-hatred: mythology of within the black family, 168–69, 174
Self-image of child, 149–50
Self-knowledge, 107, 109, 190 n.63; for Oedipus, 30, 32, 155; road to in *The Color Purple*, 170, 172, 174, 175
Self-made man, 65, 70, 144; portrayal in *Uncle Tom's Cabin*, 70–71, 76, 90–91
Self/object relationship between infant and parent, 59–60, 186 n.131
Self-respect, 75; in Cassatt's portrayals of women, 124, 146, 148
Semiotic chain (Chain of meaning), 140–41, 164, 171
Semiotics, 11, 14, 36, 83, 151; infant, 9, 21, 22–23, 24, 59, 92; Silver on formation of, 57–59; visual structures, 157
Sémiotique, le, 18–19, 23, 24, 52, 131
Sensory experience, 56–57, 133, 198 n.36
Sensuality, 100–101, 110, 133, 194 n.20; ex-

Sensuality—continued
plored in Alcott's Gothic tales, 112–14,
116, 121; as offered in The Color Purple,
169–70; in parent-infant relationship, 18,
61; seen in Cassatt's paintings, 134, 143,
147, 150
Separation, xv, 11, 12, 13, 49, 111; as part of
adolescence, 103, 110, 123
Separation/individuation, xii, 5, 9, 60–61, 92;
Chodorow on effects of, 3, 5–6, 8. See also
Individuation
Sexes, relations between, 67, 69, 75–76; separation, 69, 152, 162–63
Sexual difference, 12–15, 26, 36, 71–72, 76;
codes of, 2–3, 132; portrayed in The Color
Purple, 168–69, 175
Sexual experiences: portrayal in The Color
Purple, 168, 170
Sexuality, 31–32, 81, 108; infantile as theme
of Oedipus myth, 32–33, 34–35; male, 10,
12–13, 34; Sphynx as reverse image of
bonding, 31
—female, 13, 15, 34, 45, 103, 106; in Alcott's
Gothic heroines, 116, 121; portrayed in
Klimt's paintings, 38; repressed in Mary's
impregnation by the Word, 132; respect
and control of, 171
Sexuality of Christ and Modern Oblivion, The
(Steinberg), 128
Sexual oppression, familial, 168, 170
Sexual play, childhood memories of Freud
interpreted as, 39–40
"Short History of the Libido, A" (Abraham),
48
Showalter, Elaine, 189 n.31
Significance, structures of, 201 n.82
Signification, xiii–xiv, 13, 57, 105–6, 187
n.138; Freud on, 32, 36
Signification processes, 32, 52, 53–54, 182
n.37, 188 n.10; development in infant, 18,
19; reworked by Olsen and Walker, 74;
working inside myth, 53
Signifier/signified (S/S) relationship, x, xiii–
xiv, 3, 11–12; relationship to an "I," x–
xi
Signifiers, xiv; Modernist madonna as, 1; of
motherhood and mothering, 23; phallus as
for Lacan, 3, 12, 13; Sphinx as, 31; of
women, 26, 62
Signs, 9, 61, 65, 89, 164, 181 n.1; Barthes on,
3–4; cultural concepts of women as, 75;
Freud's Oedipal theory seen as theory of,
35–36; Gothic heroines' function as, 121;
images of in Cassatt's mother-child portrayals, 141–42, 150, 152; as part of triadic
structure, 91–92; relationship to object,
57–59, 60, 186 n.120; the semiotic as primitive, 18; Silver on, 57–58, 202 n.104;

in Uncle Tom's Cabin, 82–84, 88, 93–94,
151
Silence, 15, 158, 160
Silences (Olsen), 158–59, 161
Silver, Alfred, 57–59, 61, 110, 152, 191 n.83,
202 n.104
Sin, 144–45, 173
Skin-to-skin contact, 59, 60, 186 n.126
Slavery, 64, 66, 69, 86, 144; portrayal in Uncle
Tom's Cabin, 67–71, 73–75, 77–80, 81, 83–
85, 86–87, 89, 90–95
Sleep, 87, 190 n.63
Sleeping Beauty, 87, 190 n.63
"Sleepy Nicole" (Cassatt), 143
"Sleepy Thomas Sucking His Thumb" (Cas-
satt), 143
Snow White, 87, 190 n.63
Social movements, political, 65
Softness, 56–57, 101, 118–19
Sophocles: interpretations of Oedipus myth,
26, 29, 32, 34, 43, 52, 53, 80, 155–56, 182
n.35, 201 n.84
Speculum de l'Autre Femme (Speculum of the Other
Woman) (Irigaray), 9, 15
Sphinx, 26, 30–31, 53
S/S relationship. See Signifier/signified rela-
tionship
Stasis: relationship to growth, 105–7, 194–95
n.40
Steinberg, Leo, 128
Stern, Daniel, 23, 138–39
Stolorow, Robert D., 189 n.30
Stowe, Harriet Beecher, 1–2, 24, 62, 64, 65–
66, 72, 85–86, 202–3 n.111; allegorical
structure of works, 174; compared with
Cassatt, 124–25; experience with myth of
female martyrdom, 81; health problems
and depression, 82, 85–86, 190 n.62; loss
of son, 87; The Minister's Wooing, 104;
quoted, 64; upbringing, 78, 85–86, 101;
as woman writer and modernist, 76. See
also Uncle Tom's Cabin
Sublimation, 10, 36; male, 3, 9, 12–13; use
of Kristeva's meaning for, 29, 182 n.25
Suicide, 85–86, 119, 121
Superego, 10, 36, 42, 49, 116
Survival, 8, 25, 30, 48–49, 128
Symbiosis, 81–83, 110, 194 n.32; as stage of
development, 60–61, 92, 192 n.105, 202
n.101
Symbolic, the, 14–16, 18
Symbolic order, 30, 38, 52, 64–65, 131;
French school on, 3, 9, 11, 15–18, 22–23;
for Lacan, xiv, 10–11, 13–14, 16, 25–26
Symbolic structures, 13, 32, 34, 61, 117
Symbolization, 32, 60, 182 n.37
Symbols, xii–xiii, 9, 65, 150, 200–201 n.76;
formation of, 57–58, 151; Freud's Oedipal

Symbol—*continued*
  theory seen as theory of, 35–36; of myths
  for Campbell, 28–29; Silver's use of term,
  202 n.104
Synchronic, 53–54, 83–84, 129
Syntax: French feminists' call for innovation
  in, 14, 16

Tell Me a Riddle (Olsen), 157–58, 161–67
"Theme of the Three Caskets, The" (Freud),
  42–43
Themis, 27, 73
Themis (Harrison), 27–28
Thetic, the, 18, 188 n.21
Thinking (Thought), 57, 144, 198–99 n.37;
  Bion on, 50–51, 181 n.1, 185 n.102
Thirdness, 58–59, 61, 152, 153, 187 n.138
Thompkins, Jane, 191 n.84
Tinbergen, Nikolaas, 29, 184 n.78
Tom Sawyer (Twain), 104, 194 n.28
Totem and Taboo (Freud), 4, 5, 34, 35–36, 43–
  44
Tower of Babel, myth of, 91
Transcendentalism, 98–99
Transcendental signifier, 3, 12
Transference, 192 n.102
Transitional objects, 28, 182 n.19
Triadic signs, 191 n.83
Triads, 57, 60–61, 82–85, 91–92, 153–55,
  156
Trilogenia, myth of, 27–28
Tustin, Frances, 184 n.79, 193 n.4, 194 n.18;
  on autosensuality, 56–57, 61, 191 n.71; on
  hardness and softness, 118–19, 190 n.58,
  196 n.78
Twain, Mark, 104, 194 n.28

Uncle Tom's Cabin (Stowe), 64, 66–71, 72–80,
  81–85, 86–95, 142, 144; concept of the
  American girl, 104; family relations in
  compared with *Little Women*, 97, 98; parallels with *The Color Purple*, 167–69, 170–
  72, 173, 174; representation of relationships, 142, 149; sales, 67; serialized version, 188 n.11; Showalter's interpretation
  of, 189 n.31; triads in, 151
Unconscious, 10, 20, 51, 54, 58, 188 n.24; and
  Freud's Oedipal theory, 32, 34–35; importance for Cixous, 17–18
Underworld in patriarchal mythologies, 71–72
Utopian society, 99

Valentinus, 132
Value systems, challenges to in adolescence,
  110, 195–96 n.56
Van der Zee, James, 140–41
Visual image, puntum as a, 141
Vulnerability, phobia of, 168–69

Walker, Alice, 121, 157–58, 167; *The Color
  Purple*, 104, 157–58, 167–75; *In Love and
  Trouble*, 168; *In Search of Our Mothers' Gar-
  dens*, 159–60
Warner, Marina, 132
"Water Snakes" (Klimt), 126
"Water Snakes II" (Klimt), 38
Wharton, Edith, 66, 121, 124, 144
Whistler, James McNeill, 144
Whitman, Walt, 65, 66, 125
Will, Bronson Alcott on child's, 100–101
Willfullness as element in female develop-
  ment, 98, 102, 121
Winnicott, D. W., 11, 22, 28, 138, 140, 182
  n.19
Wish fulfillment, 42–43
Woman, 2–8, 47, 201 n.81; for French femi-
  nists, 14–15, 16; as mythic character, 65, 66
"Woman in Black at the Opera, A" (Cassatt),
  147
Womb: male, 131; myths as second, 28–29
Women, 9, 27–28, 62, 89, 145; Cassatt's portrayals of, 124, 126–27, 143, 146–48, 151,
  154; Cassatt's sense of interior lives of, 124,
  126, 143, 145–46, 151; cultural concepts
  of portrayed in *Uncle Tom's Cabin*, 68–69,
  70, 71, 72–73, 76, 82, 85, 87–88, 92, 95;
  in Freudian theory, 35, 36, 38–39, 42–44;
  in *Little Women* as dramatizing cultural
  changes and conflicts, 96–97, 101–3, 104–
  7, 108–9, 112, 121; in Oedipus myth, 26,
  189 n.40; Olsen's concepts of, 157–59,
  161–67; portrayal in Alcott's Gothic tales,
  111, 112–16, 118, 121; portrayal in Klimt's
  paintings, 37–38; position and concepts of
  in 19th century, 64–66, 72, 74–75, 81;
  Walker's concepts of, 157–58, 167–75
Women's liberation, 9, 154
Woolf, Virginia, 160
Writers, male: in 19th-century America, 65,
  66
Writers, women, 114, 158–59; position in
  19th-century America, 65–66, 76
Writing, 14, 17–18, 86, 107, 108–9. *See also*
  Écriture féminine

DATE DUE
